GINA BUTLER, who obtained her degree at the University of London, has taught in France in addition to Britain where she has held posts in schools, language centres and colleges of education. She was head of the Faculty of Modern Languages at Codsall Comprehensive School and is at present deputy headmistress of Highfields School, Wolverhampton, and an examiner in French at O-level. She is the author of *French for the Businessman II* (Interlang).

GCE O-Level Passbooks

GEOGRAPHY, R. Knowles, M.A.

ENGLISH LANGUAGE, Robert L. Wilson, M.A.

MODERN MATHEMATICS, A. J. Sly, B.A.

HISTORY (*Social and Economic*, 1815–1939), M. C. James, B.A.

CHEMISTRY, C. W. Lapham, M.Sc., A.R.I.C.

BIOLOGY, R. Whitaker, B.Sc. and J. M. Kelly, B.Sc., M.I.Biol.

PHYSICS, B. P. Brindle, B.Sc.

GCE O-Level Passbook

French

G. Butler, B.A.

Published by Intercontinental Book Productions
in conjunction with Seymour Press Ltd.
Distributed by Seymour Press Ltd.,
334 Brixton Road, London, SW9 7AG

Published 1976 by Intercontinental Book Productions, Berkshire House, Queen Street, Maidenhead, Berks., SL6 1NF in conjunction with Seymour Press Ltd.

1st edition, 1st impression 2.76.0
Copyright © 1976 Intercontinental Book Productions
Made and printed by C. Nicholls & Company Ltd
ISBN 0 85047 904 5

Contents

Introduction

During the years leading to a GCE O-level or CSE examination in French teachers aim to develop their pupils' skills of comprehension and their response to both the spoken and written forms of the language. A set syllabus, in terms of facts to be memorised, is not applicable to language examinations, but what *will* be tested by all examining boards is the candidate's ability to manipulate certain fundamental structures, and to employ the kind of vocabulary most commonly found in everyday speech in France.

The material in this book should be regarded as a point of reference during the course as well as a useful means of revision. The basic framework of the language is presented together with explanations (including short cuts where possible) and examples throughout. In certain grammatical sections will be found asterisks (**) indicating that the points following are more relevant to GCE O-level than to CSE examination requirements. Otherwise it is safe to assume that the information given is core material relevant to both kinds of examination.

After each chapter, as listed on the Contents page, is a self-test section. This will test whether the information given has been fully absorbed.

Thorough knowledge of the contents of this book will give you, the candidate, a secure foundation for the examination set by your particular board. However, it must be emphasised that good results cannot be achieved overnight. The key to examination success is steady application over a long period, with attention to detail from the beginning. In practice this means respect for such apparently bothersome trivia as **accuracy in spelling**, especially of common words like 'plusieurs', 'rencontrer', etc.; **noun genders**, which must be learned as part of each new noun; **accents**; **nouns** which appear **similar** to English ones like 'télévision', 'adresse', 'objet', etc.

Traditionally the British have indulged a reputation for being 'bad' at languages. However justified in nurturing this unenviable characteristic we may have felt in the glorious past, such linguistic isolation makes no sense in the modern world. Nowadays ease of travel and increased opportunities for all make 'foreign countries' much more accessible, and, more important, give them greater reality. We are all entitled to have our own language spoken in our own country – and we are justified in expecting foreign visitors to make some effort to speak it while they are here. The more fluid the channels of contact, the greater the need for meaningful communication, bringing with it better understanding of other people's ways of life and the abolition of wild preconceptions ('It's all garlic, frogs' legs, and snails'). This can only be fostered by meeting people in their own country and talking to them in their own language.

On a personal (and selfish) level, this kind of human exchange offers an experience to the visitor which is both more enjoyable and more rewarding. Also, it could well be that a qualification in French will one day be a desirable requirement for an interesting job. For instance, a scientist or a secretary who has such a qualification can usually command greater attention from prospective employers than one without.

Fortunately language-teaching these days places greater emphasis on oral communication, so that while hard work and application are nevertheless essential, a great deal of enjoyment and satisfaction can be obtained through using the language in active situations. Happily, too, examinations are beginning to reflect the newer styles of language teaching and the ability to communicate verbally is gradually being recognised as an extremely important aspect of learning French, along with the skills of comprehension. Indeed, for CSE candidates the examination emphasis lies on this side of language learning.

Finally, do try if at all possible to visit France, **not** on a day-trip to Calais, which will probably prove disappointing, but into a situation which is genuinely French, where no one panders to your own 'foreignness'. The best solution is to stay with a family. Remember that there is nothing quite as good for morale and future motivation as your own successful experience, no matter how limited, in managing to communicate with people in their own tongue.

Chapter 1
Articles

Of the three articles (**definite, indefinite**, and **partitive**) it is usually the partitive which causes English students the most problems. However each article has a number of idiomatic uses which differ from English usage.

The definite article

Its basic use is similar to that in English: = **the**: e.g. **le** robinet = **the** tap, **la** gorge = **the** throat; **les** robinets, **les** gorges in the plural forms.

The 'l'' form of the definite article is used for both masculine and feminine nouns **either** when the noun begins with a vowel, **or** begins with a **mute 'h'**. The full 'le' or 'la' form is used before a noun beginning with an **aspirate 'h'**; e.g. l'herbe = **the** grass, but **le** hibou = **the** owl.

When you meet a noun beginning with an 'h', you must make a point of learning if that 'h' is mute or not. This is part of the spelling of that word.

Mistakes are frequently made when the definite article is preceded by the prepositions 'à' and 'de'. You must take great care over this. Remember that: *à + le always contracts to 'au'*
à + les always contracts to 'aux'
de + le always contracts to 'du'
de + les always contracts to 'des'.

The following examples will illustrate the point:

Le monsieur a perdu ce parapluie? – Oui, c'est le parapluie **du** monsieur = Yes, it's the gentleman's umbrella.

Les filles ont perdu ces billets? – Oui, ce sont les billets **des** filles = Yes, they are the girls' tickets.

Le Maire, s'il vous plaît. Monsieur voudrait parler **au** Maire = The gentleman would like to speak to the mayor.

Les chanteurs, s'il vous plaît – Monsieur voudrait parler **aux** chanteurs = The gentleman would like to speak to the singers.

Note that before 'l'' there is **no** contraction of preposition and article. L'invité a perdu ces gants? – Oui, ce sont les gants **de** l'invité. L'hôtelier, s'il vous plaît. Monsieur voudrait parler **à** l'hôtelier = The gentleman would like to speak to the hotel-owner.

Idiomatic use of the definite article in French

Description of personal characteristics, including parts of the body

(1) With '**avoir**':

Elle a **les** cheveux blonds = She has fair hair. Il a **le** dos courbé = He has **a** stoop. As you can see the English usage either omits the article or has the indefinite article.

(2) With '**à**' in phrases often using the prepositions 'with', 'in' in English:

C'était un homme **au** nez pointu = He was a man **with a** pointed nose. La dame **au** chapeau extravagant = The lady **in the** fantastic hat.

(3) In **adverbial phrases** describing how someone is doing something: Il se promenait lentement, **les** mains dans les poches = He was walking along slowly, **with his** hands in his pockets. Incidentally you should also note how the definite article is also used here with 'poches' on the principle that he is hardly likely to be walking along with his hands in someone else's pockets! Thus a possessive adjective is unnecessary.

Marie regardait les fleurs, **l'**air absent = Mary was looking at the flowers, **with a** faraway look in her eyes.

Note that from the last example (and also the one with the fantastic hat!) it is not necessary that the personal description should be a permanent feature! You **never** translate 'with' in these cases.

(4) To denote **movement** of a **part of the body**:

Elle ouvrit **les** yeux = She opened **her** eyes. Il haussa **les** épaules = He shrugged **his** shoulders. This is really the same point as the one made above under (3): the definite article is used when the ownership (his eyes, etc.) is clear. But in cases like washing hands, faces, cleaning teeth or in any other expression where it is possible to do the action to another person, a **pronoun** is added to show whose hands are being washed or teeth cleaned.

Here are two examples to show this exactly:

Elle **se** lave les mains = She is washing **her** hands. Here a **reflexive** pronoun is used to show she is washing **her own** hands. Elle doit **lui** laver les mains tous les jours = She has to wash **his/her** hands every day. Here an **indirect object pronoun** is used to show she is washing **someone else's** hands.

*See also the section on **reflexive verbs**, page 65.*

In expressing prices for a stated quantity

Here again you should be thankful that in French there is only one possible construction, whereas in English there are several possibilities.

Dix francs **la** bouteille = Ten francs **a** bottle. Trois francs **les** cent grammes = Three francs **for** 100 grams. Les oeillets? Cinq francs **la** pièce = The carnations? Five francs **each**. (C'est cher!)

When giving someone's title or form of address

In English the title is given without any article. **Le** roi Louis Quatorze = King Louis the Fourteenth. Mon ami, **le** docteur Lebrun = My friend, Doctor Lebrun.

When making generalisations and before abstract nouns

Les singes aiment **les** bananes = Monkeys like bananas. **Le** bonheur est rare = Happiness is rare. **La** colère est une passion dangereuse = Anger is a dangerous passion.

In these cases it is considered that any monkey is likely to be fond of any banana he comes across, that happiness and anger as abstract ideas have the particular quality mentioned and so on.

Before names of countries

La Belgique est un pays où l'on parle français = Belgium is a country where French is spoken. Mon beau-frère connaît bien **le** Japon = My brother-in-law knows Japan well.

However **no** article is used with names of **feminine countries** after the prepositions **en** and **de**, which are used to express the idea of 'going to' (en) or 'coming from' (de) one of these countries.

Il est arrivé **d'**Allemagne et il s'en va demain **en** Espagne = He arrived from Germany and is going off tomorrow to Spain.

*See also chapter 16, **Use of Prepositions**, page 135.*

Miscellaneous uses

These phrases must simply be acquired through practice.

La semaine dernière = last week; **l'**année prochaine = next year; vers **le** soir = towards evening; avez-vous **le** temps de = have you time (to do something)? Incidentally, avez-vous l'heure? = have you got the time (by the clock)? **Le** lundi = on Mondays (as a regular thing); **le** matin = in the mornings (regularly). J'apprends **le** français = I learn French; arriver **le** premier = to arrive first; partir **le** dernier = to leave last.

The indefinite article

Its basic use is of course similar to that in English: = **a** (**some** in the plural); e.g. **un** manteau = **a** coat (or perhaps **one** coat as a number); **une** jupe = **a** skirt (also **one** skirt).

The **plural of the indefinite article** is the form '**des**': e.g. un appareil, **des** appareils = a camera, **some** cameras (also **cameras**); une abeille, **des** abeilles = a bee, **some** bees (also **bees**).

Idiomatic use of the indefinite article in French

Here the situation is that French frequently **omits the indefinite article** which is present in English. Typical cases are the following:

When stating someone's trade, profession or nationality
Il **est avocat** = He is **a** lawyer. Mon père est **devenu député** = My father became **an** M.P. Cette dame-là **est anglaise** = That lady is **an** Englishwoman.

You should note that the article **is included** in phrases which begin 'c'est', or 'c'était', etc., where the idea is rather more that of a definition, than a simple fact stated about someone.
Monsieur Dufour? C'est **un** avocat = Mr Dufour? He's **a** lawyer (and not, for instance, a doctor or a teacher).

See also the section on '**Ce**' *v.* '**Il**', *page 43.*

Before 'cent', 'mille' and after 'quel!'
It is very tempting to add the indefinite article in French as you would do in English, but it is such a favourite grammatical point for examiners to pick on that you really should be able to avoid making it if you keep your wits about you!
Cent fois = **A** hundred times. Mille excuses = **A** thousand excuses. **Quel** imbécile! = What **a** fool!

Before nouns in apposition
Although that sounds an alarming phrase, a noun in apposition is merely one which explains or defines another immediately preceding it in the sentence.
Nous avons visité **Tokyo, capitale** du Japon = We visited Tokyo, **the** capital of Japan. Le coupable était **Monsieur Dur, ancien épicier** = The guilty party was Mr Dur, **a** former grocer.

After 'ni . . . ni' (= 'neither . . . nor')

Il n'a mangé **ni** pomme **ni** pêche = He ate **neither an** apple **nor a** pear. Je n'ai **ni** voiture **ni** moto = I have **neither a** car **nor a** motor-bike.

See also chapter 15, **Negatives,** *page 130.*

The partitive article

One of the principal translations in English of the French partitive article is '**some**', not in the sense of 'more than one', but in that of 'a certain quantity' of a stated noun. But as we have already noticed, the article is often omitted in English and you must take great care to recognise the occasions in French which will demand the partitive article. Look at the following example: Il a demandé **du** pain et **du** fromage = He asked for bread and cheese. If you stop to ask yourself, of course he only wanted 'some', but in English it is more often than not taken for granted and omitted. The occasions on which you will not require an article are so few in French that you should always check that you have an excellent reason (good enough for the examiner!) if you find yourself omitting it before any noun you write. Generally speaking, **nouns need articles** – the choice of which particular article will be a matter for your judgement and (hopefully) your experience.

The form of the partitive article is exactly the same as the form of the preposition '**de**' + **definite article** combination mentioned earlier (page 9). That is to say '**du**', '**de la**', '**de l'**', or '**des**'. Common sense should tell you when you come across this form whether in the context the English meaning is 'of the' or 'some'. Here are some examples of the partitive article in use.

Je voudrais **du** pain, **des** fruits, et **de l'**eau minérale, s'il vous plaît = I would like some bread, fruit and mineral water, please. Le samedi elle achetait toujours **de la** crème fraîche et **des** oeufs au marché = On Saturdays she always bought fresh cream and eggs at the market.

There are **three** principal circumstances in which the partitive article (whether you expect it to be 'du', 'de la', 'de l'', or 'des') **is reduced to 'de' or 'd'' alone**. These are:

(a) **in expressions of quantity**, where fortunately the Englisl is often very similar. Cinq cents grammes **de** beurre = Five hundred grams (a pound) **of** butter. Un pacquet **de** biscuits = A packet **of** biscuits. Here it should be quite obvious what is required.

13

There are many set phrases of quantity which should be learned so that they become second nature. They are **always** met in this form: beaucoup de ..., trop de ..., plus de ..., moins de ..., combien de ..., peu de ..., e.g. très **peu de** gens apprennent l'arabe en Angleterre = very **few** people learn Arabic in England. **Combien d'**animaux se sont échappés du zoo? = **How many** animals escaped from the zoo?

In this last example you are reminded of the 'd'' form, which must occur before a vowel or a mute 'h'.

Exception: the expression '**la plupart**' = the most, the biggest part always has the **full partitive** article following. La plupart **des** milliardaires ne sont pas heureux = **Most** millionaires are not happy. La plupart **du** temps il ne faisait strictement rien = **Most of the** time he did absolutely nothing.

'**Bien des**' = **many** (a moderately colloquial expression) is also an exception in this same way. **Bien des** gens ont peur de l'avenir = **Many** people fear the future. (Et vous?)

(b) **following a negative expression** ('ne ... pas', 'ne ... jamais', 'ne ... plus') Il ne vend jamais **de** pommes = He never sells apples. Mais il vend toujours **des** fruits exotiques! = But he always sells exotic fruits! (In this case there is a normal partitive article.)
Il n'y a plus **de** confiture, mais il y a du miel, si vous en voulez = There is no more jam, but there is some honey, if you would like some.

Something frequently forgotten is that this also occurs when the idea of 'a' or 'an' is preceded by a negative. Il n'a pas **de** vélo = He hasn't got **a** bike.

The one important exception to the negative rule concerns the expression '**ne ... que**' (= only), when partitives are quite normal: Je n'achète que **des** livres d'occasion = I only buy second-hand books. It is suggested that this negative is not really a genuine case and for this reason it breaks the rules!

(c) '**de**' is used (not 'des') when an adjective whose position is normally in front of the noun is in the plural form: Il m'a apporté **des** fleurs, **de** très jolies fleurs = He brought me **some** flowers, **some** very pretty flowers. J'ai **de** bons gâteaux = I have **some** good cakes.

14

Test section

(i) First **write down from memory those commonly mis-spelt words** mentioned on page 7.

(ii) Cover the right-hand side of the following pages while you work out your answers. Decide which is **the correct form of the article** to fit in the following sentences. Remember that just occasionally there may be no need for any article.

1. Le voleur était un petit homme — yeux perçants.
   Le voleur était un petit homme aux yeux perçants.

2. Les roses sont 2 francs — pièce.
   Les roses sont 2 francs la pièce.

3. Tu as pris le chapeau — monsieur?
   Tu as pris le chapeau du monsieur?

4. C'était une route bordée — arbres.
   C'était une route bordée d'arbres.

5. M Duchesne? Il est — professeur.
   M Duchesne? Il est professeur.

6. — France est un beau pays.
   La France est un beau pays.

7. Mon frère détestait — chocolat.
   Mon frère détestait le chocolat.

8. Tu connais l'adresse — homme là-bas?
   Tu connais l'adresse de l'homme là-bas?

9. Cette dame ravissante, c'est — Française, non?
   Cette dame ravissante, c'est une Française, non?

10. Mon père a téléphoné — médecin.
    Mon père a téléphoné au médecin.

11. La victime s'est tourné — tête.
    La victime s'est tourné la tête.

12. Taisez-vous! Il y a trop — bruit.
    Taisez-vous! Il y a trop de bruit.

13. La plupart — élèves sont bêtes comme chou!
    La plupart des élèves sont bêtes comme chou!

14. Donnez-moi un litre — vin, s'il vous plaît.
    Donnez-moi un litre de vin, s'il vous plaît.

15. C'est un homme qui a beaucoup — énergie.
    C'est un homme qui a beaucoup d'énergie.

16. Je n'ai jamais bu — champagne.
    Je n'ai jamais bu de champagne.

17. — éléphants — Afrique ont — grandes oreilles.
    Les éléphants d'Afrique ont de grandes oreilles.

Chapter 2
Nouns

It has already been mentioned that new nouns must be learned with the appropriate gender. This will save a lot of problems later. Nonetheless, whereas logic is certainly no great help in determining gender, and there are always exceptions for any rules you might formulate, some guidelines do exist which relate to those noun endings which are typically masculine or feminine.

Characteristic **masculine** endings are:
– ment; – oir; – eau (2-syllable words); – age (2-syllable words); – ège; – acle; – ou.

Characteristic **feminine** endings are:
– (t)ion; – té (tié) (abstract nouns); – ance; – ence; – ée; – esse.

Some nouns obviously have both masculine and feminine forms. For instance:

–ier	(un fermier);	–ière	(une fermière);
–eur	(un acteur);	–rice	(une actrice);
	(un flatteur);	–euse	(une flatteuse);
–an	(un paysan);	–anne	(une paysanne).

These forms tend to relate closely to trades or professions and a few animal species. In these cases, when meeting a new word in the masculine form you will be able to give the feminine.

Plural

Nouns which already end in –s, –x, or –z do not add the usual **s**; le nez, les nez; le prix, les prix.

Those nouns which end in –eau or –eu add **x** in the plural: le rideau, les rideaux; le jeu, les jeux.

Nouns ending in –ou tend to add **s** in the same way as ordinary examples, but there is a list of 'old favourites' which add an **x** to form the plural. They are le bijou (les bijoux), le caillou (les cailloux), le chou, le genou, le hibou, le joujou.

Compound nouns made up of two or more words need extra care in the plural form.

(1) The very common ones which are really an adjective and a noun, or two nouns together must add plural endings to both parts:

e.g.   le grand-père   (les grands-pères);
        le chou-fleur   (les choux-fleurs).

(2) Words such as the following, where there is one basic idea which has an additional descriptive word merely make the basic noun plural:

e.g.   un sac **à main** = a
        hand-bag   (des sacs à main);
        une robe **du soir** = an
        evening dress   (des robes du soir).

(3) Compound nouns where the first element describes the use made of the second generally remain unchanged in the plural:

e.g.   un porte-clefs   = a key-ring. i.e. for carrying keys
                          (des porte-clefs);
        un coupe-papier   = a paper-knife, i.e. for cutting paper (des coupe-papier).

However with all nouns which are not strictly 'normal' you are advised to make sure of the plural when you first meet them.

(4) **Proper names**

The French do not add anything to a family name in the same way as we do in English:

e.g.   the Smiths   = les Smith;
        the Duponts   = les Dupont.

(5) You should make a special note of the plural of Mademoiselle, Madame, and Monsieur. You are likely to hear these for instance at the start of a formal speech: 'Mesdames, Mesdemoiselles, Messieurs...'

Test section

(i) Cover the right-hand side of the page while you work out your answers. **Which gender** would you guess would be correct for the following French nouns?

destination		**la** destination
voleur		**le** voleur
méchanceté	(wickedness, nastiness)	**la** méchanceté
parlement	(Parliament)	**le** parlement

ivresse	(drunkenness)	**l'**ivresse (f)
courage		**le** courage
entonnoir	(funnel)	**l'**entonnoir (m)
privilège		**le** privilège
prudence		**la** prudence

(ii) **What would be the likely feminine forms** of these masculine nouns?

un infirmier	(a male nurse)	une infirm**ière**
un patron	(a boss)	une patr**onne**
un promoteur	(a promoter)	une promot**rice**
un chanteur	(a singer)	une chant**euse**
un cochon	(a pig)	une truie (well, you can't expect miracles!)

(iii) **What would be the likely plural** forms of these phrases?

le vieux bois	les **vieux bois**
le hibou est fou	les **hiboux** sont **fous**
un cheval intelligent	des **chevaux intelligents**
un pourboire	des **pourboires**
le beau-père	les **beaux-pères**
un ver à soie (a silkworm)	les **vers** à soie
un essuie-mains (a hand towel)	des **essuie-mains**
un travail difficile	des **travaux difficiles**
un bijou exotique	des **bijoux exotiques**
le premier prix	les **premiers prix**
le nouveau pneu (the new tyre)	les **nouveaux pneus**
un monsieur mou! (a feeble man)	des **messieurs mous**!
un chapeau bleu	des **chapeaux bleus**
chez Lebrun	chez les **Lebrun**

Chapter 3
Adjectives

The first golden rule is that **adjectives must agree in number and gender** with the noun or pronoun they describe, wherever they are placed. If one adjective refers to both masculine and feminine nouns, the **masculine plural** form is always used. E.g. Jean et ses trois soeurs sont toujours **prêts** à tout (ready for anything).

The importance of being aware of the unusual position of adjectives in certain long and complex sentences is illustrated by the two sentences which follow:

Malheureuse, car un autobus venait d'écraser son chien, **la jeune fille** s'enferma dans sa chambre.

Je regrette, mais **les enfants** dont vous m'avez parlé en termes si chaleureux, ne sont vraiment pas **innocents** du crime.

Here you can see that the adjective in each sentence is very far removed from its noun.

See also the section on **dictation**, *page 186.*

The basic form of an adjective, as listed in a dictionary, is always the masculine singular. **For the feminine singular form** the basic rule is to add –e to the masculine form. But:

(1) Those already ending in an –e remain the same, e.g. malad**e** (ill), although those ending in –é add the normal extra **e**, e.g. fatigué, fatigu**ée**.

(2) Those ending in –er change to –**ère**, e.g. cher, ch**ère**; fier, fi**ère** (proud).

(3) –f becomes –**ve**: vif, vi**ve**; bref, br**ève**.

(4) –x becomes –**se**: heureux, heur**euse**; jaloux, jal**ouse** (jealous).

(5) –el, –eil, –il, –en, –on, –et endings all double the consonant for the feminine: cruel, cru**elle**; gentil, gent**ille**; bon, b**onne**; muet, mu**ette** (dumb).

(6) –s becomes –sse, except where the masculine form is the past participle: gros, gr**osse**; las, l**asse** (tired).

(7) Here are a list of independent feminine forms, which you will have to learn separately:

long (longue);
blanc (blanche);
faux (fausse);
favori (favorite);

sec (sèche);
doux (douce);
frais (fraîche);
fou (folle);

roux (rousse) (= red-haired);　　　　*beau (belle);
*nouveau (nouvelle);　　　　　　　　*vieux (vieille).

The adjectives preceded by an asterisk * are specially to be noted since they have two masculine singular forms, the second one ('bel', 'nouvel', and 'vieil') being used before nouns beginning with a vowel or mute 'h'.

E.g. un **bel** homme　　　　　but l'homme est beau;
son nouv**el** album　　　　　but l'album est nouveau;
le vi**eil** artiste　　　　　　but l'artiste est vieux.

For the feminine plural forms you merely have to add an –s.
For the masculine plural forms you usually add an –s, but as with the plurals of nouns, one or two cases require a plural –x form. These coincide exactly with the rules for nouns, and so we get –eau becoming –**eaux** (beau, beaux); –al becoming –**aux** (loyal, loyaux); and adjectives already ending in –s, or –x remaining the same.

Position of adjectives

Usually in French adjectives are placed after the noun – the opposite from English. So you must get used to the idea of saying:

　un imperméable **gris** = a grey raincoat;
　un vin **français** = a French wine.

It is usual to think of these adjectives as **distinguishing** this noun from another. In the examples quoted above the idea is of a **grey** raincoat, not a blue one, a **French** wine, not a Spanish one.

There are, however, some very common adjectives which **always** precede the noun. These are:

beau	grand	jeune	mauvais
bon	gros	joli	petit
gentil	haut	long	vieux

Occasionally you may see an adjective preceding the noun, when you would expect to find it in the normal following position. There are two possible reasons for this.

(1) If the adjective merely emphasises characteristics you would expect of the noun, so that you take the quality for granted: e.g. un savant professeur = a learned professor or une charmante Anglaise = a charming English girl (but of course!).

20

(2) If the adjective in no way adds to the impression given by the noun already: e.g. cet affreux spectacle = this dreadful sight (referring to a battle-scene or road accident, in which case the scene is unlikely to be anything other than dreadful).

Adjectives whose meaning varies according to their position

You must be quite sure of these as they crop up very frequently.
un **ancien** élève = a **former** pupil; une ville ancienne = a **very old** town;
mon **cher** Pierre = dear Peter; une montre très **chère** = a **very dear** (expensive) watch.

Other examples are **grand**: before the noun = great, important, after the noun = big in size; **pauvre**: before the noun = poor (to be pitied), after the noun = poor (no money); **propre**: before the noun = own, after the noun = clean; **même**: before the noun = same, after the noun = very (actual); **nouveau**: before the noun = new (not old), after the noun = novel (original).

You will notice that when these adjectives come after the noun they do have the literal meaning, so that in this sense they conform exactly to the point mentioned earlier, that adjectives following the noun **distinguish** it from some other.

Two other adjectives in constant use whose sense varies with their position are 'prochain' and 'dernier'. When these are **after** the noun you are seeing things very much from the point of view of the present time and referring to 'next week' or 'last year': e.g. la semaine **prochaine**; l'année **dernière**.

When put in front they simply mean 'the next' or 'the last' in a sequence: e.g. la **prochaine** fois je l'aurai!; le **dernier** jour du trimestre.

Where a noun has more than one adjective you generally keep to the normal order for each: e.g. un joli petit jardin = a pretty little garden; une vieille église belge = an old Belgian church; des rues étroites et tortueuses = narrow, winding streets. You can see from this last example how two adjectives following the noun are usually connected by 'et'; they can be considered as two ideas which reinforce each other.

Test section

(i) Cover the right-hand side of the page while you work out your answers. Remember that the adjective form given will always be masculine singular, as in a dictionary. In each instance **give both the correct form and the correct position** in relation to the noun.

dernier (= last)	le mois	**le mois dernier**
intéressant	une discussion	**une discussion intéressante**
travailleur	un garçon et une fille	**un garçon et une fille travailleurs**
cher (= expensive)	une robe	**une robe chère**
long	une route	**une longue route**
doux	une nature	**une nature douce**
vieux	un aristocrate	**un vieil aristocrate**
propre (= clean)	une nappe	**une nappe propre**
sage	une petite fille	**une petite fille sage**
ancien (= former)	une vedette (film star)	**une ancienne vedette**
frais	la crème	**la crème fraîche**
nouveau	une histoire	**une nouvelle histoire**
rose (= pink)	des éléphants	**des éléphants roses**
ancien (= old) historique	une église	**une église ancienne et historique**
pauvre (= penniless)	des gens	**des gens pauvres**
dernier (= the last)	la fois	**la dernière fois**

(ii) Now try the test the other way round, by looking at the answers on the right-hand side and **translating their meaning into English**.

(iii) **What difference in meaning** would there have been if you had placed the adjective wrongly in the examples where the position changes the meaning? Give the English meaning for these phrases.

le dernier mois	**the last month** (that I was there . . .)
une chère robe	**an affectionate (?) dress!**
ma propre nappe	**my own tablecloth**
une vedette ancienne	**an ancient filmstar**
une ancienne église	**a former church**
de pauvres gens	**poor (pitiable) people**
la fois dernière	**last time** (compared with **this**)

Chapter 4
Pronouns

Subject pronouns

It should only be necessary to remind you of one or two features of **subject pronouns. First the forms**:

je	nous	il	elle	ils	elles (used as in English)
(I)	(we)	(he)	(she)	(they)	(they)

Remember that in French **all** nouns have a gender, so that 'il', 'elle', 'ils', 'elles' can just as easily refer to inanimate objects as to people, e.g. Voilà ma nouvelle robe. **Elle** est belle.

Remember also that 'il' can be completely impersonal (= it), e.g. il pleut = it's raining. *See also chapter 5, '**Ce**' v. '**Il**', page 43.*

The remaining **subject pronouns** (that is, governing the verb) are 'tu' and 'vous' (you), and 'on'.

On does have the direct equivalent (= one), but as 'one' well knows, 'one' does not always choose to use this form in English, often preferring 'they', 'people' or 'we' used without any precise personal reference.

Tu/vous Most candidates know in theory where the 'tu' form is used and where the 'vous', but frequently appear to forget (often in mid-sentence), particularly when a subsequent subject pronoun or a corresponding possessive adjective or pronoun is needed. This is one of the principal pitfalls in letter-writing and in translating from English to French (there are of course many others) and you **must** make very sure you stick to the same form throughout. Even if the pronoun you choose in the first place is wrong it is better to be consistent about it, otherwise you merely give an impression of not knowing anything very thoroughly.

Résumé of the 'tu' and 'vous' situations

'Tu' can only be addressed to **one person**.

That one person is likely to be: a close relative;
a close friend;
a child;
a fellow pupil or student or fellow worker;
an animal.

'Vous' can be addressed to **either one person or several people**. As a plural, it is therefore the plural form of 'tu', as well as the plural form of 'vous' singular.

'Vous' is the normal polite form of address, and should be used in all circumstances other than those mentioned above. Remember that you will never give offence if you use the 'vous' form, where it would have been appropriate to use the 'tu' form, but you might do so if you are too liberal with your 'tu'!

Object pronouns

Object pronouns seem to be a very common victim of error, but this is really quite unnecessary.

Error no. 1 concerns the **position** of object pronouns. This should give very little trouble if you remember the usual rule that **object pronouns precede the verb**. English is the other way round.
E.g. Je l'ai tué avec un marteau = I killed **him** with a hammer.
François, ne **lui** a-t-il pas offert un cadeau? = Didn't François give **him** a present?
These two examples show that where the verb form has two parts (an auxiliary verb and past participle) the rule still holds good – pronouns **immediately** precede the verb.

N.B. Only when object pronouns are used with a **positive command** (e.g. eat it! give it to them!) is the order ever varied. **In this case only the pronouns follow the verb**, and are **joined** to the verb **by hyphens**.
E.g. mange-le! donne-le-leur!

Error no. 2 concerns the **choice** of object pronouns.

le (l')		
la (l')	are **direct object pronouns only** =	him, it / her, it / them
les		

E.g. Je connais Henri, je **le** verrai demain = I know Henry, I shall see **him** tomorrow.

lui	are **indirect object pronouns only** =	to him, to it / to her / to them
leur		

E.g. Catherine est malade? Mais je **lui** ai parlé ce matin même = Catherine is ill? But I spoke **to her** this very morning.

me (m')		
te (t')	can be both **direct and indirect**	me, to me / you, to you / us, to us / you, to you
nous	**object pronouns**	
vous		

24

E.g.   **Vous** aime-t-il à la folie?   = Does he love **you** madly?

Il **m**'écrit tous les jours   = He writes **to me** every day.

N.B. In the positive command form, 'me' and 'te' (following the verb) have the forms 'moi', 'toi', e.g. Ecris-**moi** bientôt = Write to me soon.

Question: Why should you be especially on your guard when using pronouns with the following verbs: (1) écrire, montrer, dire, donner, envoyer, offrir, téléphoner, prêter; (2) regarder, écouter, attendre, payer, chercher?

Answer: Because their English form is often misleading. Consider these English examples:

(1) John sent **me** a parcel.   Grandma gave **her** a sweet.

We told **them** the truth.   They telephoned **us** this afternoon.

Things are not as they seem! These sentences do **not** have two direct object pronouns as might appear the case – the words in **bold** type are **indirect** object pronouns (= to me, to them, to her, to us) and so you must be particularly careful to use the correct **indirect object pronoun** in French.

(2) He looked **at her** for a long time.

We were listening **to them** attentively.

You must wait **for her** every day at the bus-stop.

Again appearances are deceptive! These verbs offer the reverse of the problem in (1): namely, they have a preposition built into them in English which leads the unwary into thinking an indirect object is required in French. **All these verbs take a *direct object* (noun or pronoun): *never* translate the preposition.**

N.B. Think about the French form of the sentences given above. They will appear in the test section, so be prepared!

Y

This pronoun (which incidentally counts as a vowel) generally means 'there', and can stand instead of a large number of expressions of place, from the simple 'à + place name' to more varied forms 'en ville', 'devant le cinéma', 'sous le lit', etc. All the normal rules on positions of pronouns apply.

E.g. Le Président a une villa **à la campagne**. Il **y** va le vendredi. Comment est-elle allée **en ville**? Elle **y** est allée en voiture. Tu vois ce sac? Les cambrioleurs (= burglars) **y** ont caché leurs affaires.

'Y' is also used with verbs where there is the built-in preposition 'à' as part of a phrase. (In these cases there is no question of 'y' having any meaning of 'there'.) Such verbs are:

penser à = to think about; s'intéresser à = to be interested in; se fier à = to trust in; croire à = to believe in.

E.g. Vous intéressez-vous **à la peinture**? Non, je ne m'**y** intéresse pas. Monsieur Bruyère, pense-t-il toujours **à son bateau disparu**? Oui, il **y** pense tout le temps.

N.B. It is just as important to be aware of this usage for translation from French to English, as for use the other way round. Get used to noting further examples in your work, and to avoiding trying to extract a meaningless literal translation into English. **Idioms should be accepted just as they are.**

En

This pronoun often proves much too versatile for many candidates, who find both the translation of it into English and its uses in French rather baffling. Again, there is no insurmountable reason for this. 'En' is principally used in phrases expressing a quantity, a number, a weight, and stands instead of 'un' or 'une' + noun, 'de' etc. + noun. The examples given below will give you an idea of some of the different English meanings of 'en'.

Vous avez **du beurre**, Madame? Oui, j'**en** ai, Monsieur.	(= some)
Et **de la crème**? Non, je n'**en** ai pas.	(= any)
Mon voisin m'**en** a parlé hier.	(= about it, them)
Il vous faut **de l'argent**? J'**en** ai beaucoup!	(= (lots) of it!)
Ce chanteur avait fait trop **de disques**. On **en** a oublié la moitié.	(= of them)

Seen in this light, it is obviously the English which is the bigger nuisance! And as you will see, in many of these examples it is often unnecessary to translate 'en' at all. However you **must** remember that when **any** expression of quantity is implied, 'en' must be supplied to replace the original noun phrase. Be particularly careful with such simple forms as the following:

Vous avez **un frère**? Oui, j'**en** ai trois = I've got three ('of them' being understood).

Vous cherchez **une place?** **En** voici une! = Here's one (of them).

Le patron n'a plus **d'argent? En** voici! = Here's some (of it).

N.B. (1) Where a **number** is mentioned, this number must be retained also, together with 'en'. (See the example above: **j'en ai trois**.) (2) This also applies where 'un', 'une' is used in a numerical sense. (See the example above: **en voici une**.)

The second main use of 'en' is exactly parallel to the second use of 'y' mentioned above. 'En' is used with verbs where there is the built-in preposition 'de' forming part of the verbal phrase. (In these cases there is not necessarily any question of 'en' having one of its normal meanings.) Such verbs are:

se servir de = to use;   avoir besoin de = to need;
se souvenir de = to remember;   s'apercevoir de = to notice;
jouer de = to play an instrument;   sortir de = to go out of.

E.g. Hélas! Il s'**en** est aperçu trop tard = He noticed **it** too late.
C'est un instrument dangereux. Ne vous **en** servez pas! Il entra
dans le château et **en** ressortit dix minutes plus tard. Le jour de
notre mariage? Je ne m'**en** souviens plus! = I don't remember (**it**)
any more.

Idiomatic uses of 'y' and 'en'

These are many and various, and must be taken as they are without
too great an attempt to dissect them. One point which you **must**
adhere to however is that if you choose to use these (or any other
idioms) in your own essay work, they must be **100 per cent
accurate**. You will gain no credit for an approximation of a phrase
or idiom. On the other hand, correct usage of such phrases **will**
earn you credit. So here are a sprinkling of the more common
idioms using these two pronouns for you to mull over:

Je n'en peux plus! = I can't stand it any more!
Il m'en veut = He bears me a grudge.
Ne vous en faites pas! = Don't get worked up about it!
Je n'en sais rien, moi! = *I* don't know anything about it!
Il en a fait de belles! = He's really been up to his tricks!
Je m'en fiche (pas mal)! = I don't care (a damn)!
Ca y est! = That's it!
Il y va de ... = ... is (are) at stake.
Vas-y (or Allez-y)! = Go on! Come on there! (encouraging)
Je m'y connais en (musique) = I know a lot about (music).

Position of two or more pronouns together

Whichever pronouns occur together the order is as follows:

me				
te	le	lui		
se	la	leur	y	en
nous				
vous				

E.g. **Vous** l'a-t-il rendu?   = Did he give it back to you?
      Il **lui en** a parlé hier   = He spoke to him (her) about it yesterday.

N.B. Where in a positive command the direct object pronoun (**le,
la** or **les**) occurs with the indirect pronouns **me, te, se, nous,** or
vous, the order is reversed, and 'me' will take the form '**moi**':
e.g. Donnez-**les-moi**! = Give them to me!
But all other combinations of pronouns remain the same:

e.g. Donnez-**m'en**! = Give me some of it (of them)!
Only the first two columns above **ever** alter their order.

Position of pronouns where there are two verbs together

Where a second verb (**always** in the infinitive) is dependent on another verb, you must be careful to place any pronouns **before** the verb to which they **logically** belong. In the vast majority of cases this will be **before the verb in the infinitive.**

E.g. J'ai essayé de **l'appeler** mais en vain = I tried **to call him** (her) but in vain.

Ils ne voulaient pas **y aller**, mais ils ont dû **le faire** = They didn't want **to go there**, but they had **to do it**.

Viendront-ils **vous chercher**? = Will they come **to fetch you**?

The pronouns in bold type above **must** all depend on the following infinitive for their sense, and so must precede it.

Stressed or disjunctive pronouns

These pronouns are also known as emphatic pronouns and in many cases this is just what they are. Even by just saying them aloud you will notice what a forceful syllable each one is.

moi (I, me)   lui (he, him)   nous (we, us)   eux (they, them)
toi (you)   elle (she, her)   vous (you)   elles (they, them)
soi (one)

The following examples illustrate the emphatic pronoun in use:
(1) C'est **toi** qui as fait cela? = **You** did that?
(2) Qui est complètement fou? **Lui**! = Who's totally mad? **He is**!
(3) Sylvie est beaucoup plus jeune **qu'elle** = Sylvie is much younger than she is.

The first two examples bring up the point that in French you cannot, as in English, give extra emphasis to the personal pronoun by underlining the written form, or by stressing the spoken form (**I, he,** etc.). This must be rendered in French by the **addition** of the emphatic pronoun form. A very simple but common example is the phrase '**I** don't know!' which must be 'Je ne sais pas, **moi**!'.

Thus the main uses of the stressed pronoun, following the examples above, are:
(1) after 'c'est', 'c'était', etc. with a relative clause following, as a means of emphasising the personal subject pronoun;
(2) for additional emphasis to the subject pronoun at the start or end of a sentence **or** as a one-word answer to a question;

(3) as the second half of a comparison.

Other uses are:
(4) after prepositions: e.g. Sans **lui** je ne saurais vivre = I couldn't live without him!
In this context it is useful to remember that the stressed pronoun after the preposition 'à' and the verb 'être' can indicate possession: e.g. A qui sont tous ces livres? Ils sont **à moi** = . . . They're mine.
(5) combined with another pronoun or noun as a double subject to a verb: e.g. **Lui et moi** sommes de bons amis = He and I are good friends;
Je vous ai vus chez Pierre, ton ami et **toi** = . . . you and your friend;
(6) with the addition of '-même' (= self) to be the equivalent of the English 'myself', etc.: e.g. **Moi-même** je ne l'aurais pas fait comme cela = Personally I wouldn't have done it like that;.
(7) with verbs of motion and the prepositions 'à' and 'vers': e.g. Il courut vers **elle**. Sans hésiter je suis allé directement à **lui**. N.B. 'courir' and 'aller' **cannot** take an indirect object pronoun.
(8) in fairly rare cases to replace the indirect object pronoun in situations where there would otherwise be two pronouns, **both** referring to people, before the verb. The two main instances of this are with the verbs 'se présenter à' (= to introduce) and 'se fier à' (= to trust, have confidence in).
E.g. Il m'a présenté **à elle** l'autre soir (**not** 'me lui').
Je suis incapable de me fier **à eux** (**not** 'me leur').

Soi Again 'one' meets 'one'. In most cases where the context refers to a specific person, it is preferable to use the 'lui' or 'elle' form, and 'soi' is therefore mostly encountered in set expressions and proverbial phrases: e.g. Chacun pour **soi** = Every man for himself. On est toujours content de rentrer chez **soi** = You're always happy to come home.

Test section

(i) **Replace the words in bold type with the correct pronoun.**

Qui a cherché **le chat**?	**Qui l'a cherché?**
Ils ont envoyé **un paquet** en France.	**Ils en ont envoyé un en France.**
(Now add 'me' to that sentence)	**Ils m'en ont envoyé un en France.**
Pourquoi ne réponds-tu jamais **au prof**?	**Pourquoi ne lui réponds-tu jamais?**
Combien **de fromage** avez-vous acheté?	**Combien en avez-vous acheté?**

Ils ont laissé **le camion devant la mairie.**	**Ils l'y ont laissé.**
Aurait-il dû envoyer **des fleurs**?	**Aurait-il dû en envoyer?**
C'est **Joséphine** qui ne viendra pas.	**C'est elle qui ne viendra pas.**
Quand s'occupera-t-il **de Pierre**?	**Quand s'occupera-t-il de lui?**
Il pensait **à la guerre**.	**Il y pensait.**
Robert écoutait **ses disques**.	**Robert les écoutait.**
Etes-vous jamais allé **en Afrique**?	**Y êtes-vous jamais alle?**
Il ne s'est pas aperçu **du danger**.	**Il ne s'en est pas aperçu.**
Je suis plus intelligent que **Marie et Suzanne**.	**Je suis plus intelligent qu'elles.**
Henri et Philippe, ils refusaient d'obéir **au chef**.	**Eux, ils refusaient de lui obéir.**

(ii) Make these phrases into commands.

Tu te rappelles?	**Rappelle*-toi!** (*Remember, no 's')
Vous ne vous levez pas.	**Ne vous levez pas!**
Vous ne lui parlez pas.	**Ne lui parlez pas!**
Tu m'en donnes.	**Donne m'en!**
Tu me les offres.	**Offre-les-moi!**
Vous y allez.	**Allez-y!**

(iii) These are to be translated into French.

John sent me a parcel.	**Jean m'a envoyé un paquet.**
We told them the truth (la vérité).	**Nous leur avons dit la vérité.**
Grandma gave her a sweet.	**Grand'mère lui a donné un bonbon.**
They telephoned us this afternoon.	**Ils nous ont téléphone cet après-midi.**
He looked at her for a long time.	**Il l'a regardée* longtemps.**
We were listening to them attentively (attentivement).	**Nous les écoutions attentivement.**
You must wait for her every day at the bus-stop.	**Vous devez l'attendre tous les jours à l'arrêt d'autobus.**
Telephone the police!	**Téléphonez à la police!**

Pay for it at once!	**Payez-le tout de suite!**
She will lend John the book.	**Elle prêtera le livre à Jean.**
Why didn't you look for him yesterday?	**Pourquoi ne l'avez-vous pas cherché hier?**

*(*regardée) See section on preceding direct object agreement, page 64.*

Possessive adjectives and pronouns

As with all other adjectives and pronouns, possessive adjectives and pronouns must **agree** with the noun. Candidates sometimes seem to be confused about **which** noun is the one in question, but the agreement is **always with the object possessed.** It never has anything to do with the possessor.

The **possessive adjectives** are shown in the table below.

	masculine	feminine	any plural
my	mon	ma*	mes
your	ton	ta*	tes
his, her, its	son	sa*	ses
our	notre	notre	nos
your	votre	votre	vos
their	leur	leur	leurs

(1) In the **feminine singular** the asterisk* should warn you to beware. Because these forms end in a vowel, they are **not used** before nouns themselves beginning with a vowel, or mute 'h'. So for these cases alone, you use the corresponding **masculine singular** form:
e.g. une histoire becomes **mon** histoire.
une orange et une pomme becomes **mon** orange et **ma** pomme.
(2) Do not forget that you must **always repeat** the possessive adjective with **each noun**, even if the form required is the same:
e.g. J'ai perdu **mon** stylo et **mon** porte-feuille = I have lost my pen and wallet.
(3) One small point is the usage in French of the possessive adjective in the following expressions:

Bonjour, **mes** enfants! = Hallo, children!
Bonjour, **mon** oncle! = Hallo, uncle!
A vos ordres, **mon** colonel! = At your command, Colonel!

Remember the French do **not** generally use the possessive adjective in situations involving a perfectly obvious movement of a part of your own body.

See the earlier section on use of the definite article, page 9.

The possessive pronoun forms are shown in the table below.
Referring to a **singular noun possessed**:

	masculine	**feminine**
mine	le mien	la mienne
yours	le tien	la tienne
his, hers	le sien	la sienne

	masculine and feminine
ours	le (la) nôtre
yours	le (la) vôtre
theirs	le (la) leur

Referring to a **plural noun possessed**:
simply add an 's' to all forms given above: e.g. **les miens** would refer to a **masculine plural object possessed by me**; **les siennes** would refer to a **feminine plural object possessed by him or her**!
N.B. (1) The circumflex accents (^) on the **first and second plural** forms.
(2) A further English translation of the French possessive pronoun is 'my own', 'his own', etc., or even, rather peculiarly, 'my one', 'his one', etc.

As pronouns they are used of course when the noun they refer to is **omitted**, but it is this noun which gives the gender and the number of the pronoun to be used.
E.g. Il lui prit la main dans **les siennes** (= ses mains).
Prenons ma voiture: il vaut mieux garer **la vôtre** (= votre voiture) = Let's take my car, it's better to park yours.

Reminder: take care with the **correct pattern of 'tu'** and the corresponding pronoun form in complex sentences.

Test section

Cover up the right-hand side of the page while you work out your answers. **Use the word(s) on the left to help you decide on the adjective or pronoun required.**

Her brother	(un frère)	**son frère**
their cousins	(les cousines)	**leurs cousines**
mine	(mon école)	**la mienne**
yours	(vos légumes)	**les vôtres**
your books and pen – 'tu' form	(les livres et le stylo)	**tes livres et ton stylo**
his	(ses soeurs)	**les siennes**
his cases and theirs	(une valise)	**ses valises et les leurs**

Demonstrative adjectives and pronouns

For the **demonstrative adjective** there are **three singular** forms and only **one plural** form.

	masculine singular	**feminine singular**
this, that	ce, cet*	cette
these, those	**plural** (masculine and feminine)	ces

The alternative masculine singular form given, '**cet**', is used before a word beginning with a vowel, or a mute 'h'. The vowel may of course be an **adjective**, not necessarily a noun: e.g. **cet** immense terrain **but** ce grand terrain.

There really **is** only one plural form, just as there is for the definite article.

Here are just a few examples of each form:
masculine singular: ce garçon, cet arbre, ce hibou (**not** mute 'h');
feminine singular: cette fille, cette orange, cette histoire;
plural: ces garçons, ces filles, ces arbres.

The French do not distinguish particularly between 'this' and 'that', except where a comparison is stated or implied, and the difference is of significance. In this case a more emphatic form of the demonstrative adjective is used, '**-ci**' being added to the **noun** to indicate '**this**' or '**these**', and '**-là**' to indicate '**that**' or '**those**'. E.g. **Cet** animal-**ci** est moins dangereux que **ce** serpent-**là**. Je prendrai **ces** tomates-**là**; elles sont moins chères.

A few commonly found phrases also use one or other of these forms; examples are:

> à ce moment-là = at that moment
> cette fois-ci = this time
> à cette époque-là = at that time

N.B. The phrase '**cette nuit**' refers to the night which has just gone, and therefore means '**last night**'.

The **demonstrative pronoun** has the following forms:

	masculine singular	**feminine singular**
this one, that one	celui	celle
	masculine plural	**feminine plural**
these (ones), those (ones)	ceux	celles

The English translation given on the left above will not really suffice as a complete guide-line, since the precise meaning will vary according to what comes afterwards in the sentence. The first and most important thing to realise about the demonstrative pronoun is that **it never stands alone**, and **is always followed by one of three alternatives**, which will be the determining factor as regards the sense.

(1) by **'-ci'** or **'-là'** (= this one, that one)

As with the addition of this suffix to the adjective form, it merely serves to distinguish more clearly between two alternatives. As you would expect it stands instead of a previously mentioned or understood noun: e.g. Vous n'avez pas de dictionnaire? Prenez **celui-ci** (= the one here being offered). Vous voulez des prunes, Madame? **Celles-ci** ou **celles-là**? (= these or those).

N.B. An additional meaning for **'celui-ci'**, **'celui-là'** is **'the latter'**, **'the former'**. It is often used to avoid ambiguity, as in this example: Le policier attrapa le criminel; **celui-ci** était sur le point de prendre un vélomoteur = The policeman caught the criminal; the latter (i.e. not the policeman!) was about to take a moped.

(2) by **'de'** + **proper name, or noun**, to show ownership. (= John's, etc.) Voici les livres de Marie. **Ceux de** Georges de sont pas là. (= George**'s** aren't there.)

(3) by a relative pronoun (**qui, que, qu', dont, etc.** = the one who, those which, etc.): e.g. Quelles fleurs sont mortes? **Celles que** vous avez cueillies ce matin (= those which you picked this morning).

Quel menuisier avez-vous choisi finalement? (= which carpenter did you choose in the end?) **Celui dont** mon voisin m'a parlé = the one of whom my neighbour spoke to me (spoke to me about).

N.B. The forms **'ceci'**, **'cela'** (= this, that) are used when there is no specific reference to a noun, in other words when 'this', 'that' are of general reference, e.g. **Cela** me paraît impossible = That (i.e. an idea) seems impossible to me.

The short form of cela (**ça**) is basically conversational and should not be used in written texts, unless conversation is specified.

Test section

Cover the right-hand side of the page while you work out your answers. **Use the word(s) on the left to help you decide on the adjective or pronoun required.**

this old monument   (un vieux monument)   **ce vieux monument**

this one	(une cathédrale)	**celle-ci**
Paul's	(un vélo)	**celui de Paul**
the former	(deux villes)	**celle-là**
this tree	(un arbre)	**cet arbre-ci**
these peaches	(une pêche)	**ces pêches**
those (ones)	(une pêche)	**celles-là**
these (ones)	(un chou)	**ceux-ci**
Mary's	(des gants)	**ceux de Marie**
that's stupid	(stupide)	**cela est stupide**
the one you bought	(un chapeau)	**celui que vous avez acheté**

Interrogative adjectives and pronouns

The **interrogative adjective forms** are as follows:

	masculine singular	**feminine singular**
which? what a . . .!	quel	quelle
	masculine plural	**feminine plural**
which? what . . .!	quels	quelles

These are totally straightforward, and the only point to note particularly is that when 'quel', etc. is used in the exclamatory sense you must remember that this word includes in its meaning the word 'a' in English: e.g. **Quel** jardin superbe! = **What a** superb garden! **Quelles** fleurs ravissantes! = **What** delightful flowers!

The **interrogative pronoun** forms are more varied.

(1)	**of people** (= who?)	**of things** (= what?)
Subject of verb	qui? (qui est-ce qui?)	qu'est-ce qui?
Object of verb	qui? (qui est-ce que?)	que (qu'est-ce que?)

E.g. **Qu'est-ce qui** se passe? = What's happening?
Que cherchez-vous? = What are you looking for? (or **Qu'est-ce que vous cherchez?**)
Qui cherchez-vous? = Who are you looking for? (or **Qui est-ce que vous cherchez?**)

Note that   (a) there is **no short form** for the **subject** form = **what?**
        (b) use of the **short form** of the question **requires inversion of the verb** (except of course where it is the **subject case** = **who?**).

(2) **To express 'which one?'** (i.e. choice) the following forms are used, the **same** forms for both **people** and **things**.

	masculine	**feminine**
singular	lequel?	laquelle?
plural	lesquels?	lesquelles?

These forms are easy to use, the only consideration being the number and gender of the noun they are replacing.
E.g. Voilà deux robes. **Laquelle** préférez-vous? = **Which one** do you prefer? Vous avez écouté les témoins (= witnesses). **Lesquels** ont dit la vérité? = **Which ones** told the truth?

(3) **When used after a preposition** (= with what? from whom?, etc.)

of people	**of things**
qui?	quoi?

E.g. **De qui** parlaient-ils? = **Who** were they talking **about**? **Avec quoi** a-t-il ouvert la boîte? = **What** did he open the box **with**?

You should have realised by now that except if you wish to say 'which one?', you may **always** use 'qui' in any circumstance when **referring to people**.

Question: Would you think it a complicated procedure to express the idioms 'What could I (she) (we) etc. do (think), etc.?' No doubt it does sound likely, but in fact any one of these alternatives can be rendered by two words.

Que faire? = **What could I do?** can equally well be made to refer to **any** subject in **any** tense (e.g. What will he do?).

The same principle applies to the idiom '**Que penser?**' and also to '**Que dire?**' = **What can we say?** or a multitude of other versions.

Test section

Cover the right-hand side of the page while you work out your answers. **Use the word(s) on the left to help you decide on the adjective or pronoun required.**

which story?	(une histoire)	**quelle histoire?**
which one?	(une histoire)	**laquelle?**
behind which ones?	(des livres)	**derrière lesquels?**
what are you saying?	(dire)	**que dites-vous?** or
		qu'est-ce que vous dites?

Indefinite adjectives and pronouns

As the name implies you do not have a definite person or object in mind when you use these forms (= some, any).

The indefinite adjective (= some, a few) has **two forms** only, **quelque** in the **singular**, and **quelques** in the **plural**. It is the plural form which you will have met most often: e.g. Il y a **quelques** années qu'il est mort = He has been dead for **some** years.

An example of the adjective in the **singular** form might be: Tu le trouveras **quelque** part = You'll find it **some**where.

To make the adjective of even vaguer significance, you may use the forms '**n'importe quel, quelle**', etc. (= any old, it doesn't matter which), indicating that it really is very unimportant which one is chosen: e.g. Je me contenterai de **n'importe quelle** voiture! = I'll be happy with **any** car **at all**.

The indefinite pronoun (= someone, some, something, anyone, any). The **singular** form of 'someone' will be well known = **quelqu'un**. (Be careful on the spelling, however!) If by chance you should meet an apparently strange feminine form of this (quelqu'une) you should not query it, since it **does** exist but is really rather rare. The **plural** form (= some people) is of course **quelques-uns**, and this too should be a familiar form: e.g. **Quelqu'un** a pris ma place = **Someone** took my seat. **Quelques-uns** sont arrivés à l'heure = **Some** arrived on time. The form **quelque chose** (= something) is again a well-worn phrase, particularly when you forget the word you really want!

As with the adjectival form above the idea of 'any one at all' can be expressed by using the additional 'n'importe'. Thus it can be adapted to many uses:

    n'importe lequel, etc. = any one at all (of things);
    n'importe qui = anybody at all;
    n'importe quoi = anything at all.

E.g. **N'importe lequel** fera mon affaire = **Any one of them** will suit my purpose. C'est très facile – **n'importe qui** pourra le faire = ... **anybody at all** will be able to do it.

Test section

Cover the right-hand side of the page while you work out your answers. **Translate these phrases into French.**

What are you looking for?	**Que cherchez-vous?** or **Qu'est-ce que vous cherchez?**
What could I do?	**Que faire?**
What fell?	**Qu'est-ce qui est tombé?**
What a man!	**Quel homme!**
Someone will come soon.	**Quelqu'un viendra bientôt.**
We'll buy some of them.	**Nous en achèterons quelques-uns.**
Anybody at all knows how to do that!	**N'importe qui sait faire cela!**

Relative pronouns

Relative pronouns are so called because they **relate** (or refer back) to a word or words in a preceding clause. In English these are the words '**who**', '**whom**', '**whose**', '**which**', '**that**', introducing a subordinate clause.

Both **qui** (the subject form) and **que** (**qu'**) (the object form) can refer to **both people** and **things**. The thorny question for candidates often seems to be: 'The subject or object of what?'

(1) **Qui** (= who, which or that) is used as the **subject of the verb following it in that clause**.
E.g. Je connais cet homme **qui fume** un cigare = I know that man **who** is smoking a cigar.

(2) **Que** (**qu'** before a vowel) (= whom, which or that) is used as the **object of the verb following it in that clause**.
E.g. La pomme **que** tu **manges** est pourrie = The apple you are eating is rotten. Nous acceptons les défauts des personnes **que** nous **aimons** = We accept the faults of the people we love.

Both of these last examples illustrate how in English we often leave out altogether the relative pronoun when it is an object. **It is never omitted in French**. There must always be the linking relative pronoun to join the separate parts of the sentence.

In spite of dutifully learning all there seems to be about the subject 'qui' and the object 'que' many candidates still seem to find difficulty in sorting them out in practice. A simple test to apply is to say to yourself: is there already a subject for the verb following in that clause? If so, then the relative pronoun **must** be the object (que, qu').

(3) **After a preposition 'qui'** is used for **people** (we have already seen this with interrogative pronouns).

E.g. Les gens avec **qui** je travaille sont sympathiques = The people with whom I work are nice.

La dame derrière **qui** je me trouvais au cinéma portait un grand chapeau = The lady behind whom I was sitting in the cinema was wearing a large hat.

Lequel, laquelle, lesquels, lesquelles (= which) are the forms used after prepositions referring to **things.** Gender and number of the noun being replaced are of course to be carefully noted.

E.g. La villa derrière **laquelle** se trouve une piscine appartient à un chanteur célèbre = The villa behind which there is a swimming pool belongs to a famous singer.

There are two occasions where you use the '**lesquels**' form (always plural) for **people**: these are following the prepositions **parmi** and **entre** (= among, between).

E.g. Les deux messieurs entre **lesquels** il se trouvait assis étaient des savants = The two gentlemen between whom he was sitting were scientists.

(4) To express '**of whom**', '**of which**,' there is no particular reason why you cannot apply the principles in (3) above, and write **de qui**, or **duquel**, etc. There is, however, a more usual way of expressing this idea, which is to use the one word (for people **and** things) **dont**. In English this could also be '**whose**'.

E.g. (a) Nous n'avons pu entrer dans le château, **dont** les portes étaient verrouillées = We were not able to go into the castle, whose doors were bolted.

(b) Voilà le garçon **dont** je connais le père = Here (or there) is the boy whose father I know.

You must be careful over two points when using 'dont', both of which are illustrated in the examples above. Have you spotted them? From example (a) you should have noticed that there must **always** be the **definite article before the noun governed by 'dont'** (not as in English – **whose doors**). If you think of the alternative translation (**of which the doors**) there should be no problem. From example (b) you should have noticed the **word order** which is peculiar to this construction. It must be the following:

dont + subject + verb (+ object, etc.)

Again this differs from English.

Since 'dont' is the equivalent of '**de qui**', or '**duquel**' it is logical to use 'dont' as the relative pronoun with those verbs which have the preposition 'de' built into them (se servir de = to use, avoir peur de = to be afraid of, etc.).

E.g. Le couteau **dont** il s'est servi était inutile = . . . of which he made use (which he used) was useless.

This example also serves to illustrate the point that you must be totally aware of the **French idiom**, and not rely on a word-by-word translation, a procedure which is doomed to failure! For instance if you try to do that on the last example you will be very likely to forget the 'de' which is an integral part of the verb, and hastily (but incorrectly) write 'qu'il . . .' (= which he???), before you stop to think of the way the phrase is used in French. It may be appropriate here to remind you that foreign languages were never intended as a perverse invention of examiners, or as mere translation of what should really be English; each language has its own patterns and structures, its own idioms and turns of phrase.

But back to the matter in hand; here are a couple more examples showing how 'dont' fits in with such verbs as those mentioned above:

Il a perdu le passeport **dont** il avait besoin pour aller à l'étranger = He lost the passport he needed to go abroad.

(5) **Ce qui, ce que (ce qu')** (= what, that which)

'Ce qui' or 'ce que' differ from all other relative pronouns in that they do not relate back to a specific word earlier in the sentence. They have **no particular noun to refer to**; the 'what' (or 'that which') is either

    (a)   **the object of the verb in the main clause,**

or (b)   **the outcome or summing-up of the whole of a preceding clause.** This is best illustrated by a few examples:

(a) Il m'a dit de faire **ce que** je voulais = He told me to do **what** (that which) I wanted.

Ils ne savaient pas **ce qui** allait bientôt arriver = They did not know **what** was soon going to happen.

It is to be hoped that you can see from these examples that the 'what' depends on the **verb** (and indeed the whole idea) in the preceding clause. To put it another way, you could not possibly use the relative 'qui' or 'que', because that would indicate that there was **one specific noun** (or pronoun) to refer back to in the main clause.

(b) **Ce que** vous dites là manque de sens = **What** you are saying there lacks sense.
Ce qui m'énerve, c'est que nous sommes beaucoup moins riches qu'eux! = **What** annoys me is that we are a lot less wealthy than they!
Il refusa d'étudier, **ce qui** était inutile aux examens = He refused to study, **which** was useless for the exams.

In these examples the 'ce qui' or 'ce que' is giving a résumé of an idea, **either** already expressed (i.e. the rubbish the person in the first example was talking), **or** as a reaction to something about to be expressed (i.e. the fact that other people are wealthier, in the second example). In the third example, the 'ce qui' is summing up the whole of the previous clause, saying in fact 'this attitude of his' was useless for the exams. However you choose to consider it, the 'ce qui', 'ce que' is referring to a whole idea, or **group of words**, not to one particular one.

One final use of 'ce qui', 'ce que' is in the phrases '**tout ce qui**', '**tout ce que**' = all that (which). Because a relative pronoun is so rarely used here in English, you will need to make a special point of recognising when it is necessary in French. Much the easiest solution is to learn as set phrases these particular three-word-phrases. Try saying them to yourself so that they become a natural 'whole': e.g. Il faisait **tout ce qu'**on lui demandait de faire = He did everything he was asked to do (all that which . . .)
Tout ce qui brille n'est pas or = All that glitters is not gold. Il rejette **tout ce qui** est raisonnable, et ne s'intéresse qu'à **ce qui** est bizarre = He rejects all that is reasonable, and is only interested in what is strange.

Test section

Cover the answer section over the page while you work out your answers. **Fill in the correct form of the relative pronoun to complete these sentences.**

1. Jean-Paul était un homme — n'aimait personne.
2. Pouquoi avez-vous choisi — vous ne pourrez jamais utiliser?
3. C'est le moulin près — nous nous rencontrions autrefois.
4. C'est ce couteau-là — j'avais besoin tout à l'heure.
5. Votre père n'aimait pas le garçon avec — sortait ma soeur.
6. Voilà les papiers — on devrait examiner avec soin.

7. — m'agace, c'est son attitude désagréable.
8. Enfin ils arrivèrent à l'église — ils avaient vu la tour au loin.
9. Tu ne pourras jamais imiter — Henri a réussi.
10. Il perdit les lunettes sans — il ne voyait rien.
11. Tout — l'intéresse, c'est la mode.
12. Les 'baked beans' sont un plat — on ne trouve pas en France!
13. Monsieur Truffeau est un homme à — je donnerais tout!
14. Cela est une histoire — elle ne se souvient pas du tout.
15. Les étudiants parmi — elle se trouvait étaient tous paresseux.

Answers

1. Jean-Paul était un homme **qui** n'aimait personne.
2. Pourquoi avez-vous choisi **ce que** vous ne pourrez jamais utiliser?
3. C'est le moulin près **duquel** nous nous rencontrions autrefois.
4. C'est ce couteau-là **dont** j'avais besoin tout à l'heure.
5. Votre père n'aimait pas le garçon avec **qui** sortait ma soeur.
6. Voilà les papiers **qu'**on devrait examiner avec soin.
7. **Ce qui** m'agace, c'est son attitude désagréable.
8. Enfin ils arrivèrent à l'église **dont** ils avaient vu la tour au loin.
9. Tu ne pourras jamais imiter **ce qu'**Henri a réussi.
10. Il perdit les lunettes sans **lesquelles** il ne voyait rien.
11. Tout **ce qui** l'intéresse, c'est la mode.
12. Les 'baked beans' sont un plat **qu'**on ne trouve pas en France!
13. Monsieur Truffeau est un homme à **qui** je donnerais tout!
14. Cela est une histoire **dont** elle ne se souvient pas du tout.
15. Les étudiants parmi **lesquels** elle se trouvait étaient tous paresseux.

Chapter 5
'Ce' *v.* 'Il'

Many candidates find it difficult to decide **which** to use **when**, and in fact anyone who has been to France will probably have heard 'ce' used more often than he might expect. In colloquial French it is indeed sometimes used where in accordance with strict literary practice it would be incorrect. Such discrepancies of course occur between the spoken and written forms of any language.

(1) The first point to remember, from an 'English' point of view, is that 'it' is by no means always to be translated by '**ce**'. If **it** refers to some **previously mentioned noun**, it will normally be '**il**' or '**elle**' according to the gender of that noun.

E.g. Où est mon cendrier? **Il** est sur la petite table = Where is my ashtray? **It** is on the little table.

Ta montre? **Elle** n'est plus là! = Your watch? **It** isn't here any more.

Having thus begun with the use of '**il**', '**elle**' meaning '**it**', the simplest method of dealing with the whole question would be to deal first with all the other situations where '**it**' is rendered by '**il**'.

(2) '**Il**' is **always** used when **telling the time** by the clock.

E.g. **Il est** sept heures moins le quart = **It's** a quarter to seven. The set question for asking the time is of course 'Quelle heure **est-il?**'

(3) Another formula concerns **the weather**. At O-level, neither this area nor the telling of the time will be anything new (we hope!) but it is worth quoting as a stated, easily-registered fact. You ask 'Quel temps **fait-il?**' and you answer '**Il** fait....'

See also the section on **weather**, *page 148.*

All the above cases are clear-cut. Now let us examine those cases where 'ce' and 'il' seem to overlap.

(4) **Description**

   Il est beau.

   C'est un beau chien.

   Qui a pris le biftek? **C'**est lui!

You may draw the following (correct!) conclusions from these three examples:

(a) '**It**' + être + **adjective** = **Il est** ... (a noun is already in your mind here)

(b) '**It**' + être + **noun, qualified noun or pronoun** = **C'est** ...

43

In the examples using '**c'est**' you should be able to detect some sense of **definition** (**what sort of** dog is he? – a lovely one. **Who was it** who took the steak? – It was him!)

Go back to your earliest days of learning French – I have no doubt that very early on you were defining objects in response to the question '**Qu'est-ce que c'est?**', saying '**C'est** (this as-yet-unidentified object) **un (une)** ....' Having defined '**it**' and therefore necessarily also its gender, you could then go on to describing it ('**Il est** bleu' or '**Elle est** grande') **or** to defining it further ('**C'est** un crayon bleu', '**C'est** une grande boîte', i.e. **that's the sort** of pencil or box it is).

Following a common-sense reasoning, such short expressions of surprise, wonderment, horror or simple remark as 'it's magnificent', 'it's ghastly', 'it's true', etc. used in general terms with no reference to a precise noun, are rendered by '**c'est** ...'.
E.g. (looking from the top of the Eiffel Tower at the vista below) C'est magnifique! (= the whole scene) **or** (hearing of some terrible disaster) C'est affreux! (= the total experience or incident).

(5) **Describing trades or nationality**
You may either say: **Il** est professeur; **elle** est italienne; **or C'est** un professeur; **c'est** une Italienne.
N.B. **Definitely** *no* '**un**' **or** '**une**' **in the phrases using 'il est' or 'elle est'.**

Having established the profession or nationality, should you wish to qualify this further, you **must** then say:
   C'est un professeur très instruit = He's a **very learned** teacher.
   C'est une jolie Italienne = She's a **pretty** Italian girl.

(6) '**It**' + **être** + **adjective** + **verb**
Here all depends on whether the sentence ends at this point or not. Consider these three examples:
Marcel a détourné un avion (= hijacked a plane). (1) **C'est difficile à comprendre.** (2) **Il est difficile de comprendre Marcel.** (3) **Il est difficile de comprendre pourquoi Marcel a agi de la sorte** (= why Marcel acted that way).

Where the **phrase or sentence is complete after the verb**, as in the **first** example, the construction is:
   ce ... + adjective + à + infinitive
Where the **phrase or sentence is not complete** without some addition to the sense beyond that verb, the construction is:
   il ... + adjective +   (de + infinitive + ...)
   **   (que + subordinate clause)**

This condition applies in both the last two examples. An example of **que + subordinate clause** might be:

Il est évident qu'elle est coupable = It is evident that she is guilty.

N.B. Obviously 'c'est', 'il est', 'elle est', etc. may be used in any tense and also in the plural. The **plural** form of '**c'est**' is '**ce sont**', the plural of '**c'était**' is '**c'étaient**'.

E.g. **C'était eux** qui faisaient peur aux moutons = **It was they** who were frightening the sheep.

L'année prochaine **ils ne seront plus** étudiants, mais médecins = Next year they will no longer be students but doctors.

One final recommendation: learn thoroughly the circumstances in which 'il' is required, and then all others should be catered for by 'ce'.

Test section

Cover the answers and **decide** from the rest of the phrase or sentence **whether 'ce' or 'il', 'elle', etc. should be used.**

— est moi qui l'ai trouvé.	**C'est moi qui l'ai trouvé.**
Oh zut! — est déjà quatre heures.	**Il est déjà quatre heures.**
Madame Lenoir? — est française.	**Elle est française.**
— était fort difficile de le prouver.	**Il était fort difficile de le prouver.**
— sera difficile à prouver.	**Ce sera difficile à prouver.**
Au Maroc — faisait une chaleur terrible.	**Au Maroc il faisait une chaleur terrible.**
Les filles? — sont impossibles!	**Elles sont impossibles!**
— sont eux! Ils arrivent!	**Ce sont eux! Ils arrivent!**
— doit être vrai.	**Ce doit être vrai.**
— est formidable!	**C'est formidable!**
La musique? — était formidable!	**Elle était formidable!**
— sera une maison superbe.	**Ce sera une maison superbe.**
Monsieur Latour un gendarme? Non, — est facteur.	**Non, il est facteur.**
— était désagréable à entendre.	**C'était désagréable à entendre.**
— est évident que la terre est ronde.	**Il est évident que la terre est ronde.**
Pauvre Isabelle. — était aimée de tout le monde.	**Elle était aimée de tout le monde.**

Chapter 6
Adverbs

Formation

As in English the formation of a large number of adverbs in French is by means of a suffix. The basic rule is to add **-ment** to the **feminine adjective**, or where the adjective in its masculine form ends in a vowel, to add **-ment** to that masculine form.

E.g. heureuse**ment** = fortunately; propre**ment** = cleanly, properly;
fière**ment** = proudly; vrai**ment** = really;
lente**ment** = slowly; absolu**ment** = absolutely.

One or two adverbs are **irregular**:
bref – **brièvement** = briefly; gai – **gaîment** (or gaiement)
bon – **bien** = well; = gaily.
mauvais – **mal** = badly;

There are one or two large groups of **exceptions** to the general rule.

(1) Adjectives ending in – **ant** or – **ent** add – **amment** and – **emment** to the stem of the adjective.

E.g. constant – **constamment** = constantly;
évident – **évidemment** = evidently.

(2) Some adverbs are embellished by the addition of '**é**' before the normal ending – **ment**.

E.g. aveugl**ément** = blindly; précis**ément** = precisely.

And then there is 'vite' = quickly (definitely **no** -ment).

Some very common adverbs are not formed from any adjective form. Examples are **beaucoup** = a lot, much; **trop** = too much; **assez** = enough; **peu** = a little; **tout à fait** = completely; **fort** (= très) = very; **toujours** = always; **souvent** = often.

You will probably already have noticed in your reading, that the French often choose to express adverbs in terms other than the straight form given above. By using the phrases:

– **'d'une façon' ('manière') + feminine adjective** or
– **'avec' ('sans') + noun**

it is often possible to achieve a more pleasing stylistic effect.

E.g. Il a agi **d'une façon décisive** = He acted **decisively**.

Il s'est battu **avec courage** = He fought **courageously**.

Here a better sound balance to each sentence is gained by the alternative forms than by 'décisivement' or 'courageusement'. Other substitutes for long adverbs are the following:

à la folie	= follement
à la légère	= légèrement (= lightly, **not** = slightly).
peu à peu	= graduellement
tout à coup	= subitement

On similar lines to 'd'une façon . . .' are the expressions related to (a) **speech** and (b) **ways of looking at** something or someone.

'd'un ton' + **adjective** } are often used to indicate the tone or
'd'une voix' + **adjective** } level of voice used.

'd'un air' + **adjective**   is often used to indicate the way in which someone is looking at something.

Il nous a regardés **d'un air louche** = He looked at us **suspiciously**. Note also the two expressions **parler à voix basse (haute)** = to speak in a low (loud) voice.

There are quite a number of expressions where an **adjective is used as an adverb**.

parler bas (haut)	= to speak softly (loudly)
chanter juste (faux)	= to sing in tune (out of tune)
voir clair	= to see straight, clearly
sentir bon (mauvais)	= to smell nice (nasty)
travailler dur	= to work hard
coûter cher	= to cost a lot
refuser net	= to refuse point-blank
s'arrêter net	= to stop dead

As you will by now have realised, there is no totally set pattern for the best rendering of an adverb.

Position of adverbs

As a general rule adverbs come **immediately after the verb**.
E.g. Il la regarda **fixement**, puis marcha **lentement** à la porte = He looked **fixedly** at her, then walked **slowly** to the door. One sure thing is that the adverb will not come, as is often the case in English, between subject and verb (he **often** does that, etc.) **Adverbs of time** are often found at the beginning of a sentence. E.g. **Aujourd'hui** je me suis réveillé à cinq heures et demie.

In **compound tenses** (where there is an auxiliary verb and a past participle), **shorter adverbs** (e.g. bien, mal, vite) tend to be placed **after the auxiliary**, but **longer** ones are placed **after the past participle. Adverbs of time and place** can also take this position in compound tenses.

E.g. Nous avons **vite** compris de quoi il s'agissait = We **soon** understood what it was about.

Ils avaient continué **aveuglément** sous la pluie = They continued **blindly** on in the rain.

Heureusement (and malheureusement) are frequently to be found at the beginning of a sentence.

E.g. **Heureusement** l'autobus avait du retard ce jour-là = **Luckily** the bus was late that day.

Test section

(i) **From the adjective given, suggest the adverb form.**

long	**longuement**
franc	**franchement**
régulier	**régulièrement**
courant	**couramment**

(ii) **Suggest ways of forming the adverb other** than by adding –ment, to fit the phrases on the left. An adjective is supplied as a clue.

Il cria (rauque = raucous)	**Il cria d'une voix rauque.**
Le voleur s'est comporté (= behaved) (bizarre)	**Le voleur s'est comporté d'une façon bizarre.**
Il répondit (satisfait)	**Il répondit avec satisfaction.**
Après l'accident le conducteur a continué (prudent)	**Après l'accident le conducteur a continué avec prudence.**
Il parlait à sa fiancée (bas)	**Il parlait à voix basse.**
L'élève a pris son travail (léger)	**L'élève a pris son travail à la légère.**
Ce repas sent (bon)	**Ce repas sent bon.**

(iii) **Place the given adverb** in the best position in the sentence.

Il reviendra ce soir (certainement)	**Il reviendra certainement ce soir.**
C'est le grand départ (aujourd'hui)	**Aujourd'hui c'est le grand départ.**
Ce soir-là nous avons mangé (beaucoup)	**Ce soir-là nous avons beaucoup mangé.**
La nouvelle était exacte (malheureusement)	**Malheureusement la nouvelle était exacte.**
Je suis revenu (vite)	**Je suis vite revenu.**

48

Chapter 7
Comparative and Superlative Forms

Comparative form (= more. . .)

The structure is the same for both: **'plus' + adjective or adverb**
adjective plus beau = more beautiful; plus rapide = quicker.
adverb plus vite = quicker; plus intelligemment = more
intelligently.

Generally speaking the **comparative adjective** occupies the
same position as usual, and of course, it **must agree**.
E.g. **de plus jolis chapeaux** = prettier hats;
  un paysage plus pittoresque = a more picturesque
    landscape.

A complete comparison with another stated noun or pronoun is by
the addition of '**que**' after the adjective or adverb:
  'plus' + adjective (adverb) + que = more . . . than
The opposite idea (**less . . . than**) is similarly formed:
  'moins' + adjective (adverb) + que.
E.g. **Il est moins sympathique que sa sœur** = He is **less nice
than** his sister.
An equal comparison (**as . . . as**) is also along the same lines:
  'aussi' + adjective (adverb) + que.
E.g. **Nous avons marché aussi rapidement (vite) qu'eux** =
We walked **as rapidly (quickly) as** they did.
See also the section on negatives, page 133.
Note When 'more' or 'less' is used of a noun in the sense of **more**
or **less quantity**, you use **'plus de', 'moins de'.**
E.g. Ils ont montré **plus de courage** (= more courage) que les
autres.

Superlative form (= the -est, most . . .)

Adjectives
The basic pattern is: **le (la, les), plus + adjective.**
E.g. **Elle est la plus laide de toutes** = She's **the ugliest** of the
lot! Where a superlative adjective is used with a noun, the pattern
depends on the normal position of the adjective.

(for the majority, coming after the noun)	**les repas les plus copieux** = the most copious meals (pattern as above).

(for the few, coming before the noun)   **sa plus belle cravate** = his most beautiful tie (here the definite article is 'lost' in the possessive form).

Example: Paris est la capitale la plus élègante d'Europe = Paris is the most elegant capital in Europe.

From this sentence you will notice that **after a superlative** adjective 'de' is used to say 'in'.

Adverbs

The pattern is quite simple: **'le plus'** + adverb.

E.g. **C'est Jean qui chante le plus agréablement** = It's John who sings **the most pleasantly.**

There are noticeably **few irregular forms** of either comparative or superlative adjectives and adverbs. These are:

adjectives: bon, meilleur, le meilleur = good, better, best;
*   **mauvais, pire, le pire** = bad, worse, worst;
*   **petit, moindre, le moindre** = little, less, least.

These * forms are reserved only for use with **abstract nouns**; for all other usage there are the completely regular forms ('plus mauvais', 'plus petit', 'le plus mauvais', 'le plus petit').

E.g. Je n'ai pas **la moindre idée** = I haven't **the slightest idea.**

Ta conduite est **pire qu'hier** = Your behaviour is **worse than** it was yesterday.

C'est **le plus petit garçon** de la classe = He's **the smallest boy** in the class. N.B. **Don't forget** '*de*' **for 'in' after a superlative.**

There are corresponding **adverbs** for the **irregular adjective forms.**

These are: **bien, mieux, le mieux**   = well, better, best;
          mal, pis, le pis   = badly, worse, worst

and in addition, **beaucoup, plus, le plus** = a lot, more, most. Be very careful about distinguishing between the adjective and adverb when expressing the idea of 'better' or 'the best'. English usage has the same words for both, but when qualifying the **verb**, you **must** remember to use the **adverb**.

Compare these two examples:

– Les joueurs Dubut et Sauvetout étaient **les meilleurs** (**best** refers to the noun 'joueurs').

– C'est l'équipe des Loups qui a le mieux joué (**best** refers to the verb 'a joué').

Finally here are one or two **idiomatic expressions**:

Que le meilleur gagne!   = May the best man win!

faire de son mieux	= to do one's best
tant pis!	= too bad!
tant mieux!	= so much the better!

Test section

(i) Give the comparative or superlative form as indicated.

le grand jardin	(comparative)	**le plus grand jardin**
Jean-Paul chante bien	(comparative)	**Jean-Paul chante mieux**
la bonne bière	(superlative)	**la meilleure bière**
la jolie maison dans le quartier	(superlative)	**la plus jolie maison du quartier**
il arrive vite	(superlative)	**il arrive le plus vite**
nous partirons tôt	(comparative)	**nous partirons plus tôt**
le plat exotique	(superlative)	**le plat le plus exotique**
elle ne m'a pas fait une petite impression	(superlative)	**elle ne m'a pas fait la moindre impression**
les Allemands mangent beaucoup	(superlative)	**les Allemands mangent le plus**

(ii) Make comparisons as indicated ('plus . . . que', 'moins . . . que', etc.) using the item in brackets as the second element of the comparison.

Les oranges sont bonnes	(les poires)	(better than)
Mon cousin est grand	(vous)	(as big as)
La giraffe est élégante	(l'hippopotame)	(more elegant than)
La petite fille a joué sagement	(sa soeur)	(more nicely than)
L'argent est précieux	(l'or)	(less precious than)
Ma mémoire est mauvaise	(la sienne)	(worse than)
Ils ont rapidement fait des progrès	(tous les autres)	(more rapidly than all the others)
Ils ont bien préparé leurs examens	(tous les autres candidats)	(better)

Answers
Les oranges sont meilleures que les poires.
Mon cousin est aussi grand que vous.
La giraffe est plus élégante que l'hippopotame.
La petite fille a joué plus sagement que sa soeur.
L'argent est moins précieux que l'or.
Ma mémoire est pire que la sienne.
Ils ont fait des progrès plus rapidement que tous les autres.
Ils ont mieux préparé leurs examens que tous les autres candidats.

Chapter 8
Verbs (Tenses and Tables)

Correct mastery of verb forms is probably the single most important element of 'success' in using a foreign language. This is the main area which separates the good candidates from the weak, where it is possible to show that you know how the language 'hangs together' by correctly manipulating time relationships (present, past, future, etc.).

If this sounds a daunting task, that is perhaps no bad thing. Too many candidates present themselves for the examination with only the haziest knowledge of the different tenses, and have not therefore the remotest chance of success. It really **is** important to be able to use verbs correctly in the right tense.

You do not need to be a genius to earn yourself a respectable command of the main tenses (and thereby a respectable commendation from the examiner). A secure knowledge of even as few as **four tenses** (**present, future, perfect** and **imperfect**) will be good enough to ensure a creditable showing at CSE level and will provide a very solid basis for most GCE O-level work. In fact once you have mastered these 'core' tenses you should in any case be able to tackle all the tenses of the indicative without too much difficulty, since all except the past historic (and past anterior) are made up of elements of the original four. In addition you may not necessarily be required to reproduce the past historic, though you must be able to recognise its forms and function. Nearly all examining boards go so far as to give specific instructions to candidates **not** to write in the past historic and will penalise those who do. It is only where prose translation into French is a part of the examination that candidates **may** use the past historic; in essay work you are usually recommended to write in the perfect tense.

There is a fair degree of truth in the idea that when it comes to exams the French language exam **should** require much less revision than some other subjects. To what may sound like an example of demented ravings, let me add another! Either the candidate knows what it is all about by the time he comes to sit the exam, and will therefore need little revision, or he does not! In this latter case a burst of wild revision is unlikely to achieve what five years of almost daily work has not. Mastery of the uses of the imperfect tense, or manipulation of object pronouns (to name but two of the points which often cause difficulty) are not facts which can be 'mugged up' at the last minute. They are linguistic habits which are only acquired through long and careful practice. It is comparatively simple to learn the endings required for the different tenses, but to **know** them, so that their use becomes reliable and instinctive in the context of normal **total** language communication (rather than as a formula on a page of a textbook) is an entirely different achievement.

Once these linguistic habits are achieved however, the candidate is unlikely to lose them (rather like riding a bicycle!).

From the point of view of the candidate who has perhaps been too nonchalant in the past and 'turns over a new leaf' with the prospect of the exam on the horizon, the situation seems bleak. A language is an acquisitive subject, constantly building on past knowledge, and if the knowledge is shaky, then the building process becomes a more difficult task.

The message is therefore simple: learn thoroughly at each stage. The pay-offs are sure – greater confidence (itself an enormous motivating force in language learning), together with the comforting knowledge that you are well prepared for the examination.

Note To aid systematic revision or simply as a reference, tables showing the **principal parts of verbs** (regular and irregular) are to be found on pages 91 to 97. In most of the test sections following each section on tenses, verbs will be restricted to those classed normally as **regular**.

Present indicative

Notes in these chapters will deal with the **formation**, **meaning** and **usage** of the various tenses. **Remember** the vast majority of verbs in French are **regular** (that is they conform to one of three main patterns (-**er**, -**ir**, -**re**). Further, the vast majority of those verbs are of the -**er** type.

Formation
As the **present tense** is the first one to be learned, there is a tendency to regard it as easier than the others, whereas in fact it is both varied and complex. All other tenses are simpler in their basic formation. For the three main verb types, the tense is formed by the **addition of the following endings** to the **verb stem** (the infinitive minus the -er, -ir, -re).

-er type	(e.g. parler);	-ir type	(e.g. finir);	-re type	(e.g. vendre).
je parl**e**	nous parl**ons**	je fin**is**	nous fin**issons**;	je vend**s**	nous vend**ons**
tu parl**es**	vous parl**ez**	tu fin**is**	vous fin**issez**	tu vend**s**	vous vend**ez**
il parl**e**	ils parl**ent**	il fin**it**	ils fin**issent**	il vend	ils vend**ent**

Reflexive verbs

Reflexive verbs behave exactly like any other as regards conjugation and can be of any of the three types (e.g. se rappeler = to remember, se divertir = to have a good time, se battre = to fight) but they always have an additional reflexive pronoun. Here is a complete example of such a verb: **se promener** = to go for a walk:

je **me** promène	nous **nous** promenons
tu **te** promènes	vous **vous** promenez
il **se** promène	ils **se** promènent

(1) It is important to remember the seemingly obvious fact that there is an appropriate reflexive pronoun for every person of the verb. It is easy to overlook this when using a new word gleaned from the dictionary. For in dictionaries and vocabulary lists reflexive verbs are always shown in the **third person** for convenience. (See also above.) All too many candidates use this pronoun 'se' indiscriminately when referring to first or second persons of the verb, largely because they have not stopped to think. **The reflexive pronoun must match the subject.** Be particularly careful in cases where the reflexive verb is in the infinitive form – even if the subject is only implied, you **must** obey the above rule. 'Vous devez **vous cacher** tout de suite – Quoi? **Nous cacher**? Jamais!' Understood in 'Nous cacher?' is the phrase **'You're saying that we must** (hide ourselves)?'.

(2) From the point of view of **word order**, the reflexive pronoun takes the same position exactly as when these same pronouns (me, te, nous, vous) are used as ordinary object pronouns. This means they precede the verb (in compound tenses this will be the auxiliary verb ('être'). If the phrase involves a second pronoun then the order is exactly as on the pronoun table given on page 27.

E.g. Il **s'y** intéresse	= He's interested in it.
Je **m'en** souviens	= I remember it.
Elle **se le** rappelle	= She remembers him.

Present tense irregularities

Apart from the recognised irregular verbs (given in the verb tables) there are several groups of verbs which offer irregularities in certain parts of the present tense only. Particular care needs to be exercised therefore when dealing with these verbs.

(1) Those verbs in which the **first and second persons plural** have a **different stem** from that of their other forms, e.g. 'boire', which gives 'je bois', etc. but also 'nous **buv**ons', 'vous **buv**ez'. It is well worth learning such verbs separately. Some are: résoudre = to resolve, croire = to believe, voir = to see, apercevoir = to catch sight of.

(2) Those verbs which have an infinitive in **-cer, -ger**. As the letters 'c' and 'g' are hard before the letter 'o', we must supply '**ç**' and '**ge**' in the 'nous' form of the verb to maintain the soft sound as in 'je man**ge**', 'il lan**ce**' for instance. Such verbs are: plonger = to dive, nager = to swim, diriger = to direct, commencer = to begin, s'efforcer = to try hard, etc.

(3) Verbs ending in '**e** + consonant + er' (such as 'lever' or 'mener') have a **grave accent** before a **mute 'e'**:

e.g. je me lève   nous nous levons
      tu te lèves   vous vous levez
      il se lève   ils se lèvent

This also happens with verbs ending in '**é** + **consonant** + **er**' (such as 'espérer'). This will give 'il espère', but 'nous espérons'.

(4) Most verbs ending in '**eler**' or '**-eter**' **double the consonant** before a mute 'e', rather than add the grave accent. This is not a hard and fast rule, and among verbs which continue to take the grave accent are 'acheter' (to buy) and 'geler' (to freeze): e.g. il ach**è**te; il g**è**le.

(5) Verbs ending in '**-oyer**' or '**-uyer**' change the '**y**' to '**i**' before a **mute 'e'**. Examples are 'nettoyer' (to clean) and 'essuyer' (to wipe): e.g. nous netto**y**ons; ils netto**i**ent.

With verbs ending in '**-ayer**' the change is optional and so we have either 'je **paye**' or 'je p**aie**'.

As you will notice, all these slight variations depend on whether the syllable involved is the **last pronounced** syllable of the word.

Meaning and usage

Basically the present tense serves the **same** purpose as the **English** present. However it has to be borne in mind that, while a **French verb** in a particular number and person has only **one**

form, e.g. '**je travaille**', the English equivalent might be '**I work**', '**I am working**', or even '**I do work**'. In the same way the question form '**Travaille-t-il**?' could be translated as '**Is he working**?' or '**Does he work**?' The present tense in French is **always** a **simple tense** (that is, consisting of **one part** only), and so is **totally complete** with the characteristic ending on the verb stem. **Never** try to imitate the English continuous present (**am** work**ing**) or the form (**do** work).

(1) If it is necessary to emphasise that someone '**is in the very act of**' the phrase '**être en train de + infinitive**' may be used: e.g. Je suis en train de préparer mon discours = I am in the process of preparing my speech.

(2) If it is necessary to emphasise the present by '**do**' as in 'I **do hope** you will be able to come' the question is easily solved by adding '**bien**' to the verb: e.g. J'**espère bien** que vous pourrez venir'. Note also the expression '**je veux bien**' = '**Yes, I would quite like that**'.

(3) As in English the present tense is used familiarly as an **immediate future**: e.g. J'arrive! = I'm just coming! Ils reviennent dans un instant! = They'll be back in a minute!

(4) There are two cases which frequently crop up and which are great favourites with examiners, where the French use the **present** and we in English use the **perfect** tense. The first is with the **preposition 'depuis'**.

Whatever the exact equivalent in English (usually '**has been doing for a length of time**') the main point is that an action begun in the past is **carrying on into the present**. The distinction between this and the perfect tense is that these '**depuis**' examples **have not yet finished**, they are continuing at this moment of speaking or writing: e.g. J'**apprends** le français **depuis trois ans** = I **have been learning** French **for three years** (i.e. and still am!).
Il **regarde** cette émission **depuis cinq heures et demie** = He **has been watching** this programme **since half past five** (i.e. and still is!). Je la **connais depuis deux mois** = I **have known** her **for two months** (i.e. and still do!).

This **relationship with the present time** is what necessitates the use of the present tense.

Do not forget the **question associated with this structure**: e.g. **Depuis quand ...?** or **Depuis combien de temps ...?** Depuis quand jouez-vous du piano? = How long have you been playing the piano?

(5) Present tense of '**venir + de + infinitive**'
In this other favourite idiom there is no thought at all of the usual meaning of 'venir' = 'to come'. The sense unit given above = **to have just done**. Thus, ils **viennent de passer** un mois en Grèce = they **have just spent** a month in Greece.

*See also the section on the **imperfect tense**, page 69 onwards.*

(6) Present tense of '**aller + infinitive**'
This is used as in English to indicate the future tense in the sense of '**am going to do**'. Thus, cet après-midi nous **allons faire** un petit tour en ville = this afternoon we are **going to take** a stroll round the town.

Imperative mood
(1) The imperative is simply the **command form** of the verb, using the 'tu' and 'vous' forms of the present tense. Just as in English, to give someone a command, you omit the subject pronoun.
E.g. Attends un peu!   = Wait a little!
Mettez votre imperméable!   = Put your raincoat on!

One point needs to be made about the **singular form of -er verbs** (and those which, like 'ouvrir', behave in the present like -er verbs). In the imperative 'tu' form the final '**s**' is omitted.
E.g. Donne-moi cette chaussette = Give me that sock.
N'ouvre pas cette boîte   = Don't open that box.

The form (tu) **vas** (from the verb 'aller') also loses the 's' when used as a command: e.g. Va voir si elle est là = Go and see if she is there. The only exception is in the expression 'Vas-y!' = Get on with it! Go on then!

(2) There is an additional form of the imperative in French, one which makes a suggestion rather than gives an order. This is the **first person plural** form (minus 'nous') and renders the English 'let us ...': e.g. Mangeons chez Maxim = Let's eat at Maxim's. N'allons pas près du pont = Let's not go near the bridge.

(3) Imperative of '**être**' and '**avoir**'
These verbs have irregular forms, which are:

sois, soyons, soyez (être); aie, ayons, ayez (avoir): e.g. Sois sage! =
Be good! N'ayons pas peur = Don't let's be afraid.

(4) The imperative with **reflexive** and other **object pronouns**
It is worth recalling that when an imperative is **positive** any object
pronouns are attached with hyphens **after the verb**. When it is
negative, however, the pronouns come in their **usual place**.
With reflexive verbs you must of course **retain** the **reflexive
pronoun** in the imperative; their position will be as above.
E.g. Rendez-moi ma serviette = Give me back my brief-case.
Ne les attendons pas ici = Let's not wait for them here.
Asseyez-vous là-bas = Sit down over there.
Ne te couche pas si tôt = Don't go to bed so early.
When 'me', 'te' are attached with hyphens after the verb they
become of course '**moi**' and '**toi**'.

Test section

(i) Give the correct **present tense** of the following verbs in the
person indicated in brackets.

vendre	(je)	**je vends**
jeter	(tu)	**tu jettes**
boire	(vous)	**vous buvez**
s'appeler	(il)	**il s'appelle**
exagérer	(ils)	**ils exagèrent**
croire	(vous)	**vous croyez**
résoudre	(nous)	**nous résolvons**
apercevoir	(je)	**j'aperçois**
choisir	(elles)	**elles choisissent**
recommencer	(nous)	**nous recommençons**
s'inquiéter	(tu)	**tu t'inquiètes**
plonger	(nous)	**nous plongeons**
se lever	(imperative -tu)	**lève-toi**
se dépêcher	(imperative negative -tu)	**ne te dépêche pas**
hésiter	(let us . . .)	**hésitons**

N.B. Translation into French *is happily becoming a rarer
exercise in the examination. This and other test sections involving
translation into French should be considered* **optional. CSE
candidates** *will* **certainly not be required to translate into
French.**

(ii) **Translate into French using the present tense only.**
Yes, he'd quite like that.   **Il veut bien.**

They've just replied.	Ils viennent de répondre.
He's just coming!	Il arrive !
I'm in the process of making a dress.	Je suis en train de faire une robe.
She'll be coming in a second.	Elle vient dans un instant.
We really hope to stay in Paris.	Nous espérons bien rester à Paris.
I'm going to write a letter.	Je vais écrire une lettre.
You've lived there for three years.	Vous habitez là depuis trois ans.
They are willing to come with us (use 'accompagner').	Ils veulent bien nous accompagner.
How long have you been smoking?	Depuis quand fumez-vous ?

(iii) **Translate into good English.**

Qu'est-ce que tu viens de manger ?	What have you just eaten?
Depuis combien de mois ce magasin est-il fermé ?	For how many months has this shop been shut?
Vous voulez bien allez au cinéma ?	You don't mind going to the cinema?
Ils sont en train de réparer le toit.	They are repairing the roof.
Nous nous connaissons depuis des années.	We've known each other for years.
Il va traverser la Manche en canoë.	He's going to cross the Channel by canoe.

Future tense

Formation

The future tense is also a **simple** (one-word) tense. **All verbs** add the **same endings**. For -er and -ir verbs the **stem** is the whole **infinitive**: for -re verbs the **infinitive minus the final 'e'**. The irregular verbs often have an individual stem, which must be learned separately, but they still add the regular endings. **Note** that for all verbs the letter '**r**' immediately precedes the ending. Candidates sometimes confuse the future and imperfect endings and this is one way of helping you remember.

Future endings:	– ai	– ons
	– as	– ez
	– a	– ont

Thus: je mang**erai** = I will eat; tu chois**iras** = you will choose; il se souviend**ra** = he will remember, etc . . .

(1) The verbs which were pointed out in the present tense as **doubling the consonant** or **adding 'è'** maintain that peculiarity throughout the future: e.g. Vous appe**ll**erez Georges; nous nous l**èv**erons; ils je**tt**eront; j'ach**èt**erai.

(2) Those verbs with '**é**', however, retain their normal form in the future: e.g. Je rép**é**terai; il accél**e**rera; vous exag**e**rerez.

Meaning and usage

(1) The future is used on most occasions just as in English: Nous les **reverrons** demain = We **shall see** them again tomorrow. Quand **viendras-tu** me voir? = When **will you come** to see me? Some care of course must be taken with the English words 'will', 'won't', 'shall' and 'shan't', for they are not always used with a simple future sense. They can, for instance, convey the idea of 'being willing' or not, as in these examples:
Voulez-vous me passer la confiture? = **Will you pass me** the jam? Mange tes légumes! **Je ne veux pas**! = Eat your vegetables! **I won't**!

(2) The only other area where the unwary fall into well-laid traps concerns the **logical expression of what is a future idea**, but which is rendered rather carelessly in English by the present. Such instances are nearly always in clauses introduced by '**quand**' or '**aussitôt que, dès que**'.
E.g. Quand je **recevrai** sa lettre, je vous téléphonerai = When I **receive** his letter, I shall ring you.
Aussitôt que j'**aurai** 21 ans, je prendrai ma retraite! = As soon as I **am** 21, I shall retire!

The French like to think of themselves as logical, rational beings, and they certainly tend to be as far as the use of tenses is concerned. In the cases mentioned here, the main action is taking place at some future time and so it is entirely logical that the subordinate clause which is the necessary condition for that action, should also be in the future. So in the two examples above, the sequence of events must be (a) the speaker **will receive** the letter and then will telephone, and (b) the speaker **will reach** the ripe old age of 21 and then will retire.

Of course the main verb does not have to be in the future for the

60

subordinate clause to need logically itself to be future. This situation arises particularly when the **main clause** is in the form of a **command**. Here therefore you have to be very alert to recognise the logic – and act on it!

E.g. Appelez-moi quand vous **serez** prêt = Call me when **you're** ready. Faites-le dès que vous le **pourrez** = Do it as soon as you **can**.

Test section

(i) Give the **correct future tense** of the following verbs in the **person indicated in brackets.**

répondre	(tu)	**tu répondras**
arriver	(je)	**j'arriverai**
remplir	(nous)	**nous remplirons**
se rappeler	(vous)	**vous vous rappellerez**
amener	(elle)	**elle amènera**
répéter	(ils)	**ils répéteront**
projeter	(je)	**je projetterai**
mettre	(nous)	**nous mettrons**

**See note on page 58 concerning sections marked with asterisks.

(ii) **Translate these phrases into French.** Beware of apparent futures which are not, and of futures which apparently are not!

We will arrive at 6 o'clock.	**Nous arriverons à six heures.**
Will you pass the bread?	**Voulez-vous passer le pain?**
She will buy some sweets tomorrow.	**Demain, elle achètera des bonbons.**
As soon as you arrive, please telephone.	**Dès que vous arriverez, téléphonez s'il vous plaît.**
... will you telephone?	**... voulez-vous téléphoner?**
It will freeze tonight (use 'cette nuit').	**Il gèlera cette nuit.**
He won't eat his ice-cream.	**Il ne veut pas manger sa glace.**
They will get up late in the holidays.	**Ils se lèveront tard pendant les vacances.**

(iii) **Translate into good English.**

Nous vous écrirons dès que nous trouverons un hôtel.	**We will write to you as soon as we find a hotel.**
Non! Ils ne veulent pas reprendre le travail!	**No! They won't go back to work!**
Quand apprendra-t-il ses leçons?	**When will he learn his homework?**
Je vous aiderai quand vous me le demanderez gentiment.	**I will help you when you ask me nicely.**

Perfect tense (passé composé)

The perfect is one of those tenses known as **compound tenses** because it consists of **two verb parts**: an **auxiliary verb + past participle** of the verb in question. This most elementary feature of the perfect is ignored all too often by candidates who (at their peril!) omit the auxiliary verb.

It is an extremely important tense, and although for some it appears to hold mighty terrors and present unfathomable depths, it really has a very straightforward pattern compared with the present tense and its wide variety of possible endings and stem patterns.

Formation

All verbs use an **auxiliary verb** ('**avoir**' or '**être**'), which is the **only part** of the verb to be **conjugated**), together with a **past participle** formed from the verb itself, and which **does not** add set endings to show the person of the verb. (N.B. Agreement of the past participle is an area which will be dealt with a little later on separately.) Thus for a verb with '**avoir**' as the **auxiliary** verb the pattern will be as follows:

j'**ai** entendu   nous **avons** entendu = I have heard, I heard, etc.
tu **as** entendu   vous **avez** entendu
il **a** entendu   ils **ont** entendu

and for a verb with '**être**' as the **auxiliary** verb:

je **suis** sorti   nous **sommes** sortis = I have gone out, I went out, etc.

tu **es** sorti   vous **êtes** sorti
il **est** sorti   ils **sont** sortis

(1) Past participles

For **irregular** verbs these must be **learned by heart** from the verb tables.

Regular verbs form their past participle according to their type pattern:

-er verbs add **é** to the verb stem (e.g. donn**é**);
-ir verbs add **i** to the verb stem (e.g. fin**i**);
-re verbs add **u** to the verb stem (e.g. vend**u**).

(2) **Avoir** or **être**?

By far the **majority** of verbs use '**avoir**' as their auxiliary. A few verbs are conjugated with '**être**'; these **must** be learned and practised a great deal so that use of '**être**' becomes an automatic reflex (hopefully!) For ease of memory most of these verbs can be put into pairs of opposites.

aller	= to go,	venir	= to come;
*monter	= to go up,	*descendre	= to go down;
arriver	= to arrive,	partir	= to leave;
entrer	= to come in,	*sortir	= to go out;
naître	= to be born,	mourir	= to die.

Also: tomber = to fall, rester = to remain and three verbs meaning 'to return': *rentrer, revenir and retourner.

N.B. All these verbs are **intransitive**, that is, they are used without an object. However the ones marked with an asterisk* can **sometimes** take an object, and in this case they will use the verb '**avoir**' as auxiliary. Their meaning when used transitively is extended to include the following:

monter	= to take, bring upstairs;
descendre	= to take, bring downstairs;
sortir	= to take, bring out;
rentrer	= to take, bring back in.

E.g.   Elle **a descendu** l'escalier = She went down the staircase.
      Il **a monté** les bagages = He took the luggage upstairs.
      J'**ai sorti** mon mouchoir = I took out my handkerchief.

(3) In addition to the verbs on the list above **all reflexive verbs** are conjugated with '**être**'. This means also that if you make an ordinary verb reflexive, it **must** use '**être**' in the perfect tense.
E.g. demander = to ask, se demander = to wonder:
Il **a demandé** son chemin à un agent = He asked a policeman the way.
Il **s'est demandé** pourquoi il était là = He wondered why he was there.

Agreement of past participle in perfect tense

The points made in this section will, of course, apply equally in the case of the other compound tenses such as the **pluperfect** and **future perfect**.

For ease of reference we will divide the verbs into **three** groups:
(1) **'avoir' group**; (2) **'être' group**; (3) **reflexive group.**
**CSE candidates: see note on page 67.

(1) **Verbs conjugated with 'avoir'**

With these the agreement is made with the **preceding direct object, never** with the **subject**. In other words, for any agreement to be possible, there has to be an **object in front of the verb**, and that object must be **direct**, not for instance a dative pronoun such as 'lui', 'leur'.

There are **three principal occasions** on which such an agreement is likely to occur:

(a) **With an object pronoun** (**direct** only)

Je les ai remarqu**és** = I noticed them.
Il nous avait aperç**us** = He had caught sight of us.
Marie? On l'a laiss**ée** à la maison = Marie? We have left her at home.

However, there would be **no agreement**, even with the object pronoun in front, if the latter were **indirect**:
Elles nous ont écri**t** = They have written to us.
Je leur ai montr**é** mes timbres = I showed them my stamps.
Note how 'them' here means '**to them**'.
Note also that the pronoun **'en' never** leads to agreement of the past participle. Remember its basic meaning is 'of them', 'of it' and so is **not** a **direct** object pronoun.

(b) **Following the relative pronoun 'que'**

'**Que**', as we have seen, is the **direct object relative pronoun** and therefore must be the **object** of the following verb (hence the agreement where necessary):
Où sont les lettres que vous avez écrit**es**? = Where are the letters (which) you have written?
La clef qu'il m'avait donn**ée** était rouillée = The key he had given me was rusty.
Les messieurs que nous avons rencontr**és** étaient très gentils = The gentlemen (whom) we met were very nice.

In each case '**que**' fulfils the requirements (as above) for agreement of the past participle. In example (1) it refers back to 'les lettres' (thus feminine plural agreement), in example (2) it refers back to 'la clef (thus feminine singular agreement) and in the last example it refers back to 'les messieurs' (thus masculine plural agreement).

Remember that object pronouns come immediately before the verb; in the case of a compound tense like the perfect, where there are two parts, the **object pronoun** always comes **before** the **auxiliary** verb.

(c) With certain types of question, where the question formula contains the direct object of the verb

Quelle robe as-tu chois**ie**? = Which dress did you choose?
Quels romans avait-il l**us**? = Which novels had he read?
Combien de vitres avez-vous cass**ées**? = How many window-panes have you broken?

As you will see from the words in bold type, the direct object is preceding the verb, and the past participle must be made to agree. It is comforting to know that the French themselves are not always totally accurate on this rule of preceding direct object agreement. Could you suggest why they would be more likely to remember the agreement in the first example given below than in the second?
Où est la voiture? Robert l'a pri**se**.
Où sont les gâteaux? Jean les a mang**és**.

The reason is because the **agreement** is **sounded** in the first example since the past participle ends in a consonant; in the second it is not. Unfortunately, though failure to make the necessary agreements is an error with which the French would sympathise, that does not prevent examiners penalising such omissions! A cruel world indeed!

(2) Verbs from the given list conjugated with 'être'

With these verbs the **past participle** quite simply **agrees with the subject**, just as an adjective would.

E.g. Elles sont déjà arriv**ées**   = They have already arrived.
      Sa tante est mor**te** cette nuit = His aunt died last night.
      Quand sont-ils n**és**?   = When were they born?

You may in fact have seen the form '**née**' dozens of times in the births columns of English newspapers, meaning 'maiden name' (literally 'born'!).

(3) Reflexive verbs

Many candidates are under the mistaken impression that reflexive verbs agree with their subject. In fact, however, this is not so. To have to un-learn something is always a painful process so that it is much better to learn the correct ruling in the first place. In this case, the ruling is that **reflexive verbs** behave exactly like '**avoir**'-conjugated verbs – they **agree** with the **preceding direct object**. More often than not the preceding direct object is the reflexive pronoun, which is identical in number and gender with the subject.

Elle s'est lev**ée** à huit heures = She got up at 8 o'clock.

Où se sont-ils cach**és**? = Where have they hidden?

Elles ne s'étaient pas lav**ées** = They had not washed.

Obviously, in example (1) 'she got **herself** up', in example (2) 'they hid **themselves**', and in example (3) what they did **not** wash was '**them**selves!' **But this is not always the case!** With the verb 'se rappeler' = to remember, the idea is that one recalls **to** oneself a particular memory and the **reflexive pronoun** is therefore **indirect**. Hence there is **no agreement** with the reflexive pronoun:

Elle s'est rappe**lé** leur adresse le lendemain = She remembered their address the following day. Here the direct object is of course 'leur adresse'.

Often, of course, reflexive verbs are used to show **reciprocal action**, or to say **(to) each other**, and the reflexive pronoun is the expression of the 'each other'. In such circumstances of course it is clearly **indirect** object, so there will be **no agreement**.

E.g. Ils se sont demand**é** pourquoi leur ami était revenu = They wondered (literally 'asked themselves') why their friend had come back. Nous nous sommes parl**é** fort dans la nuit = We talked (to each other) far into the night.

The same degree of vigilance is therefore necessary for spotting the **indirect reflexive pronoun** as was demanded earlier in the book in the section on indirect object pronouns. In fact the problems are identical:

Ils **lui** ont envoyé de nombreuses lettres = They sent **her** numerous letters, **or** Ils **se** sont envoyé de nombreuses lettres = They sent **each other** numerous letters.

Such unusual cases of agreement must of course be pointed out, and understood by the candidate, but in case it should appear that the unusual is the norm, let us end this section by 'recapping' the most commonly found situation with reflexive verbs in the perfect. With **most** of them the **reflexive pronoun** is the **direct object** and therefore the **past participle** will **agree** with that.

E.g. Elles se sont assis**es** pour lire = They sat down to read.
Nous nous sommes dépêch**és** = We hurried up.

**Note to CSE candidates

Usually you are required simply to **recognise** the preceding direct object agreement, **not** to reproduce it yourself in your writing. **Reflexive verbs** Usually you will only be required to use in the perfect tense those reflexive verbs where agreement is with the reflexive pronoun. Naturally you will gain extra credit in the examination if you are able to use the more complicated agreements **accurately**.

Meaning and usage

The perfect tense is one of the most frequently used in the French language and is the basis for several others. It is therefore absolutely essential to any serious study, and all its many aspects, as outlined in the preceding section, **must** be mastered.

(1) To put it at its simplest, the **perfect** is the tense used in **spoken French**, or in **letters**, to relate what **has happened in the past**. It tells of facts or events which have been **completed** and are **finished**. In general terms therefore it corresponds to the English '**I did**', or '**I have done**', or even '**I have been doing**' *provided* that the action referred to has now stopped. (See example (iv) below.) It is clear-cut: an event began at a particular point in time, it ended at a particular point in time, and this is recorded in French by the **perfect** tense. In short: **something happened = perfect tense.**

E.g. (i) Hier nous sommes allés au cinéma = Yesterday we went to the cinema. (ii) Ce matin, Claude a rencontré le curé au supermarché = This morning Claude met the vicar in the supermarket. (iii) Il y a cinq ans nous avons passé de très belles vacances au nord de l'Espagne = Five years ago we spent a very good holiday in the north of Spain. (iv) Il a travaillé toute la matinée = He has worked all morning.

It is extremely important to respect the fact that the perfect is the tense used when **speaking** and in **letter-writing**. Once you have met the other narrative past tense, the past historic, you may well acquire a tendency (which you must guard against) to use **that** in your work. Unless you are asked to do so, the use of the past historic in O-level work will be **inappropriate and incorrect**.

(2) The **perfect** must **always** refer to **single and complete events** and not to happenings which were still going on at the time in question. Study the following three examples which make this point:

(i) Pendant sept ans il a travaillé à la banque = For seven years he worked in the bank.

(ii) A ce moment-là il bourrait sa pipe = At that moment he was filling his pipe.

(iii) De temps à autre il allait voir ses amis à la campagne = From time to time he went to see his friends in the country.

In **example (i)** we know as a self-contained fact that for a stated block of time (seven years) he worked in the bank – it is a **complete episode**. You should note that the **length of time** taken by an event **has nothing to do with the tense** used to relate it. Everything depends on whether the speaker or author chooses to view the event as **complete** or not. Equally valid as a time statement would be the one word 'longtemps', instead of the period 'pendant sept ans' – the statement about the 'bank' is still a completed past event.

In **example (ii)** you cannot use the perfect because there is no indication of a completed action at the time in question (hence the imperfect tense).

In **example (iii)** you cannot use the perfect either because it is describing repeated events, which again necessitate the imperfect.

If you remember these two basic characteristics about the perfect tense, then you should have little difficulty distinguishing it from the imperfect, which is the next tense we shall meet.

Test section

(i) **Give the corresponding perfect** tense of the verbs listed on the left in the present tense.

Ils se battent.	**Ils se sont battus.**
Je regarde la télé.	**J'ai regardé la télé.**
(Now the same phrase, making 'la télé' a pronoun)	**Je l'ai regardée.**
Nous choisissons des bonbons.	**Nous avons choisi des bonbons.**
(Now the same phrase, making 'des bonbons' a pronoun)	**Nous en avons choisi.**

Suzanne entre dans la cuisine.	**Suzanne est entrée dans la cuisine.**
Nous descendons les valises.	**Nous avons descendu les valises.**
Combien d'animaux dessine-t-il?	**Combien d'animaux a-t-il dessinés?**
Ils s'en vont tout de suite.	**Ils s'en sont allés tout de suite.**
Ils descendent déjà.	**Ils sont déjà descendus.**
Quels verres remplis-tu?	**Quels verres as-tu remplis?**
Elles se parlent en classe.	**Elles se sont parlé en classe.**
Tu rejettes les disques que j'apporte.	**Tu as rejeté les disques que j'ai apportés.**
Vous rentrez tôt, vous deux.	**Vous êtes rentrés tôt, vous deux.**
Papa lui vend sa moto.	**Papa lui a vendu sa moto.**
'Il m'insulte', dit Chantal.	**'Il m'a insultée,' a dit Chantal.**
Vous vous couchez tard.	**Vous vous êtes couché tard.**
Elle se rappelle l'histoire.	**Elle s'est rappelé l'histoire.**

(ii) Which of the following English phrases could be rendered by the perfect tense in French? Answer **yes** or **no**.

Last Sunday we decided to go for a walk,	**yes**
since the sun was shining brightly.	**no**
Just as we were about to set off,	**no**
the cat crawled in very sorrowfully.	**yes**
She had been in a fight;	**no** (pluperfect)
one ear was bleeding.	**no**
Father bathed the ear,	**yes**
gave her a saucerful of milk with a dash of brandy!	**yes**
and the cat promptly went to sleep.	**yes**
When we lived in our old house,	**no** (= used to)
she was always fighting.	**no**
We have only been here two weeks	**no** (depuis)
– nothing has changed!	**yes**

Imperfect tense

Formation

We have now come to the last of the four basic tenses. Fortunately its formation is extremely straightforward. It is a **simple tense** (i.e. consisting of one word) and therefore endings are added direct to a verb stem. In this case the **verb stem** consists of the '**nous**' form of the **present** tense, without the '**-ons**'. For our three regular types of verb, this would leave us with:

-er type = parl-; **-ir type = finiss**-; **-re type = vend**

To these stems the following endings are added:

je parl**ais**	nous parl**ions**	je finiss**ais**	nous finiss**ions**
tu parl**ais**	vous parl**iez**	tu finiss**ais**	vous finiss**iez**
il parl**ait**	ils parl**aient**	il finiss**ait**	ils finiss**aient**
	je vend**ais**	nous vend**ions**	
	tu vend**ais**	vous vend**iez**	
	il vend**ait**	ils vend**aient**	

You will be able to see why it is important to take the 'nous' form of the present tense, rather than the infinitive stem: for all **-ir verbs** the characteristic '**iss**' syllable would not be included in the infinitive stem, and for a fair number of other verbs we have seen that the 'nous' form of the present offers individual peculiarities.

Thus the imperfect of **boire** would be:
Stem: **buv**-   **je buvais**, etc.
and of **voir**:   **je voyais**, etc.

There is **one exception** to this rule, the verb '**être**':

j'**ét**ais	nous **ét**ions
tu **ét**ais	vous **ét**iez
il **ét**ait	ils **ét**aient

While the endings are normal, the stem is a form '**ét**-'.
All other verbs form their imperfect tense using the formula above.

N.B. Verbs with infinitives in -cer, -ger

You will remember that in the present tense, '**ç**' and '**ge**' had to be supplied to avoid a hard sound before the ending of the 'nous' form **-ons**. A similar adjustment must be made in the imperfect before **all** endings **except** the 'nous' and 'vous' persons, where the '**i**' of the endings (**-ions**, **-iez**) provides the soft sound.

E.g. Il commen**ç**ait à pleuvoir   = It was beginning to rain.
Je na**ge**ais tous les jours   = I used to swim every day.

Meaning and usage

A lot of mistakes are made concerning the choice of imperfect or perfect tenses, but just as we have seen for the perfect, so for the imperfect there are easily definable circumstances where the imperfect is called for. Provided the candidate knows these thoroughly, there should be very few cases indeed where there could be a genuine doubt about the past tense required.

In the context of tenses the word **imperfect** means '**unfinished**', and this throws considerable light on its use in French. In the section on the perfect we already came across two instances where the imperfect was the tense required, and both of these illustrated the most frequent uses of this tense.

(1) To describe **what was in progress** at the time when some other event took place (in other words, an **incomplete action**, the time and duration of its occurrence not pin-pointed). In English this often takes the meaning '**was doing**': e.g. La vieille dame **traversait** la chaussée quand elle fut renversée par un camion = The old lady **was crossing** the street when she was knocked down by a lorry.

In this and similar sentences it is easy to visualise the **imperfect part (a)** as a **continuous line**, and the **event which happened (b)** as a **vertical line** interrupting that.

(b) **elle fut renversée par un camion**
(a) **elle traversait │ la chaussée . . . . . .**

Try 'plotting' these examples in a similar way, noticing how the action which took place (**b**) (and which is therefore in the **perfect** tense, cuts into the unfinished action going on at that time (**a**). The unfinished action is therefore **imperfect**.

Le tonnerre éclata alors que je rentrais à la maison = The thunder rang out as I was coming home.
Grand-père était en train de manger son petit déjeuner quand les rideaux prirent feu = Grandfather was eating his breakfast when the curtains caught fire.
Nous jouions tranquillement au jardin quand soudain notre oncle est arrivé et nous a invités à l'accompagner au zoo = We were playing quietly in the garden when suddenly our uncle arrived and invited us to go with him to the zoo.
(Here you should plot **two (b) strokes** along the (**a**) line.)

In all of these examples the imperfect is used in conjunction with the perfect (or past historic, as the case may be) – **the two tenses are complementary**.

71

(2) To recount **habitual or repeated action** in the past.

Here the English is often expressed as '**used to**' or sometimes '**would do**'.

E.g. Tous les ans nous **passions** les vacances chez une tante à Bordeaux = Every year we **would spend** the holidays at an aunt's house in Bordeaux.

Mon père **jouait** beaucoup au football quand il **était** jeune = My father **used to play** football a lot when he **was** young.

In these examples the **actions** were all **taking place on numerous occasions in the past**.

(3) A further name for the **imperfect** tense is the **past descriptive** and this summarises very neatly the third function of the tense. It is used to **describe people, things or scenes** as they appeared in the past. **Description** here can refer to **physical appearance** (elle **avait** les cheveux blonds = she **had** blond hair), including **clothes worn** (il **portait** un chapeau melon = he **was wearing** a bowler hat), and **size** (la maison **était** énorme, et **comprenait** cinquante pièces principales = the house **was** enormous and **consisted** of fifty main rooms). It may describe **general aspects** (le paysage **dormait** tranquille sous le soleil éclatant = the landscape **slept** peacefully under the blinding sun), or **status or role** in the past (en 1735 Louis XV **était** roi de France = in 1735 Louis XV **was** King of France), or **geographical location** (la petite église **se trouvait** près de la place = the little church **was situated** near the square). Although the descriptive imperfect is frequently rendered by 'was doing' in English you must be careful to recognise the simple past tense (i.e. she wore) as a descriptive imperfect in the same way.

In all the examples quoted above you are being given **descriptive** (background) information (**not** factual information about an event which took place).

For these reasons the imperfect will often provide the **background details** at the beginning of a story, **setting the scene** against which the actual events (related in the perfect or past historic) will occur:

Un jour que le vent hurlait et que les feuilles d'automne dansaient sur l'herbe sèche, Françoise traversait la prairie. Elle se sentait seule et commençait à avoir peur. Soudain un cri se fit entendre . . . = One day when the wind was howling and the autumn leaves were dancing on the dry grass, Françoise was crossing the meadow. She felt lonely and was beginning to feel scared. Suddenly a cry was heard . . . Here at last is the point at which **the action begins**!

Did you notice incidentally that the imperfect is used to describe **feelings** or **state of mind** in the past? Here it was the phrase she **felt** lonely = elle **se sentait** seule.

(4) There are the same **two** cases as in the present tense where the English and French tense usage differs fundamentally. Firstly with the preposition '**depuis + imperfect**'. You will remember that when used with the present tense 'depuis' represented actions which 'have been going on' and 'still are'. The imperfect takes the event further back into the past – **what had been happening** and **still was happening** at the time the writer or speaker refers to.

E.g. **Depuis** le départ de sa mère il **pleurait** sans cesse = Since his mother's departure he had been crying incessantly (and presumably still was!).

Again do not forget the question form associated with this structure; 'Depuis quand . . . ?' or 'Depuis combien de temps . . . ?'

(5) Imperfect tense of 'venir + de + infinitive'

Exactly the same time relationship operates with this idiom as with the previous one. If the present tense means 'has just', the **imperfect** translates '**had just done**'.

E.g. Elle **venait de sortir** = She **had just gone out.**
Ils **venaient d'arriver** = They **had just arrived.**

Note With these four tenses well under control, you should feel able to deal confidently with the remaining tenses of the indicative.

Test section

Since any difficulties encountered with the imperfect tense mainly concern its usage in relation to other tenses, especially the perfect, there will only be a very short test section on its formation.

Cover the right-hand side of the page while you work out your answers.

(i) **Give the corresponding imperfect** tense of the verbs listed on the left in the infinitive.

s'appeler	(il)	**il s'appelait**
croire	(je)	**je croyais**
faire	(nous)	**nous faisions**
être	(ils)	**ils étaient**
boire	(tu)	**tu buvais**
prendre	(vous)	**vous preniez**

(ii) **Give the correct form of the verb** (imperfect **or** perfect) to fit the following phrases.

Comme il (retourner) à la maison en voiture, un pneu (éclater).
A cette époque-là nous (aller) souvent au bord de la mer.
La petite fille (être) charmante; elle (avoir) les yeux bleus et les cheveux bouclés.
Vous (téléphoner) au moment où je (arriver).
En 1967 Monsieur Leroy (exercer) les fonctions d'ambassadeur.
En 1968 il (mourir).
Nous (faire) nos exercices depuis dix minutes lorsqu'on (sonner) l'alarme.
Vous (apprendre) très peu quand vous (fréquenter) ce college-là.
Tu (se laver) la tête quand Georges (tomber) de l'échelle.
Dans la forêt les petits oiseaux (chanter), les animaux (courir) partout; rien ne (pouvoir) détruire la beauté de cette scène.
Je (venir) d'envoyer le télégramme à Sophie, quand une lettre (annoncer) son arrivée.

(ii) **Answers**
Comme **il retournait** à la maison en voiture, un pneu **a éclaté.**
A cette époque-là **nous allions** souvent au bord de la mer.
La petite fille **était** charmante; **elle avait** les yeux bleus et les cheveux bouclés.
Vous téléphoniez au moment où **je suis arrivé.**
En 1967 Monsieur Leroy **exerçait** les fonctions d'ambassadeur.
En 1968 **il est mort.**
Nous faisions nos exercices **depuis** dix minutes lorsqu'**on a sonné** l'alarme.
Vous appreniez très peu quand **vous fréquentiez** ce collège-là.
Tu te lavais la tête quand Georges **est tombé** de l'echelle.
Dans la forêt les petits oiseaux **chantaient**, les animaux **couraient** partout; rien ne **pouvait** détruire la beauté de cette scène.
Je venais d'envoyer le télégramme à Sophie, quand une lettre **a annoncé** son arrivée.

**See note on page 58.

(iii) **Translate** the following phrases **into French**, using the **imperfect** or **perfect**, as appropriate.

I was beginning to understand the problem, when the lesson (le cours) finished.

How long had he known Jacques when the latter went to America?
The sky was blue, the grass was green!
The restaurant was situated in a little street behind the church.
We had just ordered (commander) a new car when the old one broke down.
You always went for a walk before breakfast.

(iii) **Answers**

Je commençais à comprendre le problème quand le cours a fini.

Depuis combien de temps connaissait-il Jacques quand celui-ci est allé en Amérique?

Le ciel était bleu, l'herbe était verte!

Le restaurant se trouvait dans une petite rue derrière l'église.

Nous venions de commander une nouvelle voiture quand la vieille est tombée en panne.

Vous faisiez toujours une promenade avant le petit dejeuner.

or **Vous vous promeniez toujours . . .**

Conditional tense

Formation

The conditional is a mixture of two tenses you know already. It is formed without exception from the **future stem** of a verb, to which the **imperfect endings** are added.

An example of a typical -er verb would be:

je mang**erais**	nous mang**erions**	= I would eat, etc.
tu mang**erais**	vous mang**eriez**	
il mang**erait**	ils mang**eraient**	

The other two regular types would give:

je fin**irais**, etc. = I would finish
je vend**rais**, etc. = I would sell

(1) **Remember** that when it is the future stem which is involved, the last letter before the ending will always be '**r**'.

(2) Any slight peculiarities of spelling ('è', or 'tt', or 'll') which were noted in the formation of the future tense will apply here too! e.g. nous nous prom**è**nerions, je je**tt**erais, etc.

Meaning and usage

(1) Conditional sentences are often known as 'if' sentences,

because the conditional tense is most frequently found in a sentence containing an 'if' clause.

E.g. S'il pleuvait, je **mettrais** mon imperméable = If it rained, I **would put** my raincoat on.

Monique **accompagnerait** les garçons au cinéma, s'ils l'invitaient = Monique **would go** to the cinema with the boys, if they invited her.

A word here about the tense of the verb in the 'if' clause. You could, in the examples above, render the English 'if it were to rain', etc., in which case the imperfect should spring readily to mind, but if rendered simply as is written above, it could be more difficult to see that the imperfect **is** required. In these kinds of sentences the pattern is always:

'if' clause – imperfect; main clause – conditional.

(It is of course possible to have the 'if' clause as a **pluperfect** tense, but in this case it will be quite obvious that this is the tense needed. 'If I **had given** him the poison, I would be very sorry!')

(2) The other main use of the conditional occurs in **indirect speech** (someone said that ...) The conditional is used in the **subordinate clause** (following 'that ...') when the **actual words** at the time of speaking would have been expressed in the **future** tense.

E.g. (words spoken by Jean) 'Je viendrai ce soir à huit heures'; (words later reported by someone else) Jean a dit qu'il **viendrait** ce soir à huit heures = John said that he **would come** ...

J'avais promis que Marie **rentrerait** avant minuit = I had promised that Marie **would be back** before midnight.

It is quite logical therefore that another name given to the conditional is **future in the past.**

(3) While on the subject of logic there is the same policy of **logical tense sequence** with the conditional as in the future tense.

Il jura qu'il lui achèterait la bague dès qu'il **aurait** l'argent = He swore that he would buy her the ring as soon as he **had** the money.

Notice the precision of the future in the past 'il aurait', when compared with the vague English past 'he had'. After all, perhaps he never did have the money!

Other meanings of the conditional in English are **'might'**, **'could'**, and **'ought'**. These will be dealt with fully later on in chapter 14, **Modal Verbs**, on 'vouloir', 'pouvoir', etc., but it is well to notice now how important it is to decide precisely what is conveyed by these words; the same also applies to **'would'** and **'should'**. They are used with a variety of meanings. '**Would**' for example can mean '**used to**' and then the tense called for is the **imperfect**.

Test section

(i) **Complete these conditional sentences**, by writing the appropriate form of the verbs given in brackets (conditional or imperfect).

Si grand'mère me (laisser) de l'argent, je (s'étonner) fort.
Si l'examen (être) difficile, il ne (réussir) pas.
Nous (préférer) aller au Portugal, si nous (avoir) le choix.
Cela (plaire) à tout le monde, s'il (faire) toujours très beau en été.
Vous (aimer) assister au concert, si Papa (obtenir) des places.
Si l'essence (devenir) encore plus chère, je (vendre) ma voiture.
Si le patron leur (fournir) des machines plus modernes, ils (accomplir) leur travail plus rapidement.

(ii) From the direct speech given **form indirect speech** by starting each sentence with the words: 'Jacques a dit que . . .'

'Ta mère préparera un gâteau au chocolat.'
'Les enfants finiront leur devoir avant de sortir.'
'Je renoncerai au vin.'
'Vous croirez tout ce qu'on vous dira.'
'Il rougira si on lui parle de Simone.'
'Nous nous mettrons en maillot de bain, s'il continue à faire beau.'
'Chantal téléphonera les résultats à ses parents, quand on les lui annoncera.'

(i) Answers
Si grand'mère me **laissait** de l'argent, **je m'étonnerais** fort.
Si l'examen **était** difficile, **il ne réussirait pas**.
Nous préférerions aller au Portugal, si **nous en avions** le choix.
Cela **plairait** à tout le monde, s'**il faisait** toujours très beau en été.
Vous **aimeriez** assister au concert, si Papa **obtenait** des places.
Si l'essence **devenait** encore plus chère, **je vendrais** ma voiture.
Si le patron leur **fournissait** des machines plus modernes, ils **accompliraient** leur travail plus rapidement.

(ii) Answers
Jacques a dit que ta mère **préparerait** un gâteau au chocolat.
Jacques a dit que les enfants **finiraient** leur devoir avant de sortir.
Jacques a dit que **je renoncerai** au vin.
Jacques a dit que **vous croiriez** tout ce qu'**on vous dirait**.
Jacques a dit qu'**il rougirait** si **on lui parlait** de Simone

Jacques a dit que **nous nous mettrions** en maillot de bain, s'il **continuait** à faire beau.

Jacques a dit que Chantal **téléphonerait** les résultats à ses parents, quand **on les lui annoncerait**.

Pluperfect, future perfect and conditional perfect tenses

Pluperfect tense: formation

This compound tense consists of the **imperfect tense** of the **auxiliary** verb ('avoir' or 'être'), plus the **past participle**.
Thus we would see:

j'**avais mangé**	nous **avions mangé** = I had eaten, etc.
tu **avais mangé**	vous **aviez mangé**
il **avait mangé**	ils **avaient mangé**

Or of an 'être' verb:

j'**étais venu**	nous **étions venus** = I had come, etc.
tu **étais venu**	vous **étiez venu**
il **était venu**	ils **étaient venus**

Meaning and usage

Quite simply the **pluperfect** translates '**had done**', just as in English, and describes events which took place **before** past happenings which are already being narrated.

E.g. Ce jour-là il revit la vieille église où **il avait** tant de fois **prié** = That day he saw again the old church where **he had prayed** so many times.

J'ai essayé de trouver Pascal chez lui, mais **il était** déjà **parti** = I tried to find Pascal at home, but **he had** already **left**.

Future perfect and conditional perfect tenses: formation

Both these compound tenses are formed as their name suggests. Both are based on the perfect tense. The **future perfect** consists of the **future of the auxiliary verb**, together with the **past participle**: j'**aurai donné**, etc. = I will have given, etc. or of an 'être' verb: je **serai arrivé** = I will have arrived, etc.

The **conditional perfect** consists of the **conditional of the auxiliary verb**, together with the **past participle**: e.g. j'**aurais accepté**, etc. = I would have accepted, etc. Or of an 'être' verb: je **serais venu**, etc. = I would have come, etc.: e.g. Si tu arrives à minuit, j'**aurai terminé** la peinture = If you arrive at midnight, I **will have finished** the painting. Nous **serions rentrés** plus tôt, si on nous avait prévenus = We **would have come home** earlier, if someone had let us know. **Reflexive verbs** of course are conjugated with 'être', therefore:

Je **m'étais levé** = I had got up (pluperfect);
Je **me serai levé** = I will have got up (future perfect);
Je **me serais levé** = I would have got up (conditional perfect).

Meaning and usage

(1) In nearly all respects the usage is just as in English. Certainly 'will have done' or 'would have done' is rendered by the future perfect and conditional perfect respectively.

(2) But in addition there is the question once again of **logical tense**. The following examples will illustrate this:

Quand **vous serez habillé**, nous sortirons = When **you are dressed** we will go out.

Il a promis de le faire dès qu'**il aurait réparé** le toit = He promised to do it as soon as **he had repaired** the roof.

The English language really is to blame here. To say 'have dressed' suggests that it has happened, whereas it has yet to do so. Similarly, in the second example it is obvious that he '**would** have completed the repair' before he tackled the second job promised.

Test section

(i) **Supply the appropriate tense** (future perfect or conditional perfect) where the verb is given in brackets.

Quand tu rentreras ce soir, nous (finir) la décoration du salon.
Dès que le soleil (se lever) nous partirons.
Si le propriétaire n'était pas revenu, ils (vendre) tous les meubles.
Les cambrioleurs décidèrent d'entrer dans la maison, quand la famille (partir)'.
Si vous arrivez à neuf heures, nous (se réveiller).

(ii) In these sentences the **pluperfect is required.**
Marie (étudier) beaucoup, quand elle était jeune.
Ils (se cacher) derrière le gymnase, pour éviter le cours de français.
Nous avons téléphoné au 'Secours Routier', parce que notre voiture (tomber en panne).
Le chat est sorti, parce que tu (oublier) de fermer la fenêtre.

(i) Answers

Quand tu rentreras ce soir, **nous aurons fini** la décoration du salon.

Dès que le soleil **se sera levé**, nous partirons.

Si le propriétaire n'était pas revenu, **ils auraient vendu** tous les meubles.

Les cambrioleurs décidèrent d'entrer dans la maison, quand la famille **serait partie**.

Si vous arrivez à neuf heures, **nous nous serons réveillés**.

(ii) Answers

Marie **avait** beaucoup **étudié**, quand elle était jeune.

Ils **s'étaient cachés** derrière le gymnase, pour éviter le cours de français.

Nous avons téléphoné au 'Secours Routier', parce que notre voiture **était tombée** en panne.

Le chat est sorti, parce que **tu avais oublié** de fermer la fenêtre.

Past historic tense (passé simple)

It has already been mentioned that for most candidates knowledge of the past historic may be confined to recognition of its forms and use. It is **not** obligatory in essay writing, and normally, on those GCE O-level papers which include a translation into French, the candidates are allowed to choose between the perfect and the past historic as their main narrative tense. It is certainly, however, a tense which candidates should know well, for they will meet it in passages for translation and comprehension, and the narrative of the story for reproduction is most often in the past historic. In fact this tense has a good deal to recommend it. It has a simple, one-word form, there are no problems of auxiliaries or agreements and word order is less complex than in the perfect.

CSE candidates are **not required to write the past historic.

Formation

Verbs in the past historic are **one of three types**, characterised by a **particular vowel**. The three groups are as follows:

(1) **All -er verbs**	(2) **Regular -ir, and -re verbs and some irregular verbs**	(3) **Remaining irregular verbs**
je port**ai**	je vend**is**	je reç**us**
tu port**as**	tu vend**is**	tu reç**us**
il port**a**	il vend**it**	il reç**ut**
nous port**âmes**	nous vend**îmes**	nous reç**ûmes**
vous port**âtes**	vous vend**îtes**	vous reç**ûtes**
ils port**èrent**	ils vend**irent**	ils reç**urent**

One point of interest is that for once **regular -ir, and -re verbs** take the same endings.

There is no easy way of deciding which irregular verbs will follow the **-is** and which the **-us** pattern, and there is no alternative but to learn them by heart.

(1) As on other occasions care must be taken to supply '**ç**' and '**ge**' in those persons where **there is a following 'a' or 'u'**: that is, in **all** parts (except third person plural) of the '**ai**' types, and in **all parts of the 'us' types.**

(2) **Two verbs** only (with their derivatives) are totally **irregular**.

venir:	je vins	nous vînmes	**tenir**:	je tins	nous tînmes
	tu vins	vous vîntes		tu tins	vous tîntes
	il vint	ils vinrent		il tint	ils tinrent

Derivatives are: revenir, devenir, se souvenir; contenir, retenir.

Meaning and usage

(1) The past historic is exactly **equivalent to the perfect tense**, in the sense that it is a **past narrative** tense, used to tell of **completed, single events** in the past.

E.g. Il **ouvrit** la porte, le meurtrier l'**attaqua** par derrière = He **opened** the door, the murderer **attacked him** from behind.

(2) The difference between the two lies in the fact that whereas the perfect is the tense for spoken French, the **past historic** is the tense for **written French**. It is in fact a **literary tense**, not to be used in conversation or in letter-writing. It will appear most of all in history books, biography and novels. As we have seen the perfect is a personal narrative tense (hence conversation and letter-writing); the past historic is a **paper tense** found on the printed page. Thus, to elaborate a rather fanciful situation, your forthcoming novel will doubtless be written in the past historic, but your discussions on it with your editor will be in the perfect!

(3) It should follow logically that the **imperfect** tense stands in exactly the **same relationship** to the past historic as it did to the perfect. Description of people or places, habitual events, continuous incomplete happenings will, as before, be expressed by the imperfect tense.

E.g. Il **mangeait** une banane lorsque le fantôme **apparut** = He was eating a banana when the ghost appeared.

D'habitude ils **revenaient** tard, mais ce jour-là ils **prirent** le train de sept heures et demie = Usually they came back late, but that day they took the half-past seven train.

A reminder here that **any stated length of time** (no matter how short) will demand the past historic. The time may be as short as a few seconds or as long as several centuries.

E.g. Pendant quelques instants elle **se sentit** vraiment malade = For a few moments she felt really ill. (Note that her indisposition is viewed as an **episode**.) La guerre entre nos deux pays **dura** longtemps = War between our two countries went on a long time. (Note that although imprecise, 'longtemps' is sufficient to indicate that the episode which took place is **now over**.)

Compare also these two examples which illustrate:
(a) the subtlety which can be achieved by judicious choice of tense;
(b) how this all depends on what the writer had in mind.
(1) Je **savais** à trois heures ce qui était arrivé. (At 3 o'clock, I already knew what had happened.)
(2) Je **sus** à trois heures ce qui était arrivé. (I learnt at 3 o'clock what had happened.)

Finally a word of caution: you will often be required in the examination to work from a passage (either read to you or written down) where the main narrative tense is in the past historic. You **must obey** the instructions concerning the tense required in your answers **implicitly**. It will almost certainly be the **perfect** which is needed. We shall return to this point later in the section on examination hints, page 175.

Test section

Note Here it will of course be necessary to use examples of verbs from all three types; some irregulars will therefore be included. It might be wise to check the verb tables first!

Transfer these sentences into literary style by altering the main narrative tense from **perfect to past historic**.

Joëlle a refermé la porte doucement derrière elle.
Nous nous sommes battus avec acharnement pour sauver notre pays.
Ils devenaient de plus en plus pauvres, alors ils ont vendu leur yacht.
Il a pâli en ouvrant le télégramme; soudain il a vu Maurice et a fondu en larmes.

J'ai reçu ces renseignements le lendemain.
Tu as commencé à crier à tue-tête.
Ils ont pris le chemin de la montagne, qui était toujours dangereux.
Nous y sommes allés en autocar.
Les cerfs, qu'on avait dérangés, ont couru comme des flèches ;
certains en ont fait tomber d'autres ; ils ont fui dans tous les sens.
Elle est venue vers moi, au moment où j'allais crier son nom.
C'est nous qui nous en sommes occupés, puisque nous l'avions déjà
fait la dernière fois.

Answers

Joëlle **referma** la porte doucement derrière elle.
Nous nous battîmes avec acharnement pour sauver notre pays.
Ils devenaient de plus en plus pauvres, alors **ils vendirent** leur
yacht.
Il pâlit en ouvrant le télégramme ; soudain **il vit** Maurice et **fondit**
en larmes.
Je reçus ces renseignements le lendemain.
Tu commenças à crier à tue-tête.
Ils prirent le chemin de la montagne, qui était toujours dangereux.
Nous y allâmes en autocar.
Les cerfs, qu'on avait dérangés, **coururent** comme des flèches ;
certains **firent** tomber d'autres ; **ils fuirent** dans tous les sens.
Elle vint vers moi, au moment où j'allais crier son nom.
C'était nous qui **nous nous en occupâmes**, puisque nous
l'avions déjà fait la dernière fois.

***CSE candidates will not be required to have an active knowledge
of the following section.*

Past anterior

Formation

This tense is formed from the **past historic** of the **auxiliary verb**
plus the **past participle**. Thus we would find :
> **j'eus mangé, fini, vendu,** etc.
and **je fus sorti**, etc.
Happily there are **no exceptions** to this.

Meaning and usage

The meaning is **exactly** that of the **pluperfect** (= **had done**). Its
use is, however, fairly restricted since there are **three conditions**
which must be met for it to operate :
(1) It is only found in **subordinate clauses**.

(2) The tense of the **main clause must be past historic.**
(3) The subordinate clause **must** be introduced by a **time conjunction** such as:

quand	= when	aussitôt que	= as soon as
lorsque	= when	dès que	= as soon as
après que	= after	à peine . . . que	= scarcely . . . when . . .

E.g. Quand il **eut terminé** son repas, nous sortîmes = When **he had finished** his meal, we went out.
Dès qu'**ils furent partis**, je téléphonai à la police = As soon as **they had gone**, I telephoned the police.

Simply from the sense of the examples above you will see that the past anterior normally describes one event followed rapidly by another.

The construction with '**à peine**' is a little more complicated. It translates the English 'Hardly had something happened when . . .' and phrases of that type and, like English, has **inversion** in the subordinate clause. The other thing to remember is that '**when**' is to be translated as '**que**'.
A peine **eut-il mis** le nez dehors **qu**'il commença à pleuvoir = Scarcely had he put his nose outside when it began to rain.

The important thing is that you should be able to recognise the past anterior and deal with it in translation as if it was the pluperfect. A very reduced test section will be necessary here.

Test section

Cover the answers while you work out **good English translations** for the phrases below.

Dès que la femme fut rentrée chez elle, l'orage éclata.
A peine se fut-il installé là-bas, qu'il fut obligé de repartir.
Aussitôt qu'ils eurent ouvert la porte d'entrée, ils se rendirent compte que quelque chose n'allait pas.
Après que nous eûmes réussi avec grande peine à pénétrer dans le hangar, la découverte d'un vieux vélo rouillé nous déçut.

Answers
As soon as the woman had got home, the storm broke.
Hardly had he settled there when he was forced to move off again.
As soon as they had opened the front door, they realised that something was wrong.

After we had succeeded with great difficulty in getting into the shed, the discovery of a rusty old bicycle disappointed us.

Present subjunctive

**CSE candidates need not know the subjunctive.

There are two common myths about the subjunctive: the first is that it is dying out so fast from the French language that you can really do without it, and secondly that it is so dreadfully complicated that candidates who try to use it run a severe risk of apoplexy! The truth is that whereas some areas of the subjunctive **are** tending to be used less and less, there is still a lot of it about!

Many ordinary (and simple) everyday expressions involve the subjunctive and would sound unnatural if you tried to avoid it: e.g. the commonly found expression in English 'What do you expect me to do (about it)?' is just as common in French, and **has to be: 'Que voulez-vous (veux-tu) que je fasse?'**

As for the second point, the subjunctive forms are very easily learned, and generally the irregular forms have a very satisfying ring to them which makes them not difficult to remember. (See 'fasse' in the example already quoted.) For GCE O-level candidates it is important that you should recognise the subjunctive and know how to render it in **genuine English**, without indulging in unnaturally tortured phrases of the type often seen in examination scripts.

It is necessary that I leave (oh! *very* English!) = **Il faut que je parte**. The translation is: '**I've got to go.**'

Formation

(1) The present subjunctive is formed by adding the following **endings** to the **third person plural** stem of the **present** indicative. (Ils parlent, finissent, attendent, etc.)

que je donn**e**	nous donn**ions**	que je fin**isse**, etc.
tu donn**es**	vous donn**iez**	que je vend**e**, etc.
il donn**e**	ils donn**ent**	

You should notice **two things**:
(a) with **-er verbs** the **present subjunctive** and **present indicative** are **identical, except** for the first and second persons plural.

(b) these **first and second plural** forms are the **same** as those in the **imperfect** tense.

(2) Where in the **present indicative** (**first and second** persons **plural**) certain verbs varied their stem:
E.g. je bois, nous buvons,
     je prends, nous prenons,
this will **again** occur in **those persons** of the **present subjunctive**, e.g. Il faut que **nous buvions** du champagne = We just **must** drink some champagne.

Incidentally this is yet another good reason for learning to recognise the subjunctive forms. You would never make good sense of that last example if you thought it was the imperfect tense (which has the same form).

The most common exceptions to the verb formation above occur in the verbs 'être', 'avoir', 'faire', 'pouvoir', 'savoir', 'aller', 'vouloir'. Make sure you learn these from the verb tables.

Meaning and usage
When people talk of the complicated nature of the subjunctive, they are usually alluding to the relative difficulty of defining its meaning.

(1) Normally there is no special or particular meaning to be detected, as with the other tenses we have studied (was doing = imperfect, had done = pluperfect, etc.) All these tenses of what is known as the indicative mood state (or **indicate**) a fact, whereas the **subjunctive** mood denotes what the speaker regards (from his **personal** point of view) as **uncertain, desirable** (or not), **regrettable, necessary** (or not), rather than a clear fact. Or it can be that he is viewing the event from the point of view of some **emotion** like **fear, joy, doubt.**

(2) Since the subjunctive statement is mostly tempered by a viewpoint, as above, it is not difficult to see why it occurs in **subordinate clauses** only (with very few exceptions). In other words the verb in the subjunctive will be **preceded by 'que** . . .'. **Certain conjunctions** and **certain categories of verbs** will therefore introduce clauses in which the subjunctive will be required.

Note What follows is not intended by any means as a complete treatise on the subject, but limits itself to the principal areas with which the O-level candidate may be expected to be familiar.

Conjunctions which will introduce the subjunctive are:

bien que = although	à moins que . . . ne = unless
quoique = although	de peur que . . . ne = for fear that
avant que = before	
pour que = in order that	pourvu que = provided that
afin que = in order that	jusqu'à ce que = until

E.g. **Bien qu'il soit** riche, ses souliers sont usés = Although he is rich, his shoes are worn out.
Je vais te l'expliquer, **pour que tu comprennes** mieux = I'll explain it to you, so that you will understand better.
Avant que je meure, racontez-moi votre vie = Before I die, tell me your life-story.

Notice from the list above how '**à moins que**' requires '**ne**' before the verb, as also does the expression '**de peur que**': e.g. **A moins que** tu **ne** me **dises** la vérité, je ne te parlerai plus = Unless you tell me the truth, I shan't speak to you any more.

(3) **Main clause verbs** which express **surprise, indignation, admiration, wish, doubt, fear, command, permission, forbidding,** or other emotion will require the subjunctive in the subordinate clause following.
E.g. **Je regrette qu'il en soit ainsi** = I am sorry that things are like this. **Nous voulons que vous ayez un véritable succès** = We want you to have a real success. **Ils ont peur que vous ne perdiez tout votre argent** = They are afraid that you will lose all your money.

(Note that the '**ne**' is not negative in function, and is needed before the subjunctive verb with expressions of fearing.) The one important **exception** to the 'emotion' rule is the verb '**espérer**' = 'to hope' – **always** followed by the **indicative**: e.g. Espérons qu'il pourra arriver à temps = Let's hope he can arrive on time.

(4) **Impersonal expressions** of possibility, doubt, denial or any of the other categories of emotion mentioned in (3) also require a following subjunctive.
E.g. **Il est douteux que nous le sachions d'avance** = It is doubtful whether we shall know about it in advance.

Il vaut mieux qu'il avoue tout de suite = It would be better for him to confess straightaway.

(5) Perhaps the most common case of all: after '**il faut que . . .**' (literally: it is necessary that . . .). It should very seldom be translated like that. The more natural English is usually 'I must', 'he had to', etc.

E.g. **Il faut que tu prennes ces comprimés = You must** take these tablets. **Il fallut qu'elle se jetât dans l'eau glacée = She had to** throw herself into the icy water.

N.B. 'il faut' is **never** used in anything but this impersonal form. *See the section on 'Il faut', page 125.*

It is worthwhile reminding you that '**il est certain**', '**il est probable**' and '**je crois que**' are followed by the **indicative**: e.g. Il est certain que le gâteau sera brûlé = It is sure that the cake will be burned.

(6) There are a very few examples of fixed expressions where the **subjunctive** occurs in the **main clause**. These are:

Vive la France! = Long live France! **Ainsi soit-il!** = So be it! **Sauve qui peut!** = Every man for himself!

(7) **The question of tenses**

The present subjunctive is by far the commonest tense. As you can see from the example here, it can be used to indicate a **future idea**. (There is no future subjunctive.) **Il est possible que nous les voyions demain** = It's possible that we shall see them tomorrow.

The perfect subjunctive is easy to form, consisting (as you might expect) of the **present** tense of the relevant **auxiliary** (subjunctive form naturally) with the **past participle**. All the normal rules of agreement apply here too: e.g. Bien qu'**ils aient déménagé**, nous les rencontrons de temps en temps = Although they've moved, we meet them occasionally. It is obvious here that you need a past tense.

The imperfect subjunctive is very rarely used these days **except** in the **third person singular**, and even then only in a literary context. It follows a main verb in the imperfect, past historic, conditional perfect or pluperfect; otherwise use the present subjunctive. It is formed by putting a **circumflex** over the last **vowel** of the **third person singular** of the **past historic**, and adding a '**t**' to the verbs of the '**-er**' type (past historic '**il donna**' becomes imperfect subjunctive '**il donnât**'). Other verb types already end in '**t**': thus '**il finît**', '**il fût**'.

Other persons of this form are recognisable by their double '**s**': 'je donnasse', 'ils vendissent', etc. but you have no need to worry greatly over them.

Avoiding the subjunctive

Often the use of the subjunctive can be avoided, and the French will usually choose to do so if the alternative construction is neater. There are **two main ways** in which this can be done.

(1) By the use of **an appropriate noun**, where one exists: Quelques jours avant **sa mort** (instead of 'avant qu'il mourût') nous étions allés au théâtre = A few days before he died we had gone to the theatre.
Jusqu'à **son départ** (instead of 'jusqu'à ce qu'il parte') nous avions joué aux cartes et causé ensemble = Until he left we had played cards and chatted together.

(2) With an **infinitive construction**. When the **subject** of the **main clause** is also the **subject** of the **subordinate clause**, this is usually a possibility – and most often preferable:
Nous avons couru **pour ne pas arriver** en retard (instead of 'pour que nous n'arrivions pas') = We ran so that we shouldn't arrive late. Il avait **peur de tomber** dans le lac (instead of 'qu'il ne tombât') = He was scared he might fall in the lake.

Test section

(i) **Turn the phrases** given on the left into **subjunctive phrases** in a subordinate clause introduced by '**Il vaut mieux que . . .**'

Nous rentrons demain.	**Il vaut mieux que nous rentrions demain.**
Tu as tout préparé avant mon retour.	**. . . que tu aies tout préparé avant mon retour.**
Il finit cela d'abord.	**. . . qu'il finisse cela d'abord.**
J'apprends sérieusement.	**. . . que j'apprenne sérieusement.**
Tu n'en bois plus.	**. . . que tu n'en boives plus.**
Vous mettez cet argent de côté.	**. . . que vous mettiez cet argent de côté.**

Ils écrivent cette lettre.	... qu'ils écrivent cette lettre.
Tu t'endors vite.	... que tu t'endormes vite.
Nous partons tout de suite.	... que nous partions tout de suite.
Je poursuis le criminel.	... que je poursuive le criminel.
Vous êtes rentré avant minuit.	... que vous soyez rentré avant minuit.

(ii) **Work out a translation** in **good, natural English** for these sentences.

Il est possible qu'il vienne ce soir.
Ta mère a peur que tu ne sois malade.
J'ai défendu que Jean vous rende visite demain.
Il faut que tous travaillent de leur mieux.
Il est bien heureux qu'on l'ait reconnue à l'aéroport.

Answers
It is possible that he will come this evening.
Your mother is afraid you are ill.
I have forbidden Jean to come and see you tomorrow.
Everyone must work to their limit.
It is very fortunate that we recognised her at the airport.

Note Verb tables follow.

INFINITIVE AND PRESENT PARTICIPLE	PRESENT TENSE		IMPERFECT	FUTURE AND CONDITIONAL	PAST HISTORIC	PRESENT SUBJUNCTIVE		PERFECT
REGULAR VERBS								
-er verb **donner** donnant *to give*	donne donnes donne	donnons donnez donnent	donnais	donnerai donnerais	donnai	donne donnes donne	donnions donniez donnent	ai donné
-ir verb **finir** finissant *to finish*	finis finis finit	finissons finissez finissent	finissais	finirai finirais	finis	finisse finisses finisse	finissions finissiez finissent	ai fini
-re verb **vendre** vendant *to sell*	vends vends vend	vendons vendez vendent	vendais	vendrai vendrais	vendis	vende vendes vende	vendions vendiez vendent	ai vendu
COMMON IRREGULAR VERBS **aller** allant *to go*	vais vas va	allons allez vont	allais	irai irais	allai	aille ailles aille	allions alliez aillent	suis allé (e)

INFINITIVE AND PRESENT PARTICIPLE	PRESENT TENSE		IMPERFECT	FUTURE AND CONDITIONAL	PAST HISTORIC	PRESENT SUBJUNCTIVE		PERFECT
s'asseoir asseyant *to sit down*	assieds assieds assied	asseyons asseyez asseyent	asseyais	assiérai assiérais	assis	asseye asseyes asseye	asseyions asseyiez asseyent	suis assis (e)
avoir ayant *to have*	ai as a	avons avez ont	avais	aurai aurais	eus	aie aies ait	ayons ayez aient	ai eu
battre battant *to beat*	bats bats bat	battons battez battent	battais	battrai battrais	battis .	batte battes batte	battions battiez battent	ai battu
boire buvant *to drink*	bois bois boit	buvons buvez boivent	buvais	boirai boirais	bus	boive boives boive	buvions buviez boivent	ai bu
conduire conduisant *to drive*	conduis conduis conduit	conduisons conduisez conduisent	conduisais	conduirai conduirais	conduisis	conduise conduises conduise	conduisions conduisiez conduisent	ai conduit
connaître connaissant *to know*	connais connais connaît	connaissons connaissez connaissent	connaissais	connaîtrai connaîtrais	connus	connaisse connaisses connaisse	connaissions connaissiez connaissent	ai connu

INFINITIVE AND PRESENT PARTICIPLE	PRESENT TENSE		IMPERFECT	FUTURE AND CONDITIONAL	PAST HISTORIC	PRESENT SUBJUNCTIVE		PERFECT
courir courant *to run*	cours cours court	courons courez courent	courais	courrai courrais	courus	coure coures coure	courions couriez courent	ai couru
craindre craignant *to fear*	crains crains craint	craignons craignez craignent	craignais	craindrai craindrais	craignis	craigne craignes craigne	craignions craigniez craignent	ai craint
croire croyant *to believe*	crois crois croit	croyons croyez croient	croyais	croirai croirais	crus	croie croies croie	croyions croyiez croient	ai cru
devoir devant *to owe*	dois dois doit	devons devez doivent	devais	devrai devrais	dus	doive doives doive	devions deviez doivent	ai dû (N.B. due)
dire disant *to say*	dis dis dit	disons dites disent	disais	dirai dirais	dis	dise dises dise	disions disiez disent	ai dit
dormir dormant *to sleep*	dors dors dort	dormons dormez dorment	dormais	dormirai dormirais	dormis	dorme dormes dorme	dormions dormiez dorment	ai dormi

93

INFINITIVE AND PRESENT PARTICIPLE	PRESENT TENSE		IMPERFECT	FUTURE AND CONDITIONAL	PAST HISTORIC	PRESENT SUBJUNCTIVE		PERFECT
écrire écrivant *to write*	écris écris écrit	écrivons écrivez écrivent	écrivais	écrirai écrirais	écrivis	écrive écrives écrive	écrivions écriviez écrivent	ai écrit
envoyer envoyant *to send*	envoie envoies envoie	envoyons envoyez envoient	envoyais	enverrai enverrais	envoyai	envoie envoies envoie	envoyions envoyiez envoient	ai envoyé
être étant *to be*	suis es est	sommes êtes sont	étais	serai serais	fus	sois sois soit	soyons soyez soient	ai été
faire faisant *to do, make*	fais fais fait	faisons faites font	faisais	ferai ferais	fis	fasse fasses fasse	fassions fassiez fassent	ai fait
falloir *to be necessary*	il faut		il fallait	il faudra il faudrait	il fallut	il faille		il a fallu
fuir fuyant *to flee*	fuis fuis fuit	fuyons fuyez fuient	fuyais	fuirai fuirais	fuis	fuie fuies fuie	fuyions fuyiez fuient	ai fui
lire lisant *to read*	lis lis lit	lisons lisez lisent	lisais	lirai lirais	lus	lise lises lise	lisions lisiez lisent	ai lu

INFINITIVE AND PRESENT PARTICIPLE	PRESENT TENSE		IMPERFECT	FUTURE AND CONDITIONAL	PAST HISTORIC	PRESENT SUBJUNCTIVE		PERFECT
mettre mettant *to put*	mets mets met	mettons mettez mettent	mettais	mettrai mettrais	mis	mette mettes mette	mettions mettiez mettent	ai mis
mourir mourant *to die*	meurs meurs meurt	mourons mourez meurent	mourais	mourrai mourrais	mourus	meure meures meure	mourions mouriez meurent	suis mort (e)
naître naissant *to be born*	nais nais naît	naissons naissez naissent	naissais	naîtrai naîtrais	naquis	naisse naisses naisse	naissions naissiez naissent	suis né (e)
ouvrir ouvrant *to open*	ouvre ouvres ouvre	ouvrons ouvrez ouvrent	ouvrais	ouvrirai ouvrirais	ouvris	ouvre ouvres ouvre	ouvrions ouvriez ouvrent	ai ouvert
plaire plaisant *to please*	plais plais plaît	plaisons plaisez plaisent	plaisais	plairai plairais	plus	plaise plaises plaise	plaisions plaisiez plaisent	ai plu
pleuvoir pleuvant *to rain*	il pleut		il pleuvait	il pleuvra il pleuvrait	il plut	il pleuve		il a plu

INFINITIVE AND PRESENT PARTICIPLE	PRESENT TENSE		FUTURE AND CONDITIONAL	IMPERFECT	PAST HISTORIC	PRESENT SUBJUNCTIVE		PERFECT
pouvoir pouvant *to be able*	peux peux peut	pouvons pouvez peuvent	pourrai pourrais	pouvais	pus	puisse puisses puisse	puissions puissiez puissent	ai pu
prendre prenant *to take*	prends prends prend	prenons prenez prennent	prendrai prendrais	prenais	pris	prenne prennes prenne	prenions preniez prennent	ai pris
recevoir recevant *to receive*	reçois reçois reçoit	recevons recevez reçoivent	recevrai recevrais	recevais	reçus	reçoive reçoives reçoive	recevions receviez reçoivent	ai reçu
rire riant *to laugh*	ris ris rit	rions riez rient	rirai rirais	riais (N.B. riions, riiez)	ris	rie ries rie	riions riiez rient	ai ri
savoir sachant *to know*	sais sais sait	savons savez savent	saurai saurais	savais	sus	sache saches sache	sachions sachiez sachent	ai su
sortir sortant *to go out*	sors sors sort	sortons sortez sortent	sortirai sortirais	sortais	sortis	sorte sortes sorte	sortions sortiez sortent	suis sorti (e)

INFINITIVE AND PRESENT PARTICIPLE	PRESENT TENSE	IMPERFECT	FUTURE AND CONDITIONAL	PAST HISTORIC	PRESENT SUBJUNCTIVE	PERFECT
suivre suivant *to follow*	suis suis suit / suivons suivez suivent	suivais	suivrai suivrais	suivis	suive suives suive / suivions suiviez suivent	ai suivi
vaincre vainquant *to conquer*	vaincs vaincs vainc / vainquons vainquez vainquent	vainquais	vaincrai vaincrais	vainquis	vainque vainques vainque / vainquions vainquiez vainquent	ai vaincu
valoir valant *to be worth*	il vaut	il valait	il vaudra il vaudrait	il valut	il vaille	il a valu
venir venant *to come*	viens viens vient / venons venez viennent	venais	viendrai viendrais	vins	vienne viennes vienne / venions veniez viennent	suis venu (e)
vivre vivant *to live*	vis vis vit / vivons vivez vivent	vivais	vivrai vivrais	vécus	vive vives vive / vivions viviez vivent	ai vécu
voir voyant *to see*	vois vois voit / voyons voyez voient	voyais	verrai verrais	vis	voie voies voie / voyions voyiez voient	ai vu
vouloir voulant *to want to*	veux veux veut / voulons voulez veulent	voulais	voudrai voudrais	voulus	veuille veuilles veuille / voulions vouliez veuillent	ai voulu

Groups of verbs and derivatives

A considerable number of irregular verbs can be divided into small groups. Thus **tenir** is conjugated just like **venir**, etc.

In the preceding tables only one verb of such groups has been given. We now list other frequently encountered verbs which take the pattern of a verb listed in the tables, together with derivatives of irregular verbs (e.g. **comprendre**, which behaves in all respects like **prendre**).

like **aller**
s'en aller	= to go away

like **faire**
satisfaire	= to satisfy

like **conduire**
produire	= to produce
réduire	= to reduce
traduire	= to translate
construire	= to build
détruire	= to destroy

like **mettre**
permettre	= to allow
promettre	= to promise

like **connaître**
reconnaître	= to recognise
paraître	= to seem
disparaître	= to disappear

like **ouvrir**
offrir	= to offer
souffrir	= to suffer
couvrir	= to cover
découvrir	= to discover

like **craindre**
plaindre	= to pity
se plaindre	= to complain
peindre	= to paint
atteindre	= to attain
éteindre	= to extinguish
feindre	= to pretend
joindre	= to join

like **prendre**
comprendre	= to understand
surprendre	= to surprise

like **recevoir**
apercevoir	= to catch sight of
décevoir	= to disappoint

like **dormir**
mentir	= to tell a lie
partir	= to depart
sortir	= to go out
servir	= to serve
sentir	= to feel, smell

like **venir**
revenir	= to come back
devenir	= to become
se souvenir de	= to remember
tenir	= to hold
retenir	= to retain
maintenir	= to maintain
contenir	= to contain

Chapter 9
The Passive Voice

Formation, meaning and usage

(1) The passive voice is less often used in French than in English, but it is important nevertheless. It is easy to learn for it is formed as in English with the verb '**to be**' ('**être**') and the **past participle**. It can be used in every tense and mood as these examples show:

Tout à coup **il fut réveillé** par un bruit étrange = All of a sudden **he was woken** by a strange noise.

Si tu continues à faire cela, **tu seras puni** = If you carry on doing that, **you will be punished**.

Il faut que les oeufs **soient bien battus** = The eggs **have to be well beaten**.

Two essential points have to be borne in mind with the passive.

(a) The **tense** and **mood** of 'être' will always be the same as those which would have been used **if the clause had been expressed actively**.

(b) The **past participle** always **agrees** in number and gender **with the subject** — which is only sensible seeing that it is, after all, the subject which is being killed, beaten, rewarded, etc.

Notice how these two points are exemplified in the following sentences.

Ces ouvriers sont employés par son père = These workers are employed by his father.

Ils ont été attrapés — They have been caught.

Les jeunes filles seront récompensées par leur professeur = The girls will be rewarded by their teacher.

Elle avait été élevée avec beaucoup de soin = She had been brought up with great care.

Ils ont peur d'être saisis par des agents ennemis = They are afraid of being seized by enemy agents.

You may check that you have the correct tense of the passive by trying to turn the verb to the active voice. If you encounter difficulty in altering your tense satisfactorily to the active form, you have probably made an error. We will return to that point in a moment.

Par/de as agent

As you can see from the examples above, the **agent** is expressed by the preposition '**par**'. This is the normal procedure **except** when the situation is more generalised: e.g. Elle était aimée **de** tout le monde = She was loved by everyone. Mon père est respecté **de** tous = my father is respected by everybody. Here the preposition '**de**' is used, and as you may deduce from the examples given, this usually occurs with verbs like 'aimer', 'honorer', 'craindre', etc. (i.e. personal feelings).

You should also note one or two established phrases which use 'de': suivi de = followed by; accompagné de = accompanied by.

(2) The **main difficulty** with **tense** in the passive comes from the translation of the English '**was**'. Some people find it hard to get the idea out of their mind that this should necessarily be the imperfect (= était). However, the latter tense would only be correct (as in the **active** form) where a state of affairs was being described which was **already in existence** at the time in question. The **criteria** for **imperfect and perfect** (or past historic) are just as they always were. *(See pages 68 and 71 where these are set out in detail.)* Compare these two examples:

Nous avons essayé d'y entrer mais la porte **était fermée** = We tried to get in but the door **was shut**. (I.e. the phrase describes **the state**.)

La porte **a été fermée** par le gardien il y a cinq minutes = The door **was shut** by the warden five minutes ago. (Clearly this second example shows the shutting of the door as **an action taking place**.)

Finally here is an example to show how the past historic exactly parallels the perfect from the point of view of recounting past events:

Le cessez-le-feu **fut annoncé** à dix heures du soir = The cease-fire **was announced** at ten in the evening.

Remember therefore to **think very carefully** before translating '**was**'.

(3) **Danger! Attention s'il vous plaît!**

There is one extremely tempting snare of which you **must beware** with the passive. As on some other occasions it is the careless phrasing of English which leads the naïve into a quagmire of error here! The kind of simple trap set is the following:

'He was given a watch for Christmas.'

According to normal practice in the passive this would mean that 'he' (subject) was given (as a present!) *(Ils sont fous, ces Anglais!)* The French precision of language could never allow such nonsense! There is no ambiguity at all in the French version of that sentence: 'On lui a offert une montre pour Noël.'

100

In French **only verbs** which have a **direct object** may be turned **passively**. This calls for special care with verbs like 'dire', 'permettre', 'promettre', 'ordonner', 'défendre', 'offrir', 'donner', 'demander', etc. where the **object** is **indirect**. We can only avoid error by using an **active form** of the verb, usually by making the subject of the verb 'on', if, of course, there is no stated subject.

E.g. On lui demanda l'heure = She was asked the time.

On m'a défendu d'y aller = I was forbidden to go there.

Son neveu lui donna une montre = He was given a watch by his nephew.

Note the following set phrases in English where a passive is used and **an active form** is usual in French:

On dit que . . .	=	It is said that . . .
Terrain à vendre	=	Land for sale (= to be sold)
Bâteaux à louer	=	Boats for hire (= to be hired)

(4) **Avoidance of the passive**

It was suggested initially that the French are not as fond of the passive as the English and they will actively (if you will allow the pun) avoid it where possible. We have already seen one way, (a) below, in which this may be done.

(a) **by using 'on'**

This is by far the most usual way of dealing with the passive and the only proviso is that **a human agent** (or animal) can be visualised as being responsible for the action. This can best be illustrated by examples:

On a fouetté les espions = The spies were whipped.

On a coupé les arbres = The trees were cut down.

(In these two examples **someone** obviously did it.)

Pendant la chute de l'arbre son pantalon fut déchiré. (Here we suppose someone did not do it, so there is no alternative but to retain the passive.)

(b) **by using a reflexive verb**

There are a whole series of useful and everyday expressions in French which include the reflexive where we would have a passive, and they are well worth committing to memory.

Les timbres **se vendent** dans les cafés en France = Stamps **are sold** in cafés in France.

La soupe à l'oignon **se fait** ainsi = Onion soup **is made** like this.

Cela (ça) **se comprend** = That **is understandable**. Cela (ça) ne **se dit** pas en allemand = That **isn't said** in German. Cela (ça) ne

se fait pas en Angleterre = That **isn't done** in England. Comment cela **s'écrit-il**? = How **is that spelt**?
Soudain un bruit étrange **se fit entendre** dans les broussailles = Suddenly a strange noise **was heard** in the undergrowth.

It is wise to note down such instances of reflexives expressing a passive idea whenever you meet them, but it is **inadvisable** to attempt to invent **instances of your own**.

Test section

(i)(a) **Turn these sentences into a passive form.**

Le frère de Louise a battu Jean.
Un des élèves lança des tomates.
Un musicien russe dirigera l'orchestre.
Tout le grand public l'estime.
Un savant américain aura bientôt développé des fusées interplanétaires (= interplanetary rockets).
Son chien fidèle avait suivi le mendiant partout.

(i)(b) Now **turn these sentences** from the present into **the appropriate past tenses**.

Le soldat est blessé par une balle.
Quand nous le trouvons, il est blessé.
Ce professeur est toujours obéi.
Les vieilles dames sont attaquées par des voyous.
Pourquoi toutes les fenêtres sont-elles entr'ouvertes?
Soudain nous remarquons des volets qui sont rapidement fermés.

(ii) ** *See note on page 58.*
Translate into French. Be very careful to avoid traps!

He will be allowed to go out.
Pâté is made like this.
We were told the story.
She has been promised a horse for her birthday.
Cigarettes are sold here.
Suddenly a cry was heard inside the locked room.
They are always forbidden to come home late.
How is that said in French?

Answers

(i)(a) Jean a été battu par le frère de Louise.

Des tomates furent lancées par un des élèves.

L'orchestre sera dirigé par un musicien russe.

Il (elle) est estimé(e) par tout le grand public.

Des fusées interplanétaires seront bientôt développées par un savant américain.

Le mendiant avait été suivi partout de son chien fidèle.

(i)(b) Le soldat a été blessé par une balle.

Quand nous l'avons trouvé, il était blessé.

Ce professeur était toujours obéi.

Les vieilles dames ont été attaquées par des voyous.

Pourquoi toutes les fenêtres étaient-elles entr'ouvertes?
or . . . ont-elles été entr'ouvertes?

Soudain nous avons remarqué des volets qui ont été rapidement fermés.

(ii) On lui permettra de sortir.

Le pâté se fait ainsi.

On nous a raconté l'histoire.

On lui a promis un cheval pour son anniversaire.

Les cigarettes se vendent ici.

Soudain un cri se fit entendre dans la pièce qui était fermée à clé.

On leur défend toujours de rentrer tard.

Comment cela se dit-il en français?

Chapter 10
Question Forms and Inversion

(1) The simplest way of **asking a question** is, as in English, merely to alter the intonation of the voice: e.g. vous viendrez ce soir? = You are coming tonight? Although this is heard a great deal, it is not recommended practice in written work (unless in written conversation of course).

(2) The next easiest way of turning a simple statement into a question is by prefacing the statement '**Est-ce que . . .?**' e.g. **Est-ce que** les soldats ont dressé leurs tentes près de la rivière? = Have the soldiers put their tents up near the river? This form of question may also be used if there is a specific question word 'quand', 'pourquoi', etc. (particularly in speech), e.g. **Quand est-ce qu**'ils vont cesser ce bruit? = When are they going to stop that noise?

N.B. '**Est-ce que . . .**' has no precise meaning of its own, which is a thing many candidates find difficult to accept. It is merely a formula used for asking questions, and so the translation will vary from question to question. Provided you supply a question format in your English version you can ignore it in your translations from French.

(3) A question may also be formed **by inverting subject and verb** and this is the most favoured method in written French and with educated Frenchmen.
E.g. **Vous a-t-il parlé** de cette affaire? = Has he spoken to you about this matter? (N.B. Here you must be careful to recognise that 'vous' is the object pronoun, **not** the subject of the sentence.)
Essayeront-ils de défoncer la porte? = Will they try to break the door down?

(a) You will notice from the first example above that '-t-' **must** be inserted if the last letter of the verb (pronounced or not) is a **vowel**. All regular '-er' verbs in the third person singular will therefore be affected in this way: e.g. Pourquoi **ne mange-t-elle pas** son chocolat? = Why isn't she eating her chocolate?

(b) The 'est-ce que . . .' form of the question is normally preferred with the **first person singular**, since inversion gives such a feeble sound (and is sometimes difficult to pronounce). An exception to this is '**Puis-je . . .?**' = '**May I?**' which is considered a slightly more polite form of request than 'Est-ce que je peux ...?' You should note incidentally the special form of the verb when used in this way.

(c) If the subject of the interrogative sentence is a **noun** (all the examples so far have dealt with pronoun subjects), then the **relevant subject pronoun must be added** in order to provide the correct inverted form: e.g. **Jean revient-il** d'Amérique cette semaine? = Is John coming back from America this week?

In other words the **inverted** (and hyphenated) **form** may **only join verb and subject pronoun**.

(4) Where a **question word or phrase** introduces the sentence, all the principles of forming questions outlined above apply. You may form your question thus:

Pourquoi **est-ce qu'ils se sont opposés** au projet? (colloquially)

Or Pourquoi **se sont-ils opposés** au projet?

But Pourquoi **tes frères se sont-ils opposés** au projet? = Why did your brothers raise opposition to the scheme?

Inversion

Apart from in questions **inversion** is also required in French in certain other cases.

(1) **After direct speech** to express 'she said', 'he replied', 'we exclaimed', etc.

E.g. 'Comment a-t-il pu faire cela!' **s'exclama-t-elle**.

'Très bien,' **répondit le professeur**.

'Les voyageurs n'arriveront pas sains et saufs,' **fit-il**.

Note how in this last example the verb '**faire**' may be used to convey the idea '**to say**'. This occurs quite often in passages to be translated into English.

(2) After '**peut-être**' = 'perhaps', '**ainsi**' = 'thus', '**sans doute**' = 'doubtless', '**aussi**' = 'therefore'.

Peut-être a-t-il changé d'avis = Perhaps he has changed his mind.

Sans doute passe-t-il la nuit chez des amis = No doubt he is spending the night with friends.

Aussi le propriétaire décida-t-il de fermer le café = And so the proprietor decided to close the café.

Note Many candidates place 'Aussi' at the beginning of the sentence hoping it will mean 'And also'. As you will see from the last example, placed in this position it means something quite different.

Note also that instead of using 'peut-être' + inversion of the verb you may use '**peut-être que**' + **normal word order**.

(3) After '**à peine . . . . que**' = scarcely . . . . when
We have already seen how this operates in the section on the **past anterior** *(see page 83)*.

You will remember that the past anterior must be used in these clauses when the main verb is past historic; of course if your main verb is perfect tense, then your verb in the subordinate 'à peine' clause may be pluperfect: e.g. À peine **avaient-ils bu** le liquide qu'ils sont tombés par terre = Scarcely had they drunk the liquid when they fell to the ground.

Test section

Since the use of 'est-ce que . . .' makes question formation very simple, the test examples will cover only **inversion**.

Turn these statements into questions using the question word where one is supplied.

Ils ont souffert énormément.   (quand)
Vous vous êtes décidé à tout abandonner.   (pourquoi)
Jean aurait refusé leur offre.
Le professeur avait interrogé ces élèves.   (combien de fois)
Les réfugiés ont débarqué en pleine nuit.
Les voleurs ont l'intention de cacher leur butin.   (où)
Les policiers seraient parvenus à découvrir la vérité.   (comment)

Answers
Quand ont-ils souffert énormément?
Pourquoi vous êtes-vous décidé à tout abandonner?
Jean aurait-il refusé leur offre?
Combien de fois le professeur avait-il interrogé ces élèves?
Les réfugiés ont-ils débarqué en pleine nuit?
Où les voleurs ont-ils l'intention de cacher leur butin?
Comment les policiers seraient-ils parvenus à découvrir la vérité?

106

Chapter 11
Present and Past Participles

Formation, meaning and usage

(1) The **present participle** has only **one form**, which may refer to any person of the verb. This form is found from the '**nous**' part of the **present tense** (minus '-ons') – in fact the same stem as the imperfect tense. To this is added the one ending '**ant**'. Thus we have:

donnant = giving; **finissant** = finishing; **vendant** = selling, and also, as examples of irregular verbs; **buvant** = drinking; **conduisant** = driving; **connaissant** = knowing.

The immediate English translation, as you will see, is '**doing**'. The only **exceptions** are the three verbs '**être**', '**avoir**', and '**savoir**'.

The present participle from these verbs is:

étant (être) = being; **ayant** (avoir) = having; **sachant** (savoir) = knowing.

Remember that with verbs with infinitives in '**cer**', '**ger**', you will need to write '**ç**' and '**ge**' before the hard '**ant**' sound: e.g. man**ge**ant = eating; lan**ç**ant = throwing.

(2) The present participle may be a simple **adjective**, e.g. charmant = charming; and as such it of course **must agree** with the noun or pronoun.

une jeune fille **ravissante**	= a delightful girl
des enfants **obéissants**	= obedient children
d'un ton **rassurant**	= in a reassuring tone of voice.

(3) The present participle may be **verbal** in function, in which case it **never shows any agreement**.

E.g. Elle était étendue sur le sable, **regardant** la mer = She was stretched out on the sand, **looking** at the sea.

Notre mère, **comprenant** que nous avions froid, nous appela = Our mother, realising that we were cold, called us.

(4) The preposition '**en**' is frequently placed before the present participle: it **must** refer to the **subject** of the **main verb** of the sentence. It is also the **only preposition** which may be **followed by the present participle**.

E.g. Le facteur passait **en sifflant** devant la maison = The postman went by the house whistling.

Elle nous répondit **en souriant** = She answered us with a smile.

N.B. A **reflexive verb** used in the present participle construction will not only (a) **retain the reflexive pronoun**, but (b) **need the correct pronoun** to match the subject of the sentence: e.g. En **nous** levant ce matin, **nous** avons vu quelque chose de curieux = Getting up this morning, we saw something strange.

The present participle with 'en' often conveys the ideas expressed in the English **'while doing'**, **'on doing'**, **'by doing'**:

Ma nièce laissa tomber son porte-monnaie **en montant** dans l'autobus = My niece dropped her purse **while getting on** the bus.

En prenant la deuxieme rue à droite vous arriverez plus vite à la gare = **By taking** the second on the right you will get to the station quicker.

Sometimes **'en'** is **preceded by 'tout'** in such constructions. This strengthens the participle and is used either:

(a) **to insist on the simultaneous nature of the two actions** (i.e. all the time he was doing this, he was . . .) or:

(b) **to express concession** (i.e. even while he was doing this, he was . . .)

E.g. Il continua à courir **tout en buvant** de l'eau dans une bouteille = He went on running **while at the same time** drinking water from a bottle.

Tout en admettant la possibilité d'une erreur, je ne dirai rien pour le moment = **While admitting** there may be an error, I shall say nothing for the moment.

(5) The participle is **used on its own without 'en'** if (a) **it is giving a reason**, and (b) **the two actions are not simultaneous**.

E.g. **Sachant** qu'ils n'arriveraient pas avant midi, elle alla faire son marché = **Knowing** they would not arrive before midday, she went to do her shopping.

Entendant un bruit dans la cuisine, il se leva = **Hearing** a noise in the kitchen, he got up.

(6) *No* **to present participle!**

Candidates are frequently moved to sprinkle present participles in unacceptable situations in French. It is **most important** not only to recognise, but to bear constantly in mind the fact that **only very rarely** may **'ing'** in English be rendered by the **present participle** in French. With the English present and imperfect continuous tenses (am doing, was doing) you need to take particular care, as we have already seen in those sections.

The French present participle form may only be used in the ways already mentioned here, plus a rarer use of the **present participle** of the **auxiliary verbs 'avoir' and 'être' + past participle**.

E.g. **Ayant accepté** l'invitation, elle se sentit obligée d'y aller = **Having accepted** the invitation, she felt obliged to go.

Etant arrivés les premiers, nous avons pu choisir les meilleures places = **Having been the first to arrive**, we were able to choose the best seats.

As you can see, the use of this construction is the equivalent of a 'because' clause giving a reason for the statement in the main clause by referring to some previous action.

This last point of usage of the present participle should not be considered an essential ingredient of the O-level 'kit' and is for information rather than for required learning.

Meanwhile, back to the **'don'ts'**!

One tempting situation for the examination candidate and his manipulation of the **'ing'** situation concerns the verbs of **seeing, sensing, hearing** (seeing someone doing something, etc.).

Alas, this is **not** an occasion in French for the present participle. There are **two possible solutions**:

(a) **'voir', 'entendre', etc. + infinitive**

E.g. **J'ai vu** nos voisins **passer** de l'autre côté de la rue = I saw our neighbours crossing the road.

Il écoutait chanter sa mère = He was listening to his mother singing.

(Notice here how the **infinitive immediately follows the verb**, when there is no further complement in the sentence.)

(b) **'voir', 'entendre', etc. + 'qui' and clause**

E.g. **Il aperçut** le voleur **qui refermait** la barrière derrière lui = He noticed the thief shutting the gate behind him.

Je l'ai entendu qui marchait de long en large dans sa chambre = I heard him pacing up and down in his room.

(In the past tense, as above, the appropriate tense in the 'qui . . .' clause is the imperfect.)

(7) *No again* to the present participle!

You may **not** use the present participle to render the English **'ing'** in the various words denoting **posture**, 'sitting', 'lying', etc. In French you must use a **past participle** (which will **agree**); thus **assis** = sitting; **couché** = lying.

It's that old French logic again! The present participle used verbally in French indicates **concurrent actions** or **state of mind**, and so 'asseyant', for example, would imply 'the action of sitting down', not 'the seated state', which is what is really intended in English. A list of the most common words of posture would include:

assis	= sitting	accoudé	= leaning (on elbows)
couché	= lying	penché	= leaning out
étendu	= stretched out	appuyé	= leaning against
agenouillé	= kneeling	(sus)pendu	= hanging

and also: debout (an adverb) = standing.

Note In cases where you wish to say that someone has 'sat for a particular length of time' and the verb will evidently be in the perfect of past historic tenses, the French feel that the phrase listed above ('être assis') does not express quite adequately the idea involved. Therefore they introduce the verb '**rester**' (= to remain) together with the **past participle**, which gives the following pattern, applicable also to 'debout': **rester debout** = to stand for a length of time.

Elle est **restée assise** sur le sable pendant trois heures = She sat (literally, remained seated) on the sand for three hours.

Pendant quelque temps nous **restâmes assis** auprès du feu = We sat beside the fire for some time.

Remember therefore that the verbal phrases listed above all describe **the stationary state**, and that use of the corresponding **reflexive verbs** will imply **the action involved**. The reflexive forms are:

s'asseoir	= to sit down	s'accouder	= to lean (on one's elbows)
se coucher	= to lie down		
s'étendre	= to stretch out	se pencher	= to lean out
s'agenouiller	= to kneel	s'appuyer	= to lean against
se pendre	= to hang oneself	se suspendre	= to hang (by feet or hands)

The contrast between the two types of construction is illustrated here:

Je me couche ordinairement vers dix heures = I usually **go to bed** around 10 o'clock.

Mon petit frère **est** déjà **couché** = My little brother is already **in bed**.

Il se leva tout de suite à notre approche = **He got up** at once as we approached.

Ton ami paresseux n'**est** pas encore **levé** = Your lazy friend isn't **up** yet.

See also chapter 12. **The Infinitive Mood**, *page 113, for further instances of non-'ings' in French.*

Past participle

The uses of the past participle have mostly been covered already in earlier chapters. Here is a brief summary to remind you:

(1) **with auxiliary verbs** to form **compound tenses** (perfect, pluperfect, future and conditional perfect, and the passive). You should consult the relevant sections for all information relating to agreements and usage.

(2) **As a normal adjective**, e.g. elle est **fatiguée** = she is **tired**; des enfants **gâtés** = **spoiled** children; nous sommes **chargés** de paquets = we are loaded with parcels.

(3) Additionally the past participle may often conveniently be used **instead of a clause** of the 'when' or 'after' type, **provided** the **subject of main and subordinate clauses** is the **same**: e.g. **Arrivés** à la gare, **nous** allâmes directement à la consigne = **When we got to** the station, **we** went straight to the left-luggage office. This is obviously a neater turn of phrase than a whole clause (= Lorsque nous arrivâmes à la gare, etc. . . . .).

(4) One or two past participles have become **accepted conjunctions**: e.g. **vu que** = seeing that; **supposé que** (+ subjunctive) = supposing that; **pourvu que** (+ subjunctive) = provided that. Expressions derived from past participles are also the following:

> **entendu!** = agreed!   **y compris** = including
> **excepté** = except for

E.g. **Excepté** l'Angleterre, tous les pays d'Europe ont un climat agréable = Except for England all European countries have a pleasant climate! (As a conjunction of course there is **no agreement** of the past participle.)

Test section

(i) Turn the phrase in brackets into a **present participle** phrase, using **'en' if necessary**.

(manger une banane) elle a glissé sur le trottoir.
Nous avons peur du rendez-vous (savoir la vérité)
Elle découvrira le trésor (ouvrir la boîte)
Vous pouvez parler aux invités (remplir les verres)
Il s'arrêta net (se rendre compte du danger)

Tu ne sais quoi faire (être stupide)
Il est tombé raide mort! (boire son café)
Je peux me permettre cette folie! (avoir de l'argent)
Ils ne pourraient jamais réussir (renoncer au projet)

(ii) * *See note on page 58.*
Present, past or ??: translate these phrases **into French**,
taking great care with your '-ings'!

Sitting at the table, she began to cry.
People (use 'on') heard them fighting in the street.
Coming into the room I noticed a broken chair.
He is smiling; he has just received an interesting letter.
The leaning tower of Pisa (= Pise) is in Italy.
I see them arriving now.
By reading this novel we shall understand the author better.
They were stretched out on the carpet.
You were singing in the bathroom.
The whole time he was coming closer (use 's'approcher') he was
    looking at us.

Answers
(i) **En mangeant une banane**, elle a glissé sur le trottoir.
Nous avons peur du rendez-vous, **sachant la vérité**.
Elle découvrira le trésor **en ouvrant la boîte**.
Vous pouvez parler aux invités **en remplissant les verres**.
Il s'arrêta net, **se rendant compte du danger.** (en se rendant
    . . . also).
Tu ne sais quoi faire, **étant stupide**!
Il est tombé raide mort **en buvant son café**!
Je peux me permettre cette folie, **ayant de l'argent**!
Ils ne pourraient jamais réussir **en renonçant au projet**.

(ii) **Assise a la table, elle commença à pleurer.**
On les entendit se battre dans la rue. or **On les entendit qui
    se battaient . . .**
En venant dans la pièce j'ai remarqué une chaise cassée.
Il sourit; il vient de recevoir une lettre intéressante.
La tour penchée de Pise se trouve en Italie.
Je les vois arriver maintenant.
En lisant ce roman, nous comprendrons mieux l'auteur.
Ils étaient étendus sur le tapis.
Vous chantiez dans la salle de bain.
Tout en s'approchant il nous regardait.

Chapter 12
The Infinitive Mood

1) Occasionally the infinitive can stand **independently** in a sentence. This is usually:

(a) **in printed instructions: s'adresser au concierge** = please apply to the caretaker; **se renseigner au bar d'en face** = details available at the bar opposite.

(b) **in interrogative phrases** of the kind we have already met: **que penser?** = what are we to think?, etc.

(c) in phrases where **the verb in '-ing' is the subject** of the sentence: **voir, c'est croire** = seeing is believing; **mieux vaut ne rien dire** = better to say nothing.

(2) Usually however, **the infinitive follows** another **verb, noun or adjective** (+ 'à' or 'de'), **or other prepositions**. This can present some difficulty, but to some extent guidelines can be established.

Infinitive after another verb

(1) The **infinitive** follows **directly** on from:

(a) common **intransitive verbs of motion** ('aller', 'venir', etc. and 'envoyer').

E.g. **Elle était venue nous voir** = She had come to see us.

Va lui dire qu'il y a du courrier pour elle = Go **and** tell her there is some mail for her. (Notice in this last example how '**go and tell**', like '**come and see**', is translated with an infinitive.)

'**Envoyer chercher**' is a verb combination beloved of examiners, meaning 'to send for'.

On a envoyé chercher le médecin = They have sent for the doctor.

(b) the so-called **modal verbs** ('vouloir', 'savoir', 'pouvoir', 'devoir', 'falloir'): e.g. **Nous devions les voir** plus tard = We were to see them later. **Sait-elle danser?** = Can she dance?

(c) **verbs of the senses** ('voir', 'entendre', 'laisser', 'sentir'): e.g. **Il nous regardait jouer** = He was watching us play. **Je l'ai entendu prononcer** son discours = I heard him make his speech. **Il s'est laissé duper** = He let himself be tricked. **Laisser tomber** is another favourite combination meaning 'to drop': e.g. **Elle laissa tomber** la cafetière = She dropped the coffee pot.

(d) the **'personal viewpoint' verbs** ('aimer', 'aimer mieux', 'préférer', 'détester', 'désirer', 'espérer', 'penser', 'sembler', 'penser + oser', 'compter'): e.g. **Comptes-tu finir** cela avant 6 heures? = Do you reckon you will finish that before 6? **J'espère te revoir** bientôt = I hope to see you again soon.

(e) the verb **'faillir'**

This is a strange verb and is only used in the **perfect and past historic tenses** (occasionally also with pluperfect). It means 'to nearly do something' which would have been disadvantageous to the person involved: e.g. **Il a failli tomber** dans le ruisseau = He nearly fell into the stream. **Je faillis manquer** le train = I nearly missed the train. (For cases of 'nearly' where there is no such idea of near-mishap, you use the usual word **'presque'**, e.g. c'est **presque fini** = it's nearly finished.)

(f) the verb **'faire'**

This use of 'faire' as a 'causative' verb (i.e. causing someone to do something, or something to happen) deserves special attention.

(i) It can be used simply to render **'to make someone do something'** or 'to have someone do something': e.g. Cette anecdote **le fit rire** = This story made him laugh.
Note The pronoun 'le' is the **object of 'faire'**, not 'rire', and so precedes **that** verb.

(ii) With these verbs of motion, 'faire' has a particular meaning. **faire entrer** = show in; **faire monter** = show up; **faire sortir** = show out; **faire venir** = send for: e.g. **Faites entrer le témoin** = Send the witness in.

(iii) It may be used in the sense of **'to have something done'**, i.e. you give instructions, someone else carries them out.
Il fait construire une villa = He is having a villa built.
Il la fait construire à coté de chez moi = He is having it built near my house. **Note again** the position of the pronoun, and also the fact that the **second verb also follows directly** on to 'faire'.

(iv) This last usage may be extended to indicate that the action being carried out is **for your personal benefit**. To do this you use the reflexive form **'se faire + infinitive'**.
Tu t'es fait couper les cheveux! = You've had your hair cut!
Je vais me faire enlever ce grain de beauté = I am going to have this beauty spot removed.

(2) The **infinitive** is **preceded by** the preposition **'de'** following:

(a) verbs which **tell, ask, command, forbid, advise,** etc. someone to do something. Note that the **person told**, etc. is **indirect object**.

E.g. **Nous leur avons dit de partir** = We told them to leave.
Je permets à mon fils de fumer = I allow my son to smoke.
Il nous a défendu de descendre en ville = He has forbidden us
   to go down into town.

This particular construction is always cropping up and it is essential to **learn by heart** the verbs most frequently involved. It is probably wise to learn them according to this pattern:

   **commander à quelqu'un de faire . . . = to order someone
   to do . . .**

conseiller . . .	= to advise;	promettre . . .	= to promise
demander . . .	= to ask;	défendre . . .	= to forbid . . .
dire . . .	= to tell;	interdire . . .	= to forbid
ordonner . . .	= to order;	permettre . . .	= to allow

The exception is '**prier**' (= to beg, pray) which is a polite way of asking and takes a **direct object**. (N.B. The verb '**persuader**' is found with **either** a direct **or** an indirect object.)
Je l'ai prié de me suivre = I asked him to follow me.

(b) these other **common verbs**:

avoir peur de	essayer de	faire semblant de
craindre de	tâcher de	(to pretend)
menacer de	oublier de	mériter de (to deserve)
décider de	remercier de	refuser de

(3) The **infinitive** is **preceded** by the preposition '**à**' following:

(a)
aider à	se décider à (to resolve to)	inviter à
encourager à	apprendre à	hésiter à
chercher à	commencer à	se mettre à
consentir à	continuer à	se préparer à
obliger à	s'occuper à	réussir à
songer à (to be thinking of)	tarder à (to take a long time)	

E.g. **Cherchera-t-il à la rencontrer en secret?** = Will he seek to meet her secretly?

(b) '**avoir**', in such expressions as:
Il avait beaucoup à faire = He had a lot to do.
J'ai des copies à corriger = I have books to mark.
Il y a tant de choses à voir = There are so many things to see.

(c) verbs denoting '**to spend**', '**to waste**' of **time**.
Il a passé toute la matinée **à réparer** le téléviseur = He spent all morning repairing the television set.
Elle gaspille tout son temps **à lire** des revues = She wastes all her time reading magazines.

Infinitive after adjective, noun

(1) In most cases the **infinitive** is **preceded** by the preposition 'de': e.g. Elle sera **contente d'entendre** ces nouvelles = She will be pleased to hear that news.

Vous êtes **certain de réussir** = You are certain to succeed.

Il est **inutile de se plaindre** = It's useless to complain.

Ils ont **le droit de traverser** notre domaine = They have the right to cross our land.

(2) Some, however, require the preposition 'à' before the **infinitive**: avoir de la peine (de la difficulté) à . . . = to have difficulty doing . . . ; prendre plaisir à . . . = to take pleasure in doing . . . The **adjectives** 'prêt', 'lent', 'léger', 'lourd', 'prompt' are also followed by 'à': e.g. Sa valise était **lourde à porter** = His suitcase was heavy to carry.

Unique, seul, le premier, le dernier and **all ordinal** numbers take 'à': e.g. Vous êtes le **seul à nous encourager** = You're the only one to give us encouragement. Il est toujours **le premier à protester** = He is always the first to protest.

Note also these expressions: bon à manger = good to eat;
bon à rien = good for nothing;
quelque chose à boire = something to drink
une maison à louer = a house for rent.

Infinitive after other prepositions

Firstly a reminder that the preposition 'en' must be followed by the **present participle** (*see pages 107, 108*). **All** other prepositions are followed by the **infinitive**. **Beware the English '-ing'!**

(1) **Sans, pour** are common examples of this structure: **sans hésiter** = without hesitating; **pour vous dire vrai** = to tell you the truth.

'**Pour**' usually indicates a **purpose** (in order to . . .), and is also used in the phrases 'assez' + adjective = . . . enough to; 'trop' + adjective = too . . . to.

E.g. Il est **trop petit pour** y monter = He is too little to climb up. Vous êtes **assez âgé pour** comprendre = You're big enough to understand.

(2) **Par** is only used following verbs of '**beginning**' and

'**finishing**' when these have the sense of 'to begin/end **by doing** something'.

E.g. Nous commencerons **par prendre** cinq oeufs = We will start **by taking** five eggs. Ils avaient **fini par me convaincre** = They ended up **by convincing** me.

(3) Avant, après

(a) **Avant** always has '**de**' before the infinitive: e.g. **avant de partir** = before leaving . . . **Avant de vous y emmener**, j'ai une question à vous poser = **Before taking** you there, I have a question to ask you.

(b) **Après** is always used with a **perfect infinitive**, formed from the auxiliary infinitive ('avoir' or 'être') + past participle.

E.g. **Après avoir remercié** son vieux serviteur, le comte se retira dans sa chambre = **After thanking** his old servant, the Count retired to his room.

Après être revenus du Portugal, ils se sentaient étrangement malades = **After returning** from Portugal, they felt strangely ill.

Après m'être renseigné auprès de la sécretaire, je m'assis pour attendre = **After enquiring** of the secretary, I sat down to wait.

Note 1 Since this is an **infinitive construction** you must be careful not to supply a subject pronoun.

Note 2 Note also that the reflexive pronoun must agree with the stated subject of the main clause.

Note 3 Both the 'avant de' and the 'après avoir' constructions **must** involve the same subject as the main verb. If this is not so, you should use a clause 'avant que + subjunctive' or 'après que'.

E.g. **Avant qu'il vous y emmène**, j'ai une question à vous poser = Before **he** takes you there, **I** have a question . . .

Après que mon frère se fut renseigné auprès de la sécretaire, je m'assis pour attendre = After **my brother** had enquired of the secretary, **I** sat down . . .

Test section

(i) **Fit the various sections of these sentences together**, adding prepositions where needed. Don't forget other necessary changes!

(Le professeur ordonna) (les élèves) (se taire)
(Nous avons décidé) (émigrer en Australie)
(J'ai commencé) (éliminer les suspects)
(Vous continuerez) (travailler, j'espère)
(Bientôt tu cesseras) (suivre ce cours)

(Demande) (la vieille dame) (te montrer le chemin)
(Yves aurait préféré) (rester chez ses parents)
(Il vaudrait mieux) (commencer) (étudier sans délai)
(Je suis trop fier) (lui demander) (nous aider)
(Viendrez-vous) (nous voir cette semaine?)
(Ils seront enchantés) (apprendre cette nouvelle)
(Tu devrais) (te préparer) (faire face à la situation)

(ii)***see note on page 58*. **Translate into French.**

'Promise me to help her.
Before deciding, consider all the possibilities.
The Leriches are having themselves a swimming pool built.
He wanted something to read.
Why are you always the first to finish?
I answered without thinking.
She spends all day waiting for his telephone call.
After arriving at the hotel, we went for a walk.

Answers
(i) **Le professeur ordonna aux élèves de se taire.**
Nous avons décidé d'émigrer en Australie.
J'ai commencé par éliminer les suspects.(à is also possible
  here, depending on whether the sense is 'begin by' or 'begin to')
Vous continuerez à travailler, j'espère.
Bientôt tu cesseras de suivre ce cours.
Demande à la vieille dame de te montrer le chemin.
Yves aurait préféré rester chez ses parents.
Il vaudrait mieux commencer à étudier sans délai. (**par** here
  is less likely.)
Je suis trop fier pour lui demander de nous aider.
Viendrez-vous nous voir cette semaine?
Ils seront enchantés d'apprendre cette nouvelle.
Tu devrais te préparer à faire face à la situation.

(ii) **Promettez-moi de l'aider.**
Avant de décider, considérez toutes les possibilités.
Les Leriche se font construire une piscine.
Il voulait quelque chose à lire.
Pourquoi êtes-vous toujours le premier à finir?
J'ai répondu sans penser.
**Elle passe toute la journée à attendre son coup de
  téléphone.**
**Après être arrivés à l'hôtel, nous avons fait une promen-
  ade.** (or **nous sommes allés nous promener.**)

Chapter 13
Government of Verbs

Many problems arise over the question of the connection between a verb and its object – where is there a preposition and where not? We have already seen some examples of this problem earlier in the book in the section on object pronouns (page 24).

(1) Here briefly is a list of the verbs which in French take a **direct object (no preposition)**:

attendre	= to wait for	espérer	= to hope for
chercher	= to look for	habiter	= to live in
demander	= to ask for	payer	= to pay for
écouter	= to listen to	regarder	= to look at

E.g. Nous les avons attendus = We waited **for** them.
L'actrice a demandé un meilleur rôle = The actress asked **for** a better part.

(2) In reverse, so to speak, here is a list of verbs which in French need the preposition à (or **indirect object pronoun**):

dire à	= to tell;	répondre à	= to reply;
obéir à	= to obey;	résister à	= to resist;
plaire à	= to please;	ressembler à	= to look like.
renoncer à	= to give up;	téléphoner à	= to telephone

E.g. Tu dois **leur** obéir = You must obey them.
Elle ressemble beaucoup **à sa mère** = She looks a lot like her mother.

(3) Verbs suggesting 'removing something from someone' also require à (or **indirect object pronoun**. Here are some examples:

prendre . . . à	= to take . . . from	voler . . . à	= to steal . . . from
acheter . . . à	= to buy . . . from	arracher . . . à	= to snatch . . . from
cacher . . . à	= to hide . . . from	emprunter . . . à	= to borrow . . . from

E.g. On **lui** a pris tout ce qu'il possédait = They took **from** him everything he possessed.
Le voleur arracha **à la pauvre vieille** le sac qu'elle portait = The thief snatched **from the poor old lady** the bag she was carrying.

(4) You should also remember carefully those types of verb where there is a 'built-in' preposition such as:
avoir besoin de = to need; s'intéresser à = to be interested in; se passer de = to do without; se diriger vers = to go towards; se souvenir de = to remember.

Examples of these in use have already been given (pages 25, 26). It is perhaps worthwhile mentioning here those two common verbs where the **meaning changes** according to the **preposition** which follows.

jouer à = to play (sport); jouer de = to play (instrument).

penser à = to think of (have in mind); penser de = to have an opinion about.

Note also **croire**: Je **le** crois = I believe him.

Je ne crois pas **aux** fantômes = I don't believe **in** ghosts.

Je crois **en** Dieu = I believe **in** God.

Test section

(i) **Complete these phrases** incorporating the noun or pronoun given in brackets in English. Take care, there are plenty of traps!

Jean-Claude regardait (at me)	**Jean-Claude me regardait.**
Je voudrais montrer mes peintures (her)	**Je voudrais lui montrer mes peintures.**
Nous aurons besoin (that book)	**Nous aurons besoin de ce livre.**
Téléphonez (your father)	**Téléphonez à votre père.**
Nous nous passerons (his advice)	**Nous nous passerons de son conseil.**
Il a décidé de renoncer (women!)	**Il a décidé de renoncer aux femmes!**
Nous devrions nous servir (a bigger hammer)	**Nous devrions nous servir d'un plus grand marteau.**
Je ressemblais (grandmother)	**Je ressemblais à grand'-mère.**
Tu pourras l'emprunter (from Jean)	**Tu pourras l'emprunter à Jean.**
Ont-ils écouté (to the programme)	**Ont-ils écouté le programme?**

Chapter 14
Modal Verbs

Vouloir, pouvoir, devoir, falloir, savoir ... old uncle Tom Cobbley and all! The collective name given to this group of verbs is modal verbs, but that is rather an awe-inspiring title. We have already seen that when used in connection with a **second verb**, this additional one follows **directly** in the **infinitive** form: e.g. Je ne veux pas l'**écouter** = I don't want **to listen** to him. Used in this sense, we have also seen that pronouns are placed before the dependent verb (here = 'écouter') because, sense-wise, that is where they belong.

In addition, **vouloir**, **savoir** and **devoir** all have a transitive function, i.e. they can take a **direct object**, in which case everything is quite normal as with an ordinary verb. Here the sense of **vouloir** is **to want, wish for**; **savoir** is **to know something**; **devoir** is **to owe** (money, etc.).

E.g. Le bébé **veut son jouet** = The baby **wants his toy.**
Moi, je **sais tout cela** = I **know all that.**
Il me **devait de l'argent** = He **owed me some money.**

In conjugation all these verbs are somewhat irregular and you must learn their forms from the verb tables. Apart from the effort involved that scarcely presents a problem.

Where there is often an area of difficulty with modal verbs is over the **question of meaning**. The difficulty occurs because English has a wealth of 'mights', 'coulds', 'shoulds' and 'ought to haves', etc. which are not easy to fit into the fairly carefully defined patterns of meaning which we have already encountered. It is more important to know how to interpret the conditional perfect of 'devoir', for instance, than it is to know simply how to form it and all the remaining tenses, since the meaning of that verb in the particular tense could well give the key to a whole phrase. Firstly therefore we will summarise all the possible English meanings which could prove problematic for the examination candidate. These are given on the table on page 122.

Note 1 Savoir is not included, since the meanings comply with the normal usage.

Note 2 The **past historic** has not been included, since its meaning is very much the same as the perfect (except that it does not normally translate '**have** done'): the **future perfect** is also omitted since this is also relatively trouble-free ('shall have wanted', 'shall have been able', etc.).

	PRESENT	FUTURE	IMPERFECT	CONDITIONAL	PERFECT	PLUPERFECT	CONDITIONAL PERFECT
VOULOIR = to want to	je veux = I wish, want to	je voudrai = I shall want to	je voulais = I wanted to	je voudrais = I should like to	j'ai voulu = I wanted to (on that occasion)	j'avais voulu = I had wanted to	j'aurais voulu = I should have liked to
POUVOIR = to be able	je peux = I can, may	je pourrai = I shall be able	je pouvais = I was able, could, used to be able	je pourrais = I might, could (if I wanted), would be able	j'ai pu = I was able, managed to, may have (on that occasion)	j'avais pu = I had been able to	j'aurais pu = I could have (if I had wanted), might have (it was possible)
DEVOIR = to have to	je dois = I must, am supposed to, have to	je devrai = I shall have to	je devais = I had to, was supposed to, used to have to, must have	je devrais = I ought, should	j'ai dû = I have had to, must have, had to (on that occasion)	j'avais dû = I had had to	j'aurais dû = I should have, ought to have
FALLOIR = to be necessary	il faut = one must, one has to	il faudra = one will have to	il fallait = one had to, was supposed to, used to have to	il faudrait = one ought, should	il a fallu = one has had to, must have, had to (on that occasion)	il avait fallu = one had had to	il aurait fallu = one should have, ought to have

Vouloir

(1) '**Vouloir**' is the most usual way of **asking someone to do something**.

E.g. **Voulez-vous baisser** la vitre s'il vous plaît? = **Will you** please lower the window?

Depending on the vehemence of the tone of voice, it can convey a fairly abrupt message: **Veux-tu** te taire! = **Will you** be quiet!

(2) The **conditional** tense offers a politely moderated approach to a request, and is particularly applicable to shopping situations.

E.g. **Je voudrais** un kilo d'oranges, s'il vous plaît, Madame = **I would like** a kilo of oranges please.

Nous ne voudrions pas vous déranger = **We wouldn't wish to** disturb you.

(3) We have already pointed out in the section on the **future** tense that '**will**' when it indicates an expression of **willingness** (or not!) is to be rendered by '**vouloir**' and not the future tense of the verb in question.

E.g. Gérard, **veux-tu mettre** la table? = Gérard, **will you lay** the table? Non, **je ne veux pas!** = No, **I won't!** (Gérard is apparently **not** willing!)

(4) The **plural imperative** is found in printed notices; in speech it would have a very superior air to it.

E.g. **Veuillez respecter** les pelouses = **Kindly keep off** the lawns.

Pouvoir

(1) As the table shows, '**pouvoir**' in its various tenses can offer a vast range of meanings and you must really question very thoroughly the **exact English equivalent** before attempting a translation.

A few examples of the verb in use in different tenses will best illustrate the difficulties and their solution – otherwise only **a lot of careful practice** will fix the verb firmly in your mind.

E.g. **Tu pourras te renseigner** demain = **You'll be able to find out** tomorrow.

Elle a pu laisser son parapluie dans l'autobus = She may have left her umbrella on the bus.

Vous pourriez le remplacer par un tuyau en plastique = **You could** (perhaps) **replace it** with a plastic pipe.

123

Il aurait pu nous prévenir avant = **He might have let us know** before.

Soudain **il ne put bouger** = Suddenly **he couldn't move.**

(2) '**Pouvoir**' is the French equivalent of the polite request in English '**may I?**'

E.g. Est-ce que **je peux entrer**? = **May I come in**? or, when in the inverted question form: **Puis-je** entrer?

(3) '**Pouvoir**' is generally **not** included in statements concerning the five senses. English usage is to supply 'can'.

E.g. D'ici **on voit** la flèche de la vieille église = From here you **can see** the spire of the old church. (Of course you **can**, or you would not be saying so!)

Entendez-vous l'hirondelle? = **Can you hear** the swallow?

Il sentait des gouttes de sueur couler sur son front = **He could feel** drops of sweat running down his forehead.

This is often a point which occurs in **translation**, so you would be wise to make a particular note of it.

(4) '**Pouvoir**' = (**physically**) 'to be able'.

'**Can**' in the sense of '**to know how to**' is translated by the verb '**savoir**'. This is also a favourite point of translation, so you must be careful to distinguish between:

I can't run 5 kms. in 30 seconds (= physically impossible) **and** I can't play chess (= I haven't learned how to).

= **Je ne peux pas courir** 5 kms. en 30 secondes *and* **Je ne sais pas jouer** aux échecs.

Devoir

(1) As with the preceding verb the exact shade of meaning of '**devoir**' used with another verb **must be studied** very closely. Again some examples in use will help to guide you.

E.g. **Nous devions toujours faire attention** aux trains = We always **had to** (or were supposed to) **look out for** the trains.

Il a dû se tromper = **He must have made a mistake.**

A quelle heure **dois-tu le voir**? = At what time **are you supposed** to see him? Oh zut! **je devais le rencontrer** il y a une demi-heure! = Oh drat! **I was meant to meet him** half an hour ago! Oui, **j'ai dû le faire** = Yes, I had to do it.

Vous devriez vous excuser auprès de Paul = **You ought to** make your apologies to Paul.

Tu aurais dû mettre d'autres chaussures = **You ought to have put on** some other shoes.
Ils durent ranger le salon = **They had to tidy** the lounge.
Elle doit avoir froid, la petite = **The poor little thing must be** cold.

(2) In short '**devoir**' can cover the following meanings, depending on the tense used:
   (a) necessity or compulsion;
   (b) duty or moral obligation;
   (c) previous arrangement;
   (d) expression of personal opinion about a fact or state.
See if you can work out in which category each of the examples above could best be placed.

Falloir

(1) This verb has much in common with 'devoir' in that it translates '**must**' and '**have to**', but it tends to be **stronger** and more **insistent** than the other. It is an **impersonal verb** (which means it is used in the **third person singular only**).

A few examples will demonstrate its use:
Il faut avoir un permis pour conduire = **You have to have** a licence to drive.
Il fallait payer à la caisse = **You had to pay** at the desk.
Il fallut enfin **traverser** un large fleuve = Lastly **we had to cross** a wide river.

The above examples show how it is very often left to the context to indicate to the listener or reader who precisely was compelled to do this or that. However it is possible to specify who was involved by the use of an **indirect pronoun**: e.g. **Il leur a fallu passer** la nuit dans l'auberge = **They had to spend** the night at the inn.

(2) You may **not** use this **infinitive** construction, however, where there is a **noun subject specified**, e.g. Monsieur Duchesne has to spend . . . In this case you **must** use the construction '**il faut que + subjunctive**' which we have already seen: e.g. **Il faut que Monsieur Duchesne passe** la nuit dans l'auberge.

Note If you **choose** to use the subjunctive clause instead of the infinitive construction, where the latter would be grammatically correct, this generally implies **an even stronger sense of necessity**.

You will have noticed that on no single occasion have we used the word 'necessary' in translating the examples. That is not to say that it would not be perfectly acceptable in some cases, but by and large you find that the most natural English is 'I had to', 'you must', etc. and the **natural expression** is what is **right** when it comes to translation.

Savoir

(1) '**Savoir**' fortunately presents few problems. It is important to remember its meaning of '**to know how to**' or 'to have learned how to', which is **always** the meaning attached to the verb when used to mean '**can**'.

E.g. Les filles! **Elles ne savent rien faire**! = Girls! **They can't** (don't know how to) **do anything**!

(2) '**Savoir**' v. '**connaître**'

'To know, or to know?' It all depends on 'whom' or 'what'!

Savoir = to know (facts, things which can be memorised)
Connaître = to know (be acquainted with – people, places, animals, books, etc.)

E.g. Lloyd George **a connu mon père** = (well, you know what!)
Tu ne connais pas cette musique? = **Do you not know this piece of music?**

Test section

(i) Cover the right-hand side of the page while you **work out the best English translation** for these phrases.

Est-ce que je dois venir demain?	**Do I have to come tomorrow?**
Il faut que je parte.	**I've got to go** (leave).
Il a pu se tromper.	**He may have made a mistake.**
Veuillez bien vous asseoir.	**Be so kind as to sit down.**
Il n'a jamais su jouer du piano.	**He has never known how to play the piano.**
Tu devais avoir faim.	**You were hungry, I expect** (you must have been in a hungry state).
Il nous faudra bientôt manger.	**We'll have to eat soon.**
J'aurais voulu les aider.	**I should have liked to help them.**

126

Nous devrions aller à la banque.	**We ought to go to the bank.**
Elle pourrait arriver tard.	**She could** (might) **arrive late.**
Je n'aurais pas dû me fâcher.	**I shouldn't have got cross.**
Il fallait y dormir.	**We** (they) **used to have to sleep there.**
Ils auraient pu changer d'avis.	**They might have changed their mind.**
Voulez-vous vous reposer un instant?	**Will you have a rest for a minute?**
Il aurait fallu que Michel prît lui-meme la décision.	**Michel really ought to have taken the decision himself.**

(ii)****See note on page 58.*
Translate these phrases into French.

You are supposed to meet Papa outside the supermarket. ('tu')	**Tu dois rencontrer Papa devant le supermarché.**
I know your little brother. ('tu')	**Je connais ton petit frère.**
We will have to drive less quickly.	**Il nous faudra conduire moins vite.**
You were able to show him the way.	**Vous avez pu lui montrer le chemin.** (on that occasion)
She would have liked to discuss that.	**Elle aurait voulu discuter de cela.**
May I smoke?	**Puis-je fumer?**
They might be bored.	**Ils pourraient s'ennuyer.**
Pierre can swim very well.	**Pierre sait très bien nager.**
I ought to do the washing-up.	**Je devrais faire la vaisselle.**
They had to come back quickly.	**Ils ont dû revenir vite.** (on that occasion)
Jean really must continue his studies.	**Il faut que Jean poursuive ses études.**

Chapter 15
Negatives

Or: the '**not never no more**' syndrome! We seem to have managed remarkably well so far to avoid mention of the negative, but the situation cannot last. So now for a little negative thinking!

(1) The most obvious difference between English and French negative forms is that in French the **negative** has **two parts**, the first of which is always '**ne** ...'. It is the second part which supplies the meaning. This first characteristic of the negative gives rise to one of **two common mistakes** made by candidates. These are:

(a) to **leave out** the small, but important '**ne**' which is only omitted when there is no verb.

(b) to **misplace** the **main part** of the negative ('pas', 'jamais', etc.).

The negatives are as follows:

(i)	**ne ... pas**	= not
	ne ... point	= not (at all)
	ne ... plus	= no longer, no more
	ne ... jamais	= never
	ne ... guère	= scarcely
	ne ... rien	= nothing
(ii)	**ne ... personne**	= nobody
	ne ... nulle part	= nowhere
	ne ... aucun(e)	= not (a single)
	ne ... nul, nulle	= not (a single), no ...
	ne ... que	= only
	ne ... ni ... ni	= neither ... nor

Back in your early carefree days of learning French you may have been told that the **negative 'sandwiches' the verb**; this in fact expresses very well how negative and verb work together.

Subject	**ne**	(obj. pron)	**verb**	**pas** (or other)
Elle	*ne*	l'	**aime**	*pas.*
Nous	*n'*		**allons**	*jamais* chez eux.

As we have seen before, particularly in respect of the position and use of pronouns in compound sentences, where there are **two**

parts to the verb, it is the **auxiliary** verb which counts as the functional part. Thus when the negatives in the section (i) above are used in compound sentences, the same will apply: the **past participle** will be added **after the 'pas'** ('rien', 'plus', etc.) to give the following pattern:

Subject	ne	(obj. pron)	auxiliary verb	pas, etc.	past participle
Elle	*ne*	l'	**a**	*pas*	**aimé.**
Nous	*ne*		**sommes**	*jamais*	**allés** chez eux.

E.g. Ils *n*'étaient *pas* revenus = They hadn't come back.
Je *ne* me suis *jamais* couché si tard = I've never gone to bed so late.
For the verbs in section (ii) above, however, the **two parts of the negative enclose the entire verb form**, past participles an'all!
E.g. Vous *n*'avez rencontré *personne* – c'est bizarre! = You met no one – that's strange!
Je *ne* les ai vus *nulle part* = I haven't seen them anywhere.
Ils *n*'ont bu *que* du champagne! = They only drank champagne!
Although it may seem rather bothersome that the negatives divide themselves into two groups in this way, for most of those in this second group (ii) – the p.p.p. types (post-past participle!), there is a fairly acceptable reason for their odd behaviour.

'Nul', 'nulle', and 'aucun(e)' evidently need completion of their sense by a noun (although 'ne . . . aucun' may also be a pronoun), and it is logical therefore that they should be placed before this noun: e.g. Après cela, je *n*'ai eu *aucune* envie de le revoir = After that I hadn't the slightest wish to see him again.

'Ne . . . ni . . . ni' offers similar excuses. The expression must be completed by a noun, pronoun or verb to make sense: e.g. Pendant neuf ans il *n*'a mangé *ni* viande *ni* poisson = For nine years he ate neither meat nor fish.

With this negative, of course, there are **three parts** to remember, and you must **always** include '**ne**' before the verb. Notice, however, that the **indefinite article** is normally **omitted** after 'ni': e.g. Il *ne* porte *ni* manteau *ni* imperméable = He is wearing neither an overcoat nor a mackintosh.

'Ne . . . que' is rather strange. Although negative in form it is really **restrictive** in meaning. 'Que' always immediately precedes whatever in the sentence is being restricted.
E.g. Je *n*'ai connu *que* lui dans la famille = I knew only him in the family.

Ils *n'*ont cueilli *que* 250 grammes de fraises = They only picked 250 grams of strawberries.

(2) English is often lax in its placing of the word 'only' and great care has to be taken in translation. In the sentence 'We only play football on Wednesdays', it is obvious that '**only**' refers to 'on Wednesdays' and ought strictly to come immediately in front of it: it means that we don't play on any other day of the week. **The French always place 'que' correctly** (how smug!): e.g. Nous *ne* jouons au football *que* le mercredi.

There is a slight difficulty when '**only**' refers to the **verb**, as in 'She only smiled'. To cope with this in French you supply the verb '**faire**' in addition to the original verb: e.g. **Elle ne fit que sourire** (i.e. the only thing she did was to smile).

(3) If '**only**' is qualifying the **subject of the sentence**, you must use '**seul**', not the 'ne ... que' structure: e.g. **Seule la police** pourra nous le dire = **Only the police** will be able to tell us.
N.B. The final 'if only' is '**if only**!' This is simply rendered by '**si seulement** ...', e.g. **Si seulement** tu nous avais écrit = If only you had written to us.

Negatives which begin a sentence

rien	aucun
personne	nul
ni ... ni ...	

may all be the subject of a sentence, just as in English.

The only **difficulty** is in remembering to place the '**ne**' in its customary position before the verb, and in **avoiding** the temptation to include 'pas' in such sentences.
E.g. **Ni** lui **ni** son frère aîné **n'était** là = Neither he nor his elder brother was there.
Aucun bienfait **ne peut** résulter de cette affaire = No good can come out of this matter.

Two negatives together

Negative expressions may be combined almost without restriction. Where 'plus' is one of them it is usually the first of the two. Otherwise 'jamais' is normally first.
E.g. Je **n'**ai **plus ni** argent **ni** amis = I have no longer either money or friends.
On **ne** voit **jamais personne** aux fenêtres = You never see anyone at the windows.
Elle **n'**a **plus rien** dit = She said nothing more.
Il **ne** ferait **jamais** mal **à personne** = He would never harm anyone.

N.B. '**Pas**' and '**point**' **cannot** be combined with any other negative. You will have seen from the examples quoted on the previous page how often one of the two negatives is translated by an English positive form ('any', 'anything', 'anyone', etc.). The French point of view here is that they are both undoubtedly negatives (take away one and you would of course express the remaining one automatically in a negative form to convey the correct idea), and so, both negatives they remain. **Remember this point** in translation. **Remember too** that you may not in French imitate the English practice of including in the same phrase 'not + anybody', 'not + ever', 'not + anything', 'not + any more', etc. You must give the corresponding **total negative** form.

E.g. anyone = quelqu'un;   not anyone = **no one = ne . . . personne**.
anything = quelque chose;   not anything = **nothing = ne . . . rien**.
ever = jamais;   not ever = **never = ne . . . jamais**.
still = encore, toujours;   **no more = ne . . . plus**.
a, some = un, des;   not a = **no = ne . . . aucun**.
either . . . or = ou . . . ou;   **neither . . . nor = ne . . . ni . . . ni**.
anywhere = quelque part;   not anywhere = **nowhere = ne . . . nulle part**.

A variation on this principle also occurs with '**sans**' which is regarded as introducing a negative phrase (After all 'without' does suggest 'you have not got'!) Thus we have:
Il partit **sans rien dire** = He left **without saying anything**.
Elle resta là **sans parler à personne** = She stayed there **without speaking to anyone**.
Sans aucun doute, il est mort = **Without a doubt** he is dead.
Ils étaient sortis **sans chapeau ni parapluie** = They had gone out **without a hat or an umbrella**.

Negatives with an infinitive
Usual phrases are of course of the type: Je ne veux pas les voir = I don't want to see them. Il n'a pas voulu y participer = He didn't want to take part. In these cases it is clear that the negative is attached to the 'wanting'.

But it is equally possible to have a **negative** which refers to the **infinitive**: 'He decided **not to play** any more' (quite different from 'He did not decide to play . . .'). This is rendered in French by putting **both parts of the negative together before the verb (infinitive)**.
E.g. Il décida de **ne plus jouer**.
Dis-leur de **ne pas revenir** trop tôt = Tell them **not to come back** too soon. Compare the following two statements:
J'ai essayé **de ne pas réveiller** les enfants = I tried **not to waken**

131

the children. **Je n'ai pas essayé de** reveiller . . . **I didn't try to . . .**

No negative!

Quite often the **negative** is used **without a verb**, usually in very short answers of the type:

Que fais-tu là? **Rien!** = **What are you doing there? Nothing**!
Personne ici? = **Nobody** at home?
Passe-t-il ses vacances à l'étranger? **Jamais!** = Does he spend his holidays abroad? **Never**!

In **literary French** and **elegant speech** you could also come across the omission of 'pas' with the verbs 'pouvoir', 'savoir', 'cesser' and 'oser', e.g. **Je ne saurais le dire** = I couldn't say.

However it is **never incorrect** to use 'pas' with these verbs.

These are the **only situations** where you may find the **'pas' omitted**, or, as in the examples above, the **'ne' omitted**.

N'est-ce pas?

It has been said that you can tell an Englishman speaking French by the number of times he lets this phrase trip ever-so-lightly off his tongue, as though this, more than any other expression, shows he is tuned in to the language on the genuine wavelength!

This is a trifle unkind since the phrase really is used a great deal by the French themselves; perhaps it is the rather unlikely intonation of the aspiring linguist which is more to blame for this derision than the use of the phrase itself. Accent and intonation are really what makes an idiom spoken by a foreigner acceptable as such to the native ear. A French lady of my acquaintance trained for months to perfect the English phrase 'Pull ze ozzer one, eet 'as got bells on eet' in an effort to appear spontaneous and idiomatic, but to her chagrin never achieved the desired result!

'Revenons à nos moutons', however. All things considered it may well be prudent not to end too many sentences with 'n'est-ce pas?'. Its correct usage is **at the end of an affirmative** or **negative statement** where the speaker expects a response 'yes' or 'no'. The various meanings are therefore manifold: 'is he?', 'isn't he?'; 'will you?', 'won't you?'; 'do they?', 'don't they?', etc.

E.g. Vous venez avec nous, **n'est-ce pas?** = You are coming with us, aren't you? ('Oui' or 'Non'?) Vous ne le ferez plus, **n'est-ce pas?** = You won't do it any more, will you? (Here the answer must be either 'Si' or 'Non'. 'Si' is used to mean 'Yes' when the **question** has been **phrased negatively**.)

Note 1 While on the subject of apparently niggling small points, here are two more connected with the negative. The first is a revision point. Your cue is 'de'.

Have you remembered that **following a negative** correct usage demands that all 'du', 'de la', 'de l' ', and 'des' forms become '**de**' or '**d**'? (The only **exception** is with that strange half-negative 'ne . . . que' which does **not** have this effect on following 'du', 'de la' or 'des'.)

Incidentally in the parallel English situation it is usual to say '**any**' (to replace 'some') after a negative.
E.g. Je **n'ai pas de** frères = I **haven't any** brothers.
Il **ne m'a pas rapporté de** fleurs, mais il **m'a envoyé des** chocolats = He didn't bring me **any** flowers back, but he sent me **some** chocolates.

Note 2 The other point concerns expressions of **negative comparison**. You will remember that the way to express a comparison is to say: **aussi + adj. (adv.) + que = as . . . as**
Should you wish to say '**not so . . . as**' your 'aussi' becomes '**si**'.
E.g. Jacqueline **n'est pas si jolie que** sa soeur = Jacqueline is **not so pretty** as her sister.
Mais elle est **aussi intelligente qu'elle** = But she is just **as intelligent** (as she is).
Hélas! votre fils n'a **pas** travaillé **si bien que** l'année dernière, Madame = Alas! your son has **not** worked **so hard as** last year, Madame.

Finally, a few negative expressions in common use:
ni moi (toi, lui, etc.) **non plus** = nor me (you, he) neither
n'importe! = no matter!
je ne sais que faire = I don't know what to do
je n'en sais rien = I know nothing about it
jamais de la vie! = never in this world!

Test section

(i)(a) **Turn these phrases into the negative** by using the expression indicated in brackets.

Pourquoi sont-ils venus?	(ne . . . jamais)
Quelqu'un pourra le prendra.	(ne . . . personne)

Jeanne, l'aime-t-elle toujours? (ne . . . plus)
En vacances il a grossi. (ne . . . que d'un kilo)
Nous avons vu quelqu'un entrer. (ne . . . personne)
Nos parents, ont-ils découvert quelque chose? (ne . . . rien)
Ou un rat ou une souris aurait pu le tuer. (ne . . . ni . . . ni)

(i) (b) Add the additional negative shown in brackets.

Ils ne sont jamais retournés. (ne . . . plus)
Vous ne répondez rien. (ne . . . jamais)
Cet homme n'a ni maison ni argent. (ne . . . plus)
Ces bêtes ne se voient plus à la campagne. (ne . . . guère)
Tu travailles toujours sans intérêt. (ne . . . aucun)

Answers
(i) (a) Pourquoi ne sont-ils jamais venus?
Personne ne pourra le prendre.
Jeanne, ne l'aime-t-elle plus?
En vacances il n'a grossi que d'un kilo.
Nous n'avons vu entrer personne.
Nos parents, n'ont-ils rien découvert?
Ni rat ni souris n'aurait pu le tuer.
(i) (b) Ils ne sont plus jamais retournés.
Vous ne répondez jamais rien.
Cet homme n'a plus ni maison ni argent.
Ces bêtes ne se voient plus guère à la campagne.
Tu travailles toujours sans aucun intérêt.

(ii) ** *See note on page 58.* **Translate into French.**

Who did that? No one, sir.	**Qui a fait cela? Personne, monsieur.**
I hope not to see him at George's.	**J'espère ne pas le voir chez Georges.**
You'll be coming back soon, won't you?	**Vous reviendrez bientôt, n'est-ce pas?**
Without saying anything, he left.	**Sans rien dire, il partit.**
I didn't see anyone.	**Je n'ai vu personne.**
He doesn't owe me anything any more.	**Il ne me doit plus rien.**
Only the doctor can help you.	**Seul le médecin peut vous aider.**
There was not a sign of life.	**Il n'y avait aucun signe de vie.**
Nothing will make him change his mind.	**Rien ne le fera changer d'avis.**

Chapter 16
Use of Prepositions

Except when used in their most obvious sense, prepositions are notoriously difficult to get right in a foreign language. For people learning English the task is just as difficult – cold comfort for the examination candidate, maybe. There is no quick way to master the idiomatic use of prepositions. As is so often the case, careful attention to printed and spoken examples is the only sure way of getting to grips with the problem. Listed here are some of the most frequently encountered idioms for learning by heart. Verbal phrases involving the prepositions '**à**' and '**de**' which have been included in earlier sections of the book have not normally been featured here. Such verbal expressions as 's'intéresser à', 'se servir de', etc. will not be found below.

The prepositions are listed alphabetically under the **English word**, to make it easier for candidates to check idioms of which they are unsure. At the end there will be a short section where the idioms are listed in random order, as the English rendering does not include a preposition. It is, of course, possible to tackle the phrases from either the French or the English side, giving the equivalent in the other language. Candidates will choose which method best suits their particular examination requirements; CSE candidates will probably prefer to work from the French side, giving English equivalents, whereas for O-level candidates there is a greater need for the French phrases to be learned by heart.

about	he spoke *about* her	**il a parlé** *à son sujet (propos)*
	about midnight	*vers* **minuit**
	about twenty kilometres	*environ* **vingt kilomètres**
	about a hundred books	*une centaine de* **livres**
	What are they talking *about*?	*De quoi* **parlent-ils?**
above	*above* all	*avant* **tout**
	above forty people	*plus de* **quarante personnes**
across	*across* the street	*de l'autre côté de* **la rue**
	to go *across* the field	*traverser* **le champ**
after	*after* some time	*au bout de* **quelque temps**
	the day *after* his death	*le lendemain de* **sa mort**
	to take *after* someone	**tenir** *à* **quelqu'un**

at	seven o'clock *at* night	**sept heures** *du* **soir**
	at my house	*chez* **moi**
	at all costs	*à* **tout prix**
	at last	*enfin*
	at first	*d'abord*
	at the same time	*en* **même temps**
	at the grocer's	*chez* **l'épicier**
	to speak *at* the same time	**parler** *à la fois*
before	(place)	
	before (= outside) the house	*devant* **la maison**
	before (= in front of) me	*devant* **moi**
	(time)	
	before six o'clock	*avant* **six heures**
	one month *before*	**un mois** *auparavant*
	the day *before*	*la veille*
	to let someone know *beforehand*	**prévenir** *d'avance*
by	*by* the seaside	*au bord de* **la mer**
	by chance	*par* **hasard**
	midday *by* my watch	**midi** *à* **ma montre**
	to recognise *by* his nose	**reconnaître** *à* **son nez**
	by the way	*à* **propos**
	side *by* side	**côte** *à* **côte**
	by boat, train	*en* **bateau**, *en* **train**
	by plane	*par* **avion**
	by bus, car, rail	*en* **autobus, voiture, chemin de fer**
	by bicycle, moped	*à* **bicyclette** (*en* **vélo**) **en vélomoteur**
down	I go *down* the road	**je descends la rue**
	to fall *down* a hole	**tomber** *dans* **un trou**
for	(connected with time)	
	for the whole week (**past**)	(*pendant*) **toute la semaine**
	for a week (**future**)	*pour* **une semaine**
	we have been playing *for* an hour	**nous jouons** *depuis* **une heure**
	to thank *for* your help	**remercier** *de* **votre aide**
	for ever	*à* **jamais**
	to be sorry *for*	**avoir pitié** *de*
	for example	*par* **exemple**
	to shout *for* help	**crier** *au* **secours**
	to weep *for* joy	**pleurer** *de* **joie**

	word *for* word	mot *à* mot
from	*from* Saturday on	*dès (à partir de)* **samedi**
	from what you say	*d'après* **ce que vous dites**
	to buy *from* the butcher's	**acheter** *chez* **le boucher**
	a week *from* today	*d'aujourd'hui* **en huit**
	tell them *from* me	**dites-leur** *de ma part*
	to take *from* the table	**prendre** *sur* **la table**
	hanging *from* the wall	**suspendu** *au* **mur**
	from 1914 till 1918	*depuis* **1914 jusqu'en 1918**
	ten kilometres *from* here	*à* **dix kilomètres** *d'ici*

in, into	(= '**à**')	
	to arrive *in* time	**arriver** *à* **temps**, *à* **l'heure**
	to have a pain *in* the head	**avoir mal** *à* **la tête**
	to hold *in* one's hand	**tenir** *à* **la main**
	wounded *in* the leg	**blessé** *à* **la jambe**
	in spring	*au* **printemps**
	in the shade, the sun	*à* **l'ombre,** *au* **soleil**
	in future	*à* **l'avenir**
	in the country	*à* **la campagne**
	in a loud voice	*à* **voix haute**
	in bed	*au* **lit**
	in July	*au* **mois de (en) juillet**
	in my opinion	*à* **mon avis**
	in London	*à* **Londres**
	in the twentieth century	*au* **vingtième siècle**
	in the distance	*au* **loin**
	in Japan, Denmark (and all masculine names of countries)	*au* **Japon, Danemark**
	in the United States	*aux* **Etats-Unis**
	(= '**dans**', '**en**')	
	in Paris (the real heart)	*dans* **Paris**
	in an hour (from now)	*dans* **une heure**
	in an hour (within that time, time taken)	*en* **une heure**
	to live *in* town	**demeurer** *en* **ville**
	in summer, autumn, winter	*en* **été, automne, hiver**
	in short	*en* **somme (bref)**
	to change *into* a frog	**se changer** *en* **grenouille**
	in Italy (all feminine names of countries)	*en* **Italie**
	(= '**de**')	
	to dress *in* a skirt	**s'habiller** *d'une* **jupe**

to fall *in love with*	**tomber** *amoureux de*
five o'clock *in* the morning, afternoon (evening, night)	**cinq heures** *du* **matin,** *de l'*après-midi, (*du* **soir,** *de la* **nuit**)
in any case	*de* **toute façon**
the best *in* the world	**le meilleur** *du* **monde**
in the course of time	*avec* **le temps**
to fall *into* the hands of	**tomber** *entre* **les mains de**
to go out *into* the rain	**sortir** *sous* **la pluie**
in the reign of	*sous* **le règne de**
in (**after**) an hour all had become calm again	*au bout d'*une heure tout était devenu calme
into the bargain	*par-dessus* **le marché**

of

a tie *of* silk (silk tie)	**une cravate** *en* **soie**
it is kind *of* him	**c'est gentil** *à* **lui**
most *of* you	**la plupart** *d'entre* **vous**
on behalf *of*	*de la part de*

on, upon (= '**à**')

on a bicycle, *on* foot, horseback, one's knees	*à* **bicyclette,** *à* **pied,** *à* **cheval,** *à* **genoux**
on purpose	*à* **dessein (exprès)**
on the contrary	*au* **contraire**
on the left, right	*à* **gauche, droite**
on that occasion	*à* **cette occasion**
to arrive *on* time	**arriver** *à* **temps**
to work *on* a farm	**travailler** *dans* **une ferme**
on my arrival, return	*à* **mon arrivée, retour**
to knock *on* a door	**frapper** *à* **une porte**
on radio, television	*à* **la radio,** *à* **la télévision**
on duty	*de* **service**
on leave	*en* **permission**
on a journey, away	*en* **voyage**
on strike	*en* **grève**
on a fine summer's day	*par* **une belle journée d'été**
on the way	*en* **route**
on holiday	*en* **vacances**
on business	*pour* **affaires**
to fall *on* the ground	**tomber** *par* **terre**
on both sides	*des* **deux côtés**
on Sundays	*le* **dimanche**

N.B. '**On**' is never translated before days and dates.

out of	*out of* breath	*à bout de* **souffle,** *hors* d'haleine
	out of politeness	*par* **politesse**
	eight *out of* ten	**huit** *sur* **dix**
	out of work	*en* **chômage**
	to jump *out of* the window	**sauter** *par la* **fenêtre**
	out of fashion	**démodé**
	out of order (broken down)	*en* **panne**
outside	to wait *outside* the door	**attendre** *devant* **la porte**
over	hanging up *over* the mantelpiece	**accroché** *au-dessus de* **la cheminée**
	to jump *over* the hedge	**sauter** *par-dessus* **la haie**
	a bridge *over* the river	**un pont** *sur* **la rivière**
	a raincoat *over* his arm	**un imperméable** *sur* **le bras**
	it's *over*	**c'est** *terminé,* **(fini)**
through	to look *through* the window	**regarder** *par* **la fenêtre**
	… *through* a curtain	… *à travers* **un rideau**
	to walk *through* the woods	**aller** *à travers* **les bois**
	a *through* train	**un train** *direct*
	to travel *through* (via)	**voyager** *par*
	through a mistake	*à la suite d'* **une erreur**
to	the road *to* Versailles	**la route** *de* **Versailles**
	the train *to* Lyon	**le train** *de* **Lyon**
	come with me *to* the crossroads	**venez avec moi** *jusqu'au* **carrefour**
	she turned *to* him	**elle se tourna** *vers* **lui**
	be kind *to* me	**sois gentil** *envers* **(pour) moi**
	to go *to* town	**aller** *en* **ville**
	from day *to* day	**de jour** *en* **jour**
	to all appearances	*selon* **toute apparence**
	he is cruel *to* his wife	**il est cruel** *envers* **sa femme**
	up *to* that time	*jusqu'alors, jusque* **là**
under	he was sitting *under* a tree	**il était assis** *sous* **un arbre**
	hidden *under* the floor	**caché** *sous le* **plancher**
-wards	afterwards	**plus tard**
	backwards	**en arrière**
	downwards	**en bas**

	forwards	**en avant**
	homewards	**vers la maison**
	upwards	**en haut**

with   *with* his hands in his pockets — **les mains dans les poches**
to compare *with* — **comparer** *à*
to shake hands *with* — **serrer la main** *à*
what can be done *with* this cardboard box? — **que faire** *de* **ce carton?**
she got angry *with* me — **elle s'est fâchée** *contre* **moi**
to stay *with* a family — **rester (séjourner)** *dans* **une famille**

black *with* soot — **noir** *de* **suie**
with all my heart — *de* **tout mon coeur**
to cry *with* sadness — **pleurer** *de* **tristesse**
to fill (up) *with* — **remplir** *de*
a girl *with* blue eyes — **une fille** *aux* **yeux bleus**
I live *with* my parents — **j'habite** *chez* **mes parents**
to speak *with* your mouth full — **parler la bouche pleine**

within   please apply *within* — **prière de s'adresser** *à l'intérieur*
within reach — *à* **la portée** *de* **la main**
within three miles of the town — *à moins de* **trois milles de la ville**
within sight — *en* **vue**

Miscellaneous

four times a day — **quatre fois** *par* **jour**
to change one's mind — **changer** *d'*avis
my (your) turn to play — *à* **moi (toi) de jouer**
80 kilometres an hour — **80 kilomètres** *à* **l'heure**
see you soon, Tuesday — *à* **bientôt,** *à* **mardi**
see you later — *à* **tout à l'heure**
early — *de* **bonne heure**
to be slow, fast (watch) by 3 minutes — **retarder, avancer** *de* **3 minutes**
*in the middle of the night — ***en pleine nuit**
*in the heart of the country — ***en pleine campagne**
*as for you! — ***quant à vous !**
*to treat as a friend — ***traiter en ami**

*(included here since a little out of line with listed prepositions.)

Test section

(i) **Supply in each case the correct prepositional phrase.**

C'est — toi de payer.

C'est **à** toi de payer.

Qu'y a-t-il — la télé ce soir?

Qu'y a-t-il ce soir **à** la télé?

Il est sorti — la pluie.

Il est sorti **sous** la pluie.

Il arrive — voiture.

Il arrive **en** voiture.

Nous sommes allés — Japon.

Nous sommes allés **au** Japon.

Elle s'est assise — ombre.

Elle s'est assise **à l'**ombre.

On l'a construit — cinq semaines.

On l'a construit **en** cinq semaines.

— secours! Aidez-moi!

Au secours! Aidez-moi!

Des vacances — Allemagne!

Des vacances **en** Allemagne!

Un monsieur — joues rouges.

Un monsieur **aux** joues rouges.

Regarde — la fenêtre!

Regarde **par** la fenêtre!

Il est parti .*(before)* mon arrivée.

Il est parti **avant** mon arrivée.

Reviens — bonne heure.

Reviens **de** bonne heure.

Au revoir! — dimanche prochain!

Au revoir! **A** dimanche prochain!

Déguisons-nous — astronautes.

Déguisons-nous **en** astronautes.

C'est — l'autre côté de la rue.

C'est **de** l'autre côté de la rue.

Il vécut — dix-neuvième siècle.

Il vécut **au** dix-neuvième siècle.

Il nous a traités — camarades.

Il nous a traités **en** camarades.

Résultats: soixante — cent!

Résultats: soixante **sur** cent!

(ii) **See note on page 58.** Translate into French.

I am going to the United States for a month.

Je vais aux Etats-Unis pour un mois.

We hope to arrive before ten o'clock.

Nous espérons arriver avant dix heures.

Let's go for a boat trip.

Faisons une promenade en bateau (or Allons faire . . .)

He has a house in the country.

Il a une maison à la campagne.

I worked hard for three years.

J'ai travaillé dur pendant trois ans.

She knew me by my hat.

Elle m'a reconnu à mon chapeau.

Try to be there on time.

Essayez d'être là à l'heure.

This dress is (made) of wool.

Cette robe est en laine.

141

Chapter 17
Everyday Basics

Under this heading will be found several small but important items which are essential in everyday conversation.

Numerals

Cardinal numbers

0 zéro	13 treize	40 quarante
1 un, une	14 quatorze	50 cinquante
2 deux	15 quinze	60 soixante
3 trois	16 seize	*70 **soixante-dix**
4 quatre	17 dix-sept	*71 **soixante et onze**
5 cinq	18 dix-huit	72 soixante-douze
6 six	19 dix-neuf	*80 **quatre-vingts**
7 sept	20 vingt	*81 **quatre-vingt-un**
8 huit	*21 **vingt et un**	*90 **quatre-vingt-dix**
9 neuf	22 vingt-deux	*91 **quatre-vingt-onze**
10 dix	23 vingt-trois	*100 **cent** (**not** 'un cent')
11 onze	30 trente	*1,000 **mille**
12 douze	31 trente et un	*1,001 **mille un**

The rest are easily formed:

> 45 quarante-cinq
> 73 soixante-treize
> 250 deux cent cinquante

999,999 = neuf cent quatre-vingt-dix-neuf mille neuf cent quatre-vingt-dix-neuf! 1,000,000 = un million!

In the list above the numbers marked with an asterisk* are particularly prone to being mis-spelt.

(1) You should note that the numbers '**vingt**' and '**cent**' take plural 's' only when standing alone: cinq cents, quatre-vingts, and **not** followed by another numeral.

(2) '**Mille**' as a noun (= a mile) may of course add an 's' if plural; as a numeral it is **invariable**.

(3) **Dates** 1917 is generally spoken 'dix-neuf cent dix-sept', but in legal documents (and also in normal use as an alternative) a form '**mil**' is used to mean 'a thousand'. Thus 1917 = **mil** neuf cent dix-neuf.

142

En quelle année est-il né? Il est né **en dix-neuf cent trente-trois** = In which year was he born? He was born in 1933.

Ordinal numbers

*1st	= **premier, première**	*9th	= **neuvième**
2nd	= second (e) or deuxième	10th	= dixième
3rd	= troisième	11th	= onzième
4th	= quatrième	*21st	= **vingt et unième**
*5th	= **cinquième**	38th	= trente-huitième

Again those numbers of special form or with slight spelling irregularities are marked with an asterisk*, and should be learned very carefully.

Ordinal numbers are of course **adjectives** and therefore **must agree**. Except for those marked above any number may be turned into an ordinal by the suffix '**-ième**' being added to the cardinal number. (If this ends in an 'e', then this vowel is removed before adding the suffix: e.g. trente – tren**ti**ème (= thirtieth.)
E.g. C'est sa **première** leçon de français = It's her **first** French lesson.
Cette année marque **le deux centième anniversaire** de l'indépendance de l'Amérique = This year marks **the two-hundredth anniversary** of American Independence.
C'est **le quatrième livre** qu'il m'a emprunté = That's **the fourth book** he's borrowed from me.

The abbreviated form of the ordinal numbers is written '**5ème**', '**1er**', etc. (or, as in the case of the postal districts in Paris, '**5e**', '**18e**').

N.B. (1) **Titles of sovereigns**
Except for '**1st**' = '**premier**' the **cardinal numbers** are used; e.g. **François premier** = **Francis I**, but **Louis quatorze** = **Louis XIV**. You should note (a) **the use of small letters** here with the numbers; (b) **the omission of 'the'** in the king's name.

(2) **Dates**
Here also French usage is the **cardinal numbers, except** for the **first** = **le premier**; thus 'the first of April' = 'le premier avril', but 'the twentieth of August' = '**le vingt août**'. You should note particularly one irregularity; '**le onze** septembre' = 'the eleventh of September'.

In French of course **no word** at all is used where in English we say '**on**' the second of July, **nor** where we say '**of**' July: e.g. Nous sommes partis **le deux juillet**.

Approximate numbers

By adding '**-aine**' to the **cardinal number** (take off the 'e' first if this is the last letter) you may indicate an **approximate** number. Thus '**une trentaine d'invités** = '**about thirty** guests'.

These approximations are most commonly found with the following numbers; some, you will see, have evolved particular meanings:

une huitaine = about a week; **une quinzaine** = about a fortnight;

une douzaine = a dozen, **une dizaine** (– not '**x**') = about ten; or about twelve;

des centaines = hundreds; **une vingtaine** = about twenty.

N.B.: **des milliers** = thousands.

As in the example at the top of the page, all these nouns need '**de**' joining them to a second noun: 'une douzaine **d'**oeufs'.

Fractions

In numerical order, so to speak, the fractions are:

$\frac{1}{2}$ = **la moitié**; $\frac{1}{3}$ = **le tiers**; $\frac{1}{4}$ = **le quart**; $\frac{1}{5}$ = **le cinquième** and so on. Hereafter the **ordinals** serve as fractions, just as they do in English, and so $\frac{5}{7}$ = **cinq septièmes**.

You should take careful note of how the **definite article** is used in French, e.g. Je lui ai donné **le quart** du chocolat; j'en ai gardé **les trois quarts** pour moi = I gave him **a** quarter of the chocolate; I kept **three** quarters for me. As you can see, the French always speak of '**the** third', '**the** fifth', '**the** five-sixths', etc.

'**Half**' offers **three** alternatives:

– **la moitié** is a noun and is used quantitatively (a total may be divided up); La moitié des cerises étaient pourries = **Half** (the total number of) cherries were rotten.

– **demi** is an adjective, and is used to mean '**a half something**': Il a bu **une demi-bouteille** de champagne = He drank **a half-bottle** of champagne. Compare '**la moitié de** cette bouteille' = 'half (the quantity contained in) this bottle'.

demi when used before a noun in this way is invariable, and always attached to the noun with a hyphen; **after the noun** it **agrees** as normal: e.g. Nous avons causé deux heures et **demie** = We chatted for two and **a half** hours.

When half = **mid** it is rendered by '**mi**', which again is invariable before a noun, and attached to it by a hyphen.

E.g. On s'était arrêté **à mi-chemin** = We had stopped halfway there. Il portait les traces d'une grande cicatrice **à la mi-jambe** = He bore the marks of a large scar **halfway** up his leg.

Dimensions

There are two possible ways of giving the dimensions of an object.

(a) **avoir + (measurement)**   **+ de long**   = to be x . . . long;
       . . . **+ de large**   = to be x . . . wide;
       . . . **+ de haut**   = to be x . . . high;
       . . . **+ de profondeur** = to be x . . . deep;
       . . . **+ d'épaisseur**   = to be x . . . thick.

E.g. La pièce **a 4 mètres de long** = The room is 4 metres long.
'**By**' is expressed by '**sur**'; and so: '. . . **sur 3 mètres 50 de large**' = **by** 3 metres 50 wide'.
Les murailles **avaient deux mètres d'**épaisseur = The walls were two metres thick.

(b) Alternatively you may use the construction with the verb '**être**':

être long + de (measurement) = to be x . . . long, etc.
   . . . **large** . . .
   . . . **haut** . . .
   . . . **profond** . . .
   . . . **épais** . . .

E.g. Ce puits **est profond de dix mètres** = This well is ten metres deep.

A second dimension is merely joined by '**et**' in this construction:
'. . . **et épais d'un mètre**' = '**by** one metre thick'.

N.B. If using the first (more usual) construction, then you will notice that for the dimensions of depth and thickness the **noun** must be used.

Time of day

'**Quelle heure est-il?**'
The main things to remember in answering this question are:
(1) The correct pronoun is '**il**'.
(2) '**Heure**' is **plural** except for 'one o'clock': e.g. **onze heures**.
(3) '**Demie**' has a **final** 'e' except after 'midi' and 'minuit'.
(4) While 'quarter past' is simply '**et quart**', the quarter before the hour is '**moins le quart**' (or 'moins un quart').
(5) The **minutes past** the hour are **not** preceded by '**and**'.
(6) '**Heures**' is **always** included except in '**midi**' and '**minuit**'.

Check these points in the following examples

Il est midi (minuit) = It is midday (midnight).
Il est une heure = It is one o'clock.
Il est cinq heures = It is five o'clock.
Il est huit heures et demie = It is half past eight.
Il est midi (minuit) et demi = It is half past twelve.
Il est neuf heures et quart = It is a quarter past nine.
Il est onze heures moins le quart = It is a quarter to eleven.
Il est dix heures moins une = It is one minute to ten.
Il est sept heures **du** soir = It is seven o'clock **in the** evening.
Il est deux heures moins vingt **de l'**après-midi = It is twenty to two **in the** afternoon.

The question '**A quelle heure ...?**' has precisely the same form for the time mentioned, preceded of course by '**à**' to indicate the time '**at which**' something took place.
E.g. Nous nous sommes couchés hier **à** quatre heures du matin = We went to bed last night **at** four in the morning.

The preposition '**vers**' is used to give approximate times (= **about**). E.g. Les fêtes prirent fin **vers minuit** = The festivities came to an end **round about midnight**.
Nous ne savons pas au juste, mais nous comptons y être **vers six heures** = We don't exactly know, but we are expecting to get there **around six o'clock**.

The 24-hour system is used extensively in France to avoid ambiguity. You must therefore be prepared to see (or hear) it in relation to traffic time-tables and in radio or television announcements. E.g. Le train de Bordeaux? Il part à **vingt et une heures vingt-cinq**, du quai numéro trois (= 21h 25) = The train to Bordeaux? It leaves at 9.25 from no. 3 platform. Les prochaines informations seront à **treize heures trente** (= 13h 30) = The next news bulletin will be at 1.30.

Age

Although giving your age is probably one of the first idioms you ever learn in French, a great number of candidates still make mistakes in this area in examinations (and therefore presumably also in non-examination conditions).

It is totally inadequate to be able to say (or write) proudly 'J'ai quinze ans' when asked if you cannot also reply correctly regarding other people's ages, or even your own in a tense other than the present.

E.g. Mon frère? Il **a** dix-sept **ans** = My brother is **seventeen**.
En 1975 **j'avais** seize **ans** = **In 1975 I was sixteen**.
So our thought for the day is this:
'*Avoir*' is *always* **used to express** *age*: '*Ans*' **is always included in the phrase**.

Comparative age is rendered:
avoir + (time period) + de plus que = to be x older than . . .
         . . . **+ de moins que** = to be x younger than . . .
E.g. Mon cousin **a deux ans de moins que moi** = My cousin **is two years younger than I**.
J'ai un mois de plus que toi = I am a month older than you.
To express '**as old as**' you may either say '**avoir le même âge que** . . .' or '**être aussi âgé(e) que** . . .'
E.g. Je crois qu'il **a le même âge que mon père** = I think he **is as old as** my father.
'Aged' simply uses this adjective form '**âgé(e) de** . . .'
E.g. Ils étaient accompagnés d'**une petite fille âgée de huit ans** = They had with them **an eight-year-old-girl**.
N.B. C'était un homme **âgé d'une quarantaine d'années** (de quarante ans environ) = He was a man **aged about forty**.

Impersonal expressions

The largest group of **impersonal expressions** concerns the **weather**. To a large extent this is therefore a question of vocabulary, and a list of the more common weather patterns is given below. It would be useful however, firstly to point out a few features common to all impersonal verbs.

(1) (a) They are used **only** in the **third person singular**, even when they (occasionally) take an object.
(1) (b) Their **past participle** in compound tenses is **invariable**.
E.g. **Il pleuvait des balles** = It rained bullets.
Il est arrivé des choses inouïes pendant mon absence! = Unimaginable things happened in my absence!

(2) **Il est** (used impersonally) + certain **adjectives** will be followed by (a) **de + infinitive construction** or (b) **que + subjunctive clause**.
E.g. Il est difficile de l'imaginer en Turquie = It is difficult to imagine him in Turkey.
Il est regrettable qu'elle soit si bête = It's unfortunate that she is so stupid.

See chapter 5, 'Ce v. Il', page 43 and the section on the **subjunctive**, *pages 85–6, in chapter 8.* **Verbs.**

(3) **Il faut** can be used (a) **with an object** (in the sense of 'something is **needed**') or (b) **with an infinitive construction** or (c) with **que + subjunctive**.

E.g. **Il faut des clous** = **We need** some nails.

Il nous faut aller à la banque = **We shall have to go** to the bank.

Il faut que tu fasses un plus grand effort = **You will have to** make a greater effort.

Again, refer back to the section on the **subjunctive**, *page 85, also chapter 14,* **Modal Verbs**, *page 121, for details of this verb.*

(4) **Miscellaneous impersonal verbs** with which you should be familiar:

il y a = there is, there are (don't forget '**il y avait**');
il s'agit de = it is a question of, it is about (of a story);
il (me) plaît de = (I) like (doing);
il (me) reste = (I) have . . . left;
il y va de = it is a question of;
il suffit (que + subjunctive) = it is enough (that . . .);
il semble
il paraît } (que + subjunctive) = it seems (that . . .);
il s'ensuit que = it follows that . . .;
il arrive (que)
il se passe (que) } = it happens (that);

(5) **Weather expressions**
'Quel temps fait-il?'.

It is surprising how many times the simple error of using the verb 'être' is made with these expressions. It is also important to know the 'weather' verbs in the **different tenses**; particularly in essay-writing, the weather is very rarely 'going on at this time'. Except where, as in the second group listed, there is a particular verb which describes a certain weather condition, the verb to use is '**faire**'. (A second thought for the day!)

(a) **il fait beau**   = it is fine (the weather is fine)
   il fait chaud   = it is warm
   il fait très chaud   = it is hot
   il fait doux   = it is mild, pleasant
   il fait frais   = it is chilly, cool
   il fait froid   = it is cold
   il fait jour   = it is daylight

il fait nuit	= it is night
il fait noir, sombre	= it is dark
il fait mauvais (temps)	= it is bad weather
il fait du soleil	= it is sunny (the sun is shining)
il fait du vent	= it is windy
il fait du brouillard	= it is foggy
(b) **il gèle**	= it is freezing
il neige	= it is snowing
il pleut	= it is raining
il grêle	= it is hailing
il tonne	= it is thundering

Considerable variety may be obtained by introducing **a noun** and **adjective** in the following way:

il fait un temps (+ adjective, e.g. 'superbe', 'atroce', 'splendide' . . .)

This may be done with the following nouns:

une chaleur = a heat; un froid = a cold; une pluie = a rain; un soleil = a sun.

Here are a few examples of expressions incorporating these nouns with an adjective (or phrase):

il fait une chaleur insupportable	= it's unbearably hot
. . . **un temps de chien**	= it's foul weather
. . . **un froid de canard**	= it's freezing cold
. . . **une pluie battante**	= it's pelting down with rain
. . . **un soleil magnifique**	= it's beautifully sunny

There should be more than enough possible phrases to be 'computed' from these elements; do not be tempted to try further inventions, however, if you cannot be sure a suitable noun exists.

Test section

(i) **Write out in full the following numbers or titles.**

5,004	**cinq mille quatre**
193	**cent quatre-vingt-treize**
400	**quatre cents**
380	**trois cent quatre-vingts**
11.09.1906	**le onze septembre, dix-neuf cent six**
01.08.1675	**le premier août, seize cent soixante-quinze**
Henri VIII	**Henri huit**

149

Charles I	**Charles premier**
(⅘) du gâteau	**les quatre cinquièmes du gâteau**
donne m'en (⅔)	**donne m'en les deux tiers**
j'ai reçu (⅙) de sa fortune	**j'ai reçu le sizième de sa fortune**
c'est une (½) tasse	**c'est une demi-tasse**
j'en ai avalé (½)	**j'en ai avalé la moitié**
l'avion arrive à 23h 10	**l'avion arrive à vingt-trois heures dix** (onze heures dix du soir)
mon train part à 18h 01	**mon train part à dix-huit heures une** (six heures une du soir)

(ii) ** *See note on page 58.*
Translate into French.

I know about ten people in Paris.	**Je connais une dizaine de gens à Paris.**
She was five then.	**Elle avait cinq ans à cette époque-là** (alors).
He will telephone about 7 pm tonight.	**Il téléphonera vers sept heures ce soir.**
The lounge is 5.50 metres long by 4 metres wide.	**Le salon a cinq mètres cinquante de long sur quatre mètres de large.**
There were thousands of people at the match.	**Il y avait des milliers de gens au match.**
It was about (concerning) a twenty-year-old elephant.	**Il s'agissait d'un éléphant âgé de vingt ans.**
It's half past twelve (midnight).	**Il est midi et demi.**
It was twenty-five minutes to four.	**Il était quatre heures moins vingt-cinq.**
It was cold but fine.	**Il faisait froid mais beau.**
I hope it won't rain.	**J'espère qu'il ne pleuvra pas.**
On Thursday it was really filthy weather!	**Jeudi il faisait un** (vrai) **temps de chien!**

Chapter 18
Vocabulary Points

In the preceding chapters we have aimed to give the student and examination candidate a complete overall picture of the fundamental structure of the French language. Of necessity the focus thus far has been on structures, since these constitute what may be termed the bare bones – or skeleton – of the language. However, knowledge of the structures alone will not create a living language. Only through an extensive range of vocabulary and idiom can linguistic expression be fully developed.

In this final chapter, therefore, we shall be concentrating on that precise area, vocabulary enrichment. There would be little point in providing long lists of specialised topic areas (professions, birds, clothes, etc.) which may be obtained easily from other sources. The chapter has **two aims**. The first is to highlight some of the regularly occurring **sticking points of vocabulary**, including some of the well-known '**faux-amis**'. 'Faux-amis' means literally 'false friends', and in the context of a language they are words or phrases apparently very similar to phrases in our own language, but in reality with a quite different meaning.

The second aim is **to provide a list** (by no means exhaustive) of **common idioms** and **everyday expressions**. How many of these phrases individual students master will, of course, vary enormously; quite obviously they will not all count as essential basic examination components, and your own response to this section will to some extent be a matter of personal requirement and ambition.

Vocabulary difficulties

across: **franchir**, to go across (frontier, line, bridge); **traverser**, to walk across; **traverser à la nage**, to swim across; **traverser en courant**, to run across.

again: usually: **encore, de nouveau; encore une fois, une fois de plus,** once more.
  With many verbs 'again' can be rendered quite satisfactorily by the prefix '**re-**': **repartir, refaire, revoir,** etc.

ask: usually: **demander; poser une question**, to ask a question.

bring: **apporter** to bring (in hand), carry; **amener**, to bring (lead) someone along; **rapporter**, to bring back.

bus: **un autobus**, a bus (in town); **un (auto) car**, a bus (in country) long-distance coach.

catch: **attraper**, to catch (hold of) ball, etc.; **prendre**, to catch a bus, train.

clock: **une pendule**, (domestic) clock (on wall or mantelpiece); **une horloge**, clock in public place (large); also **une montre**, a watch.

come: usually: **venir; entrer en courant**, to come running in; **descendre en courant**, to come running down.

day: **le jour**, day (i.e. not night); **faire jour**, to be daylight; **la journée**, daytime (i.e. the period of time) all day long.

enjoy: usually (anything you can take pleasure in) **jouir de; nous nous amusons bien**, we enjoy ourselves; **passer de bonnes vacances**, to enjoy one's holidays.

evening: **le soir**, the evening (i.e. not morning); **la soirée**, the (whole) evening (i.e. period of time).

girl: **une petite fille**, a little girl; **une fillette**, girl (about 5–10 years old); **une jeune fille**, a teenage girl.

go: usually: **aller**; also **se rendre à; s'approcher de**, to go up to; **entrer dans**, to go into; **sortir de**; to go out of; **monter**, to go up; **descendre**, to go down; **aller se coucher**, to go to bed; **rouler**, to go (vehicles); **marcher**, to go, work (mechanical).

hear: usually: **entendre; entendre dire que**, to hear (it said) that; **entendre parler de**, to hear about (something, someone).

just: **c'est juste**, it's just (fair) **or** it just goes, fits; **je viens de le dire**, I've just said it; **il ne fit que sourire**, he just (only) smiled; **nous sommes sur le point de partir**, we are just about to go.

keep: usually: **garder; surveiller**, to keep an eye on; **faire attendre**, to keep waiting; **tu ne cesses (pas) de parler**, you keep on talking.

know: **savoir, connaître** (*see page 126*).

language: **une langue; un langage** (specialised) language; **un patois**, local language, dialect.

late: **tard** late (late hour); **en retard**, late (for a time given).

leave: **quitter**, to leave (someone, something); **partir**, to leave (**no** object); **laisser**, to leave behind (forget).

live: **habiter**, to live at (certain address); also **demeurer**, to live (dwell); **vivre**, to live (be alive).

look: usually: **regarder**, to look **at**; **chercher**, to look **for**;

ressembler à, to look like (someone); **avoir l'air** ... to look (expression); **avoir bonne mine**, to look well; **avoir mauvaise mine**, to look ill; **Attention!** Look out!

man: usually: **un homme; un vieillard**, an old man; **un vieux**, an old fellow; **un bonhomme**, a bloke, man; **un bonhomme de neige**, a snowman.

moment: **en ce moment**, at this moment; **à ce moment-là**, at that moment.

much: **beaucoup** (also a lot, a great deal); **trop**, too much; **tant**, so much; **autant qu'avant**, as much as before; **autant de gens**, as many people.

party: **un parti**, a (political) party; **une soirée**, a (formal, elegant) party; **une surprise-partie**, a (young people's) party; N.B. **une partie** = a game (tennis, cards), also a part.

people: usually: **les gens; des personnes**, people (especially if a number given); **Il y avait beaucoup de monde**, there were a lot of people.

rest: **se reposer; le reste**, rest (remainder).

return: **revenir**, to come back (to here); **retourner**, to go back (to there); **rentrer**, to come (go) back home; **rendre** to give (something) back.

road: **une route**, a road (in country); **une rue**, a road (in town); **un chemin**, a way, the road to somewhere (i.e. direction).

room: usually: **une pièce; une chambre**, a bedroom; **une salle**, a (public) room, compare 'une salle de classe' = classroom.

school: usually: **une école; une école primaire**, a primary school; **un collège**, secondary school; **un lycée** (grammar school, or sixth-form college).

shop: **un magasin**, large shop; **un grand magasin**, a department store; **une boutique**, a small shop; **un supermarché**, a supermarket.

sit: see pages 109, 110.

sleep: **dormir; s'endormir**, to go to sleep; **endormi**, asleep.

so: (before adjective, adverb) **si, tellement; si grand**, so big; **alors**, so, in that case; **aussi** (+ inversion), therefore, and so; also **donc**.

take: **prendre**, to take (in the hand); also 'to catch trains', etc.; 'take road, direction'; **faire attention, etre prudent**, to take care; **emmener**, to take (people); **emporter**, to take (carry) away; **sortir**, to take (out of); **enlever**, to take off, take away from.

then: **alors**, at that time, then in that case; **donc**, therefore; **puis**, then (after that) **must** be at the start of the sentence, and relate

153

a series of events; **ensuite**, afterwards, next (in series of events).

things: **les choses** (f. pl.); **les effets** (m. pl.), personal effects; **les affaires** (f. pl.), belongings.

visit: **visiter**, to visit (sight-see) of buildings, towns; **rendre visite à**, to visit (people); also **aller voir**, to go and see.

walk: **marcher**, to walk (+ phrase or adverb to describe **how**); **aller à pied**, to walk (i.e. not ride or fly!); **se promener**, to go for a walk (pleasure); **s'en aller**, to walk (go) away; **la marche à pied**, walking (the exercise); **une promenade**, walk (outing).

window: usually: **une fenêtre**; **une vitrine**, shop window; **la vitre**, window pane, car window; **un vitrail** (pl. **vitraux**) church window.

word: **un mot**, written or spoken word; **une parole**, spoken word.

year: **l'an** (m.), **l'année** (f.) – the distinction is often unclear; it is best to learn examples as they occur. '**An**' is always used in people's ages and in 'le jour de l'an', New Year's Day.

Faux-amis

These words are sources of many errors, either through mis-spelling or through the candidate's persistent refusal to fix the true meaning firmly in his mind. Discipline yourself to conquer the brutes now!

A. Actuellement = at the present time; **vraiment, vérit-ablement** = actually.

A cet âge-là = at that age; **à cette époque-là** = at that time, in those days.

Aider = to help; **assister à** = to be present at (to attend performance, game, etc.).

L'argent = money; **la monnaie** = change.

Aussi = also; at beginning of sentence = therefore.

Un avis = a notice, opinion; **un conseil** = a piece of advice.

B. Une balle = a (small) ball (tennis, etc.), a bullet; **un ballon** = an (inflatable) ball (football etc.); **une boule** = bowl (for game of bowls), also a pellet, ball.

La banque = bank (for money); **le bord de la rivière, la rive** = the river bank.

C. La campagne = the country (side); **le pays** = the country (of France, etc.).

Casser — to break (dishes, etc.); **briser** = to break, tear down (also hearts!); **rompre** = to break in two, break off relationships.
La chance = luck, (often good) fortune; **le hasard** = chance; **l'occasion** (f.) = opportunity.

F. La face = side (record, coin); **le visage, la figure** = face.
Fameux = notorious, infamous; **célèbre** = famous.

H. L'humeur (f.) = mood, **de bonne, mauvaise humeur** = in a good, bad mood; **l'humour** (m.) = (sense of) humour.

J. La journée = the daytime; **le voyage** = the journey.

L. La librairie = the bookshop; **la bibliothèque** = the library.
Une livre = a pound (money, weight); **un livre** = a book.

N. La nouvelle = piece of news, **or** a short story; **un roman** = a novel; **un roman policier** = a detective story.

O. Occupé = engaged (not free), busy.

P. Une part = a share; **une partie** = a part (*see also 'party', page 153*). **Les parents** = parents, **or** relations; **les rapports** (m.pl.) = relationships.
Passer = to pass by, sit an exam., spend time (N.B. **dépenser** = to spend money); **réussir à, être reçu à** = to pass an exam; **se passer de** = to do without.
Pêcher = to fish; **pécher** = to sin; **une pêche** = a peach; **un péché** = a sin; **un poisson** = a fish.
Une pièce = a room; **un morceau** = a piece; **une tranche** = a slice.
Une place = a seat (cinema, train, etc.), a public square, a job, a situation; **un endroit** = a place, location, also **un lieu.**
La poste = the Post Office; **le poste** = set (radio, TV), appointment, job; **le poste de police** = the police station.
Prévenir = to let know, forewarn; **empêcher** = to prevent.

R. Raconter = to recount, tell stories; **dire** = to tell, say to someone; **rencontrer** = to meet.
Rester = to remain, stay; **se reposer** = to have a rest.

S. Un spectacle = a show (theatre) sight, scene; **des lunettes** (f. pl.) = glasses; **des lunettes de soleil** = sun-glasses.
Une station (de métro) = an underground station; **une gare** = railway station.

T. Une tache = a stain, spot; **une tâche** = a task, job; **tâcher** = to try.

U. User = to wear out (shoes, etc.); **se servir de, utiliser** = to use.

V. Des vacances (f. pl.) **always** = holidays; **un congé** = short holiday, period of time off work, leave of absence; **des congés payés** = paid holidays.
La veille = the day before; **la vieille** = the old woman.
Vilain = ugly; **un escroc, un scélérat** = a villain.
La voie = the track; **la voix** = the voice.

Idioms

A word of warning here: it is essential not only to learn these phrases thoroughly if you intend to make use of them, but also to be quite sure of precisely how they function, how they fit into a sentence. An idiom inappropriately placed or incorrectly formed is worse by far than none at all!

Clearly the expressions listed here are destined partly for use in personal writing and conversation. It is also likely of course that they will find their way into passages you may meet as comprehension pieces or which you may be required to translate; in this case too, therefore, the section should provide useful material for examination practice.

Some expressions should already be very well known, others totally new, and for these a 'ration' of a few per week, spread over a fairly lengthy period, should ensure gradual absorption into the system!

A. *d'abord*	first of all, at first
un accident: **par accident**	by accident
d'accord: **je suis d'accord avec . . .**	I agree with . . .
une affaire: **un homme d'affaires**	a businessman
faire de bonnes affaires	to do good business
une aiguille: **chercher une aiguille dans une botte de foin**	to look for a needle in a hay-stack
ainsi: **s'il en est ainsi**	if that's the way it is

et ainsi de suite	and so on
pour ainsi dire	so to speak
un air: **dans (en) l'air**	in the air
en plein air	in the open air
un courant d'air	a draught
avoir l'air triste, etc.	to look sad, etc.
aller: **comment allez-vous?**	how are you?
je vais très bien	I am very well
ça va	OK, that's OK, I'm fine
cela vous va bien	that suits you (clothes)
un billet aller et retour	a return ticket
appuyer sur le champignon	to step on the gas
après: **après-demain**	the day after tomorrow
l'argent: **tu en as pour ton argent**	you've got your money's worth
arriver: **cela (m')arrive tout le temps**	that's happening (to me) all the time
il lui est arrivé un accident	he has had (met with) an accident
assez: **j'en ai assez!**	I'm sick of it! I've had enough!
une assiette: **manger dans une assiette**	to eat **off** a plate
je ne suis pas dans mon assiette	I'm not feeling too good
attention: **fais attention!**	look out!
attention à la peinture!	careful of the paint!
autant: **d'autant plus que...**	all the more so since...
autant qu'il m'en souvienne	as far as I can remember
autre: **autrement**	otherwise
parler de choses et d'autres	to talk about this and that
vous autres Français	you French
ni l'un ni l'autre	neither (one nor the other)
c'est tout autre chose	that's quite a different matter
en avance: **tu arrives en avance**	you're early (before time)
avant: **avant tout**	above all
en avant!	forward! Go on!
un avis: **changer d'avis**	to change one's mind
à mon avis (à votre avis, etc.)	in my (yours, etc.) opinion
avoir: **il m'a eu!**	he had me there!
qu'est-ce que tu as? (qu'as-tu?)	what's the matter with you?

j'en ai pour deux minutes	I'll be ready in two minutes
qu'est-ce qu'il y a?	what's the matter?
il n'y a pas de quoi	please don't mention it

B. *la barbe*: **quelle barbe!** — what a nuisance! how irritating!

rire dans sa barbe	to laugh up one's sleeve
bas: **à bas les examens!**	down with exams!
à bas les mains!	hands off!
un enfant en bas âge	a very young child
battre: **battre des mains**	to applaud
beau: **j'ai beau parler**	it's no use me talking (wasted effort, since it comes to nothing)
besoin: **au besoin**	if needs be, in an emergency
bien: **je me porte bien**	I feel well
je suis très bien avec eux	I get on well with them
c'est bien fait pour toi!	it serves you right!
c'est bien lui?	is it really him?
bien des fois	many times
tant bien que mal	somehow or other
blanc: **passer une nuit blanche**	to have a sleepless night
bon: **a quoi bon?**	what's the use?
bonne année, bon voyage	Happy New Year, have a good trip
bon appétit!	enjoy your meal!
le bord: **au bord de la mer**	at the seaside
la bosse: **rouler sa bosse**	to knock around a fair amount
le bras: **il a le bras long**	he is very influential
à bras ouverts	with open arms
bras-dessus bras-dessous	arm in arm

C. *ça*: **ça y est!** — that's it! there we are (go)!

ça alors!	well I never! stone the crows!
le cafard: **avoir le cafard**	to be feeling down, depressed
la cause: **à cause de**	because of
pour cause	for good reason
cent: **cent pour cent**	100 per cent
faire les cent pas	to pace up and down
la chance: **tu as de la chance!**	you lucky dog!
je n'ai pas de chance	I'm out of luck
quelle chance!	what a stroke of luck!

chanter: **faire chanter quelqu'un**	to blackmail someone
un chat: **j'ai un chat dans la gorge**	I've a frog in my throat
je donne ma langue au chat	I give up (e.g. guessing the answer)
chaud: **avoir chaud**	to feel hot
pleurer à chaudes larmes	to weep bitterly
le cheval: **monter à cheval**	to ride (horses)
les cheveux: **j'ai mal aux cheveux**	I've got a hangover
couper les cheveux en quatre	to split hairs
chez **les Français**	in the character of French people
faire comme chez soi	to make oneself at home
un chien: **entre chien et loup**	at dusk
clair: **il ne fait pas clair**	it's dark, dismal
bleu clair (invariable)	light blue
la clé (clef): **fermer à clé**	to lock
tenir quelque chose sous clé	to keep under lock and key
le clou: **rester cloué sur place**	to stand rooted to the spot
le coeur: **avoir mal au coeur**	to feel sick
avoir le coeur gros	to be sad at heart
si le coeur vous en dit	if you feel like it
apprendre par coeur	to learn by heart
à contre-coeur	against one's will
faire contre mauvaise fortune bon coeur	to put a brave face on things
la colère: **se mettre en colère**	to lose one's temper
combien: **c'est combien?**	how much is it?
le combien sommes-nous?	what date is it?
le compte: **en fin de compte**	all things considered
se rendre compte	to realise
conduire: **se conduire bien(mal)**	to behave well (badly)
coucher: **coucher à la belle étoile**	to sleep beneath the stars
le coup: **donner un coup de pied à**	to kick
donner un coup de main à	to give a helping hand to

donner un coup de poing à	to punch
donner un coup de télé-phone à	to ring up
arriver en coup de vent	to arrive in a great rush
jeter un coup d'oeil à	to glance at
faire d'une pierre deux coups	to kill two birds with one stone
tout à coup; tout d'un coup	suddenly; all of a sudden
la course: **faire des courses**	to go shopping
coûter: **ça coûte cher** (invariable)	that costs a lot, expensive
coûte que coûte	at all costs
le cri: **pousser un cri**	to utter a shout
croire: **je crois que oui (non)**	I believe so (not)
je ne pouvais en croire mes yeux	I couldn't believe my eyes
le cuisine: **faire la cuisine**	to do the cooking
la cuisine est excellente	the cooking is excellent
D. *dans*: **boire dans un verre**	to drink **out of** a glass
de: **du matin au soir**	from morning till night
de jour en jour	from day to day
manquer de (courage), etc.	to lack (courage), etc.
changer de (chemise), etc.	to change (shirt), etc.
se débrouiller:	to manage, find a way; to get by OK, fend for oneself
dernier: **ces derniers temps**	lately
la semaine dernière	last week
descendre: **descendre du train**	to get off the train
descendre dans un hôtel	to stay in a hotel
deux: **en moins de deux**	in less than no time
deux fois; tous les deux	twice; both of them
entre deux âges	middle-aged
tous les deux jours	every other day
dire: **à vrai dire**	to tell you the truth
cela va sans dire	that goes without saying
dis (dites) donc!	I say!
cela vous dit quelque chose?	does that idea appeal to you?
donner: **donner sur**	to look out on to
je vous le donne en trois	I'll give you three guesses
dormir: **dormir à poings férmés**	to sleep soundly

je n'ai dormi que d'un oeil	I slept with one eye open
le dos: 'Voir au dos'	see over
le drap: être dans de beaux draps	to be in a right pickle
droit: avoir droit à	to be entitled to
avoir le droit de	to have the right to
allez tout droit	keep straight on
à droite! Tenez la droite!	on the right; Keep to the right!
drôle: une drôle d'idée!	a funny idea!
quel drôle d'homme!	what a funny man!
dur: travailler dur	to work hard
avoir l'oreille dure	to be hard of hearing
E. une école: faire l'école buissonnière	to play truant
encore: pas encore	not yet
encore une bière, etc.	another beer, etc.
quoi encore?; encore une fois	what else?; once more
non seulement ... mais encore	not only ... but also
envie: avoir envie de	to feel like
je meurs d'envie de	I am dying to
un étage: au premier étage	on the first floor
être: c'en est trop!	this really is too much!
il était une fois ...	once upon a time there was ...
où en sommes-nous?	where did we get up to?
un exemple: par exemple	for instance
ah ça, par exemple!	well, that's the limit!
F. la façon: de toute façon	in any case
sans plus de façons	without more ado
la faim: avoir (très) faim	to be (very) hungry
j'ai une faim de loup!	I could eat a horse!
faire: faire la vaisselle	to do the washing up
faire la lessive	to do the washing
faire le ménage	to do the housework
faire une promenade	to go for a walk
faire son marché	to do one's shopping
cela fera bien mon affaire	that will suit me very well
ne t'en fais pas!	don't worry so!
falloir: il m'a fallu deux heures pour y arriver	I took two hours to get there
une personne comme il faut	a respectable person

161

fauché: **être fauché**	to be 'broke'
la faute: **c'est à lui la faute**	it's his fault
faute de; faute de quoi	for lack of; failing which
la fièvre: **avoir de la fièvre**	to have a temperature
filer: **filer à l'anglaise**	to take French leave
file! (filez!)	buzz off! hop it!
une fille: **une vieille fille**	a spinster
une fois: **une fois pour toutes**	once and for all
foncé: **bleu foncé** (invariable)	dark blue
le fond: **au fond de; au fond**	at the bottom of; fundamentally
fou: **plus en est de fous plus on rit**	the more the merrier
la fourmi: **avoir des fourmis dans les jambes**	to have pins and needles in the legs
frais: **'peinture fraîche'**	'wet paint'
mettre (tenir) . . . au frais	to put (keep) . . . somewhere cool
froid: **avoir froid (aux pieds)**	to feel cold (have cold feet)
G. *un garçon*: **'Garçon!'**	'Waiter!'
un garçon manqué	a tomboy
un gâteau: **c'est du gâteau!**	it's a piece of cake, a cinch
grand: **en grande partie**	to a large extent
les grandes personnes	grown-ups
gras: **Mardi Gras**	Shrove Tuesday
faire la grasse matinée	to have a lie-in
H. *une habitude*: **d'habitude**	usually
comme d'habitude	as usual
haut: **regarder de haut en bas**	to look up and down
haut les mains!	hands up!
l'heure: **tout à l'heure**	just now, **or** soon, in a while
de bonne heure	early
hier: **hier soir; hier au soir**	last night; yesterday evening
je ne suis pas né d'hier	I wasn't born yesterday
avant-hier	the day before yesterday
huit: **huit jours**	a week
I. *ici*: **d'ici peu**	before long
jusqu'ici	up till now
par ici, messieurs 'dames!	this way, ladies and gentlemen!

162

J. *la jambe*: **à toutes jambes** — as fast as possible
à grandes enjambées — with big strides
jouer: **jouer un tour (une farce)** — to play a trick

le jour: **au grand jour** — in broad daylight
le plat du jour — 'today's special' (on a menu)
de nos jours — nowadays
vivre au jour le jour — to live from hand to mouth
voir sous un autre jour — to see in another light
du jour au lendemain — overnight
juger: **à vous d'en juger** — you be the judge of that
à en juger par — judging by
juste: **trois heures juste** — three o'clock exactly
ne pas savoir au juste — not to know exactly

L. *là*: **oh là là!** — dearie me!
qu'est-ce que tu entends par là? — what do you mean by that?
viens là! — come here!
là-bas — down there (vague; any distance)

la langue: **avoir la langue bien pendue** — to have the gift of the gab
les langues vivantes — modern languages
large: **au large de Marseille** — off Marseilles (at sea)
se promener de long en large — to walk up and down
se lever: **se lever du pied gauche** — to get out of bed on wrong side
un lieu: **au lieu de** — instead of
avoir lieu — to take place
en premier lieu — in the first place
long: **le long de** — along
à la longue — in the long run
à longueur de journée — all day long
un loup: **à pas de loup** — stealthily

M. *la maison*: **à la maison** — at home
le mal: **avoir le mal de mer** — to be seasick
avoir mal (à la tête, à l'estomac) — to have a headache, stomach-ache
se faire mal; avoir le mal du pays — to hurt oneself; to feel homesick
se donner beaucoup de mal pour — to take a lot of trouble to

pas mal de	lots of
un malheur: **par malheur**	unfortunately
un malheur ne vient jamais seul	troubles never come singly
le marché: **par-dessus le marché**	into the bargain
acheter bon marché (invariable)	to buy something cheaply
la médaille: **c'est le revers de la médaille**	that's the other side of the story
midi: **le Midi (de la France)**	the South of France
mieux: **je ne demande pas mieux**	I shall be delighted
faute de mieux	for want of anything better
faire de son mieux	to do one's best
la mine: **avoir bonne (mauvaise) mine**	to look well (ill)
faire grise mine	to pull a long face
moins: **moins . . . moins . . .**	the less . . . the less . . .
du moins	at least (with reservations)
au moins	at least (minimum number)
en moins de rien	in no time at all
la mouche: **faire mouche**	to hit the bull's eye
quelle mouche te pique?	what's eating you?
un mouton: **jouer à saute-mouton**	to play leapfrog
revenons à nos moutons	let's get back to the point *(see page 132!)*
les moyens: **les moyens de transport**	means of transport
avoir les moyens de	to be able to afford to
vivre au-dessus de ses moyens	to live beyond one's means
N. *le nez*: **fourrer le nez partout**	to poke one's nose everywhere
la nouvelle: **vous m'en direz des nouvelles**	you'll be surprised how good it is (be delighted with it)
O. *un oeuf*: **va te faire cuire un oeuf**	get lost!
un oeuf à la coque	a boiled egg
des oeufs brouillés	scrambled eggs
des oeufs sur le plat	fried eggs

une oreille: **faire la sourde oreille**	to turn a deaf ear
un os: **mouillé jusqu'aux os**	soaked to the skin
P. *la page*: **être à la page**	to be 'with it'
un panier: **un panier à salade**	a Black Maria
pareil: **c'est du pareil au même**	six of one and half a dozen of the other
parler: **parler boutique**	to talk shop
parler petit nègre	to talk pidgin French
tu parles!	you bet! and how! you're telling me!
passe: **être en passe de devenir**	to be about to become
être dans une mauvaise passe	to be in a tricky situation
une patte: **à quatre pattes**	on all fours
graisser la patte à quelqu'un	to oil someone's palm
la peine: **ce n'est pas la peine**	it's not worth it
faire de la peine à	to hurt (upset) someone
pendre: **pendre la crémaillère**	to have a house-warming party
perdre: **perdre le nord**	to go bonkers
peu: **peu à peu**	gradually
peu de gens; un peu de fromage	few people; a little cheese
peu intéressant, peu important, etc.	**un**interesting, **un**important, etc.
peu après; à peu près	shortly afterwards; nearly
la peur: **avoir peur (une peur bleue)**	to be afraid, (scared stiff)
le pied: **frapper du pied**	to stamp one's foot
c'est un casse-pieds!	he's a ghastly bore!
pile: **pile ou face?**	heads or tails?
plein: **faire le plein** (d'essence)	to fill up with (petrol)
en plein visage	right in the face
la pluie: **parler de la pluie et du beau temps**	to talk about nothing much
plus: **de plus en plus** (de + noun)	more and more
plus . . . plus . . .	the more . . . the more . . .

plus que	more than (comparison)
plus de; en plus	more than (quantity); what's more
la poche: **connaître comme sa poche**	to know like the back of your hand
le point: **au point de vue de**	from the point of view of
au point du jour	at day-break
la pomme: **tomber dans les pommes**	to faint
le pot: **dîner à la fortune du pot**	to take pot-luck
tourner autour du pot	to beat about the bush
pouvoir: **je n'y peux rien**	I can't do anything about it
je n'en peux plus!	I can't stand it any more!
sauve qui peut!	every man for himself!
prendre: **à tout prendre**	by and large
prendre feu	to catch fire
prendre ses jambes à son cou	to take to one's heels
pressé: **être pressé**	to be in a hurry
le progrès: **faire des progrès**	to make progress
Q. *quand même!*	after all! I mean to say!
quatre: **tire à quatre épingles**	dressed very smartly
un de ces quatre matins	one of these fine days
se mettre en quatre pour	to go out of one's way to
descendre l'escalier quatre à quatre	to come tearing down the stairs (literally: four by four)
quelque chose: **quelque chose de bon**	something good
quelque chose d'autre	something else
la question: **ce n'en est pas là la question**	that's not the point
la queue: **faire la queue**	to queue up
quinze: **quinze jours**	a fortnight
quitter: **ne quittez pas!**	hold the line! (telephone)
quoi: **de quoi vivre**	enough to live on
de quoi manger, etc.	something (enough) to eat, etc.
R. *la raison:* **avoir raison**	to be right
raison de plus	all the more reason
regarder: **ça ne vous regarde pas**	that's none of your business

remonter: **remonter une montre**	to wind a watch up
rendre: **rendre heureux**, etc.	to make happy, etc.
rendre service à quelqu'un	to do someone a favour
rentrer: **la rentrée**	return to school
rentrer dans le garage	to put away in the garage
répondre: **Répondez s'il vous plaît**	R.S.V.P.
répondre de	to answer for, guarantee
rester: **reste à savoir**	it remains to be seen
rester tranquille	to keep still
retard: **avoir du retard**	to be late (trains, etc.)
arriver en retard	to arrive late
réussir: **bien (mal) réussir**	to turn out fine (badly)
réussir un gâteau	to make a good cake
revenir: **cela revient au même**	it comes to the same thing
je n'en reviens pas!	I can't get over it!
rien: **cela ne fait rien**	that doesn't matter
(il n'y a) rien à faire	nothing to be done
de rien! (said after 'merci')	please don't mention it!
rire: **il (n') y a (pas) de quoi rire**	it's (no) laughing matter
un rouleau: **être au bout de son rouleau**	to be at the end of one's tether
rouler: (of vehicles)	to go, drive along
rouler sur l'or	to be rolling in money
S. *le sac*: **l'affaire est dans le sac!**	it's in the bag!
saint: **jusqu'à la Saint-Glinglin**	till the cows come home
sans: **sans blague!**	no kidding! you're joking!
sans doute; sans aucun doute	probably; no doubt
la santé: **avoir une santé de fer**	to be as strong as a horse
à votre santé!	cheers!
sauter: **faire sauter**	to blow up (explosives)
cela saute aux yeux	it stands out a mile
savoir: **en savoir long sur**	to know a lot about
pas que je sache	not that I know of
la séance: **'Prochaine séance à ...'**	'Next performance at ...' (cinema)

le sens: **sens unique**	one way (street)
avoir du bon sens	to have a lot of common sense
sens interdit	no entry (street)
être sens dessus dessous	to be upside down, topsy-turvy
le service: **à votre service**	at your service
servir: **cela ne sert à rien (de)**	it's no use (doing)
à quoi cela sert-il?	what's the use of that? (*or* what is that used for?)
servez-vous	help yourself
seul: **se sentir seul**	to feel lonely
faire . . . tout seul	to do . . . all by oneself
le soin: **etre aux petits soins pour**	to wait on hand and foot
se soigner	to take care of oneself
la somme: **somme toute; en somme**	on the whole; in short
suivre: **à suivre**	to be continued (story)
sûr: **bien sûr**	of course

T. *la table*: **mettre la table;**	to lay the table
à table!	the meal is ready!
tant: **tant mieux!**	jolly good! so much the better!
tant pis!	too bad! can't be helped!
taper: **il me tape sur les nerfs**	he gets on my nerves
tard: **mieux vaut tard que jamais**	better late than never
une tartine:	a piece of bread with butter
tu en fais toute une tartine	you're going on and on about it
tas: **un tas de choses à faire**	heaps of things to do
une tasse: **une tasse à café**	a coffee cup
une tasse de café	a cup of coffee
tel: **un tel homme; de tels gens**	**such a** man; such people
à tel point que	to such an extent that
Mademoiselle une telle	Miss So-and-so
le temps: **à temps**	in time, on time
de temps en temps, de temps à autre	from time to time
entre temps	meanwhile
tenir: **tenir un magasin**	to run a shop
tenir à quelque chose	to think a lot of something

tenir à faire quelque chose	to be very keen on doing
la tête: **faire un signe de tête**	to nod
une femme de tête	a businesslike woman
tête nue	bare-headed
de la tête aux pieds	from head to toe
tomber: **tomber pile**	to come just at the right time
tomber par terre	to fall on the floor
tort: **avoir tort**	to be wrong
être dans son tort	to be in the wrong
tôt: **plus tôt**	sooner
tôt ou tard	sooner or later
toucher: **toucher un chèque**	to cash a cheque
un tour: **faire un petit tour**	to go for a little walk
faire le tour du monde	to go round the world
tout: **tout à fait**	completely
tout de suite	immediately
pas du tout	not at all
tous les jours	every day
à toute vitesse	at top speed
tout le monde	everybody
travers: **regarder de travers**	to give a funny (black) look
trente: **avoir trente-six choses à faire**	to have millions of things to do
voir trente-six chandelles	to see stars
il n'y a pas trente-six façons de le faire	there's only one way to do it
se mettre sur son trente et un	to dress up to the nines
se tromper:	to make a mistake
se tromper de chemin	to take the wrong road
trop: **être de trop**	to be in the way
un truc:	a thingummy, a whatsit
avoir le truc; c'est un truc	to have the knack; it's a knack
U. *à la une des journaux*	main headlines
V. les vacances: **aller en vacances**	to go on holiday
les grandes vacances	the summer holidays
une vache: **elle est vache!**	she's a bitch!
parler français comme une vache espagnole	to speak the most awful French
manger de la vache enragée	to have a really tough time of it

venir: **je vous vois venir!**	I see what you are driving at!
un va-et-vient continuel	a continual to-ing and fro-ing
d'où vient-il que	how does it happen that
soyez le bienvenu!	welcome!
le vent: **dans le vent!**	'with it'
un verre: **un verre à vin**	a wine glass
un verre de vin	a glass of wine
la vie: **c'est la vie!**	that's life!
il est toujours en vie	he is still alive
gagner sa vie	to earn one's living
vieux: **c'est vieux jeu**	it's old hat
mon vieux!	old chap! (not old in years)
se faire vieux	to be getting on a bit
vite: **au plus vite**	as quickly as possible
faire quelque chose en vitesse	to do something speedily
la voie: **être sur la bonne voie**	to be on the right track
voir: **cela se voit**	that's quite obvious
voyons!	come now!
fais (faites) voir!	let's have a look!
un voleur: **au voleur!**	stop thief!
vrai: **pour de vrai**	for real, well and truly
la vue: **avoir la vue faible**	to have weak eyesight
avoir la vue bonne	to have good eyesight
à perte de vue	as far as the eye can see
Y. *y*: **j'y suis maintenant**	now I understand
pendant que tu y es	while you're about it
les yeux: **faire les yeux doux à**	to make eyes at
cligner des yeux	to blink
coûter les yeux de la tête	to cost a packet
loin des yeux, loin du coeur	out of sight, out of mind
entre quatre yeux	just between you and me

Du courage! Cheer up!

Avis important!

'Le test section de ce chapitre est abandonné, en raison du **travail excessif** déjà effectué par les étudiants!'

Index

Examination Hints

Examining boards differ quite significantly in their choice of examination exercises: some offer a more traditional pattern than others, with greater emphasis on written manipulation of French than on oral or aural interpretations; some offer alternative syllabuses where the emphasis tends to be more on oral and comprehension skills than on (for instance) translation from English to French. All boards demand some kind of free writing in French, whether at CSE or GCE O-level. This area is often the one which causes most panic in candidates but it is foolish not to try to pull out all the stops here, since the exercise always carries a considerable proportion of marks. An incredible number of candidates simply seem to give up at this point, either repeating themselves stupidly in an effort to 'pad out' the number of words, or writing the most inexcusably careless errors, apparently forgetting all they have ever known. The difficulties which undoubtedly exist in connection with this exercise **can** be indentified and dealt with and this will be done in the section on essay work (page 182).

It is in the interests of each student to find out the exact details of the examination his or her particular board is setting, not only as regards the form of the examination, but also if possible the proportion of marks allotted to each part. He or she must then be intelligent enough to divide his or her energies accordingly!

In this section of the book we shall deal with the major areas tested, giving advice and (where practicable) worked examples. These areas are:
Translation from French to English (unseen translation)
Translation from English to French (prose translation)
Comprehension (aural and written)
Essay work
Oral and dictation
Background knowledge

Translation: French to English

This is often felt to be an easier task than some of the others, presumably because candidates are producing their own language on paper. However, the question of 'their own language' is precisely the stumbling block in many cases! The candidates who are guilty (and they are many in number) of writing English which sounds as though it were penned by Javanese natives are probably acting from the best of motives, imagining that they must translate every word as it stands there in French. (This should at least illustrate as clearly as anything else how dissimilar are the idioms of two languages!)

Translation into English has **two basic requirements**:
(a) **accuracy** (in tense, vocabulary, and 'completeness')
(b) **natural English**

Accuracy

(1) Here what needs to be underlined is the **importance of absolute accuracy**. To recognise 'il buvait' as a past tense of the verb 'to drink' is no good at all if you do not translate accurately the **imperfect tense**. The context will tell you whether this is 'he was drinking', 'used to drink', or even 'he drank'.

'Il pourrait le faire' **must** be recognised as the conditional tense (= he might, could possibly do it). Too hasty an approach to the sentence could well cause a candidate to miss the nuance.

'Un verre à vin' is **not** 'a glass of wine'; although three of the four French words are accurate, the phrase is quite wrong.

Examine the text very carefully indeed, so as to avoid rushing into mistakes like these, to which even the better candidates (who may be over-confident or slap-happy) are prone.

(2) A device used by quite a few candidates is to miss out the bits they are not sure of, possibly in the misguided hope that the examiner will not notice!

It is not intended that all vocabulary should be known – there is considerable scope in this exercise for **intelligent guesswork**. Consider the following phrase: 'Après avoir monté six étages, il dut s'arrêter pour **reprendre haleine**, et arrivé chez lui, il se laissa tomber sur une chaise, **épuisé**.' In bold type are the phrases you may not know, but what guesses might you make from the parts you **do** know? 'After he had climbed up six storeys, he had to stop to . . . and when he got to his room, he dropped down on to a chair, . . .' How about 'get his breath back' and 'exhausted'? Splendid! Full marks! No one need ever know you guessed if you try – and succeed!

Natural English

(1) Having made sure your interpretation of the French is accurate you must polish that translation to read like good English. It is often a good idea to do this without looking at the French text,

which can exert a hypnotic influence which blocks the English turn of phrase. Work therefore on your rough-draft translation, trying to find the natural English equivalent for that situation. When satisfied that what you have produced sounds like English, check back to the original to make sure that you have not distorted what was meant there. **Think of English style and meaning**.

(2) **Pitfalls!**
Some words simply cannot be translated as they stand and still read well; for instance:
(a) **on** (very rarely 'one': try 'we, they, someone');
(b) **il faut** (very rarely 'it is necessary': try '. . . must' and take your cue for the subject from that given elsewhere in the sentence);
(c) **n'est-ce pas?** *(see page 132)*;
(d) **cela me plaît** (very rarely 'to please': try 'I like', etc.);
(e) **traverser à pas de loup** (and similar 'verb + descriptive adverbial phrase' structures: often to be translated as though adverb is the verb and the verb is the adverb, i.e. 'to steal across'. Compare 'monter en courant' = 'to run up', etc.).

(3) **Beware!**
(a) **Faux-amis** – our old (false) friends! (e.g. 'les assistants' = bystanders: 'il est sympathique' = he is nice);
(b) pronouns **'en', 'y', 'le'** (often not to be translated at all, e.g. 'il me l'a demandé' = he asked me; 'rentrez-**y**' = go in!; 'j'**en** ai cinq' = I have five);
(c) long question forms ('Qu'est-ce que tu manges?' – **never** 'What is it that you are eating!' but 'What are you eating?').

Exercise: Translate into French
Notre guide était mort, j'en étais sûr, mais il fallait le faire confirmer par un médecin. On nous avait donné, la veille de notre départ, le nom d'un vieux médecin, maintenant en retraite, qui habitait cette montagne, isolé de tous. Il pourrait nous aider au besoin, nous avait-on dit.

Après avoir recouvert le corps du guide avec un sac de couchage, nous descendîmes en direction de la petite rivière, qui devait nous conduire à la baraque délabrée de l'ancien médecin. La nuit tombait, nous ne voyions plus clair, bientôt nous nous égarâmes.

Je m'en rendis compte le premier, mais je ne dis rien, craignant la réaction de mon compagnon. Peu de temps après, celui-ci, laissant tomber tout à coup son sac à dos, se retourna vers moi pour me crier, furieux, 'Mais tu es fou, toi? Ça fait au moins une heure qu'on marche. On devrait être déjà arrivés. A quoi bon continuer comme ça?'

Possible answer

Our guide was dead, I was sure of it, but we had to have it confirmed by a doctor. The day before we left we had been given the name of an old doctor, now retired, who lived on this mountain, far away from anyone. We had been told he might help us in an emergency.

After covering over the body of the guide with a sleeping bag, we went down in the direction of the little river which was supposed to lead us to the tumbledown shack belonging to the former doctor. Night was falling, we could no longer see clearly, and soon we got lost.

I was the first to realise it, but said nothing, afraid of what the reaction of my companion would be. Soon afterwards, dropping his rucksack on the ground suddenly, he turned towards me shouting at me in fury, 'Are you mad then? We've been walking for at least an hour. We should be there already. What's the use of going on like this?'

Translation: English to French

As indicated earlier this exercise, once obligatory in GCE O-level, has in many cases been dropped altogether or else is offered as an alternative to a short essay. If you have successfully completed the optional parts of the test sections involving translation into French, then you are likely to be able to deal quite satisfactorily with prose translation at this level. For obvious reasons (one of which being that nowadays, hopefully, students are taught French via the living language, not via translation from English) prose translation is kept fairly simple. It is very much **a contrived affair** – those turns of idiom you have struggled with over the years are carefully formed into a story of sorts for the examination. You may be quite sure that the 'depuis', 'venir de' or similar joys of structure will feature somewhere, and success in prose translation largely hinges on whether you are astute enough to recognise the constructions lurking there amid the English.

Never translate each word as it comes along; **always** (a) **look at the whole phrase**; (b) **identify the structure involved**; (c) **decide on the tense required** (and if a compound tense, note to yourself which **auxiliary verb** is needed); (d) **check you have considered all the possibilities of agreement**.

Now write your version of that phrase and go on to the next. Constantly look at **the way each phrase fits in with those around it** – a revised version may be necessary in the light of previous or following phrases. **View the passage as a whole**.

178

Leave ample time for **checking systematically**. Make sure you have practised the art of checking on all your work before you come to sit the exam, so that by that time it is an automatic process.
Check these six points:

(1) that every **verb** is **correct in number and person**;
(2) that every **tense** is **consistent**;
(3) that every **past participle agrees if it should do so**;
(4) that the use of '**tu**' and '**vous**' (with corresponding adjective or pronoun) is **consistent**;
(5) that every **adjective agrees** with its **noun** or **pronoun**;
(6) that **accents** are **correct** and also **general spelling**.

Don't leave alternatives for the examiner to choose from – he will ignore both.
Don't cross out errors in such a way as to obscure your final version.
Do make a rough copy first but **take care** in **recopying** it.

As a preliminary exercise before trying the translation which follows, try to list all the points you think are being tested there. You should find a minimum of **twenty major grammatical points** which you will have been practising regularly during your O-level course.

Exercise: Translate into French

It was half past midnight. I went back to the hotel but the three people had just left. A dog was asleep in front of the fireplace, his head on his paws. Catching sight of the proprietor of the hotel I went over to him and asked to speak to him alone. 'Of course, Sir,' he replied. 'This way, please. Have you found what you were looking for?' he asked me. 'Unfortunately, no,' I replied. 'No one is willing to help me. The men whom I saw yesterday have disappeared from the town!' I was tired and hungry and suddenly I fell to the floor.

Possible answer

Il était minuit et demi. Je rentrai (suis rentré) à l'hôtel, mais les trois personnes venaient de partir. Un chien était endormi devant la cheminée, la tête sur les pattes. Apercevant le propriétaire de l'hôtel, je m'approchai (me suis approché) de lui pour demander de lui parler seul à seul. 'Mais certainement, Monsieur,' répondit-il (a-t-il répondu). 'Par ici, s'il vous plaît. Avez-vous trouvé ce que vous cherchiez?' me demanda-t-il (m'a-t-il demandé). 'Hélas, non,' répondis-je (ai-je répondu). 'Personne ne veut m'aider. Les trois hommes que j'ai vus hier ont disparu de la ville!' J'étais fatigué et j'avais faim; soudain je tombai (suis tombé) par terre.

Comprehension

This is becoming an increasingly popular test, fortunately so in the view of many French teachers since it concentrates on the French language in a context.

Comprehension is the test which most closely relates to the actual use of language you might experience in France.

The comprehension test takes a variety of forms; usually a longish passage of French, either printed or on tape is followed by printed **questions**. These may be either **in French or English**. Normally the questions follow the order of the material in the passage.

Aural comprehension (*a passage on tape or read by the teacher*)
This demands a very alert ear. Often an answer depends on one word of the text, and so a high degree of concentration is demanded. This is certainly an exercise which needs a good deal of classroom practice beforehand.

Frequently the questions are of the **multiple-choice** type, but you may be required to give **longer answers** (**French or English**). In any case there will be pauses after each question to give time for the writing of the answers.

Longer answers in English Here, be **concise** and **accurate**. Usually only one or two points are required: irrelevant additions will waste your time and earn nothing extra in the way of marks.
If, for instance, part of the piece were to read '*Elle avait vingt ans – le teint frais, de beaux yeux – et elle allait à Paris rencontrer son fiancé*', and a question asked for information on her age and appearance: you would mention that she was twenty, had a fresh complexion and beautiful eyes, but you would not mention that she was going to Paris, nor that she was going to meet her fiancé.

Longer answers in French **Relevance and accuracy** of information are of course equally important here, but in addition you must pay **very great attention to tenses**. Frequently the **original passage** is in the **past historic** but the **questions** will be in the **perfect**. Usually you must give a complete answer (with verb) which **must** concur with the **tense of the question**.

(a) Obviously this will involve **radical changes** from the original, particularly if a 'pourquoi?' question has been asked. This will most often involve transposing the original tense to the **pluperfect** (the reason why was because of something someone **had done**).

(b) A favourite type of **question** is one phrased in the **singular** requiring a **plural answer** – here you must not only **check the tense** but also the **number and person** of the verb.

Written comprehension (*passage and questions printed on the paper*) Emphasis is on manipulation of the information given in the passage and less on factual information (since you are not relying on your memory here). **Questions** may be **in English** in which case you can expect them to be reasonably **searching**, asking for conclusions to be drawn and so on. The questions may be **multiple-choice in French** or they may demand **longer answers in French**. All advice given above is applicable here. With regard to **longer answers in French**, the following two examples will illustrate the points (a) and (b) made above.

(i) '*Le général arriva en retard. L'interrogation, qui aurait dû avoir lieu à neuf heures, commença à neuf heures et quart et ne se termina qu'à midi moins le quart.*'

Questions
1. Pourquoi l'interrogation a-t-elle commencé plus tard que prévue?
2. Combien de temps l'interrogation a-t-elle duré?
1. Think! **Pluperfect required**, because the general **had arrived** late; '**arriver**' is conjugated with '**être**'.
2. **Perfect** is required (as in the question): **subject of answer** is the **same** as of the **question**, **verb form** can remain the **same** (which is half the work done for you!) – all you need do is calculate the **length of time** involved.

Answers
1. **Elle a commencé plus tard que prévu parce que le général était arrivé en retard**.
2. **Elle a duré deux heures et demie**.

(ii) '*Marie raconta ensuite: "Je travaillais à la cuisine avec ma mère quand le facteur arriva." Il est vrai qu'il leur apporta une lettre recommandée ce jour-là.*'

Questions
1. Qui se trouvait à la maison à ce moment-là?

2. Que faisait Marie?

3. Quelle sorte de lettre le facteur a-t-il apportée?

1. Think! Two people were there, **verb** must therefore be **plural**.

2. **Tense** of the verb (se trouver) will be the **same** as in the original, but must change from **first to third person**.

3. **Past participle agreement** in the **question** because of the direct object (quelle lettre) at beginning of sentence. This should **not** be imitated in the **answer**. The **subject** of the answer corresponds to the subject of the question, so **verb form** can remain the **same** otherwise.

Answers

1. Marie et sa mère se trouvaient à la maison (s'y trouvaient) à ce moment-là.

2. Elle travaillait.

3. Il leur a apporté une lettre recommandée.

Most mistakes occur in this sort of test through candidates copying blindly from the original, without stopping to consider exactly what changes need to be made.

Note 1 You will gain credit for use of **pronouns** in your answers, but only if these are **accurate**, with **all** necessary agreements.

Note 2 You will find it to your advantage to learn a **formula** for **question-and-answer patterns**.

E.g. '*Qu'est-ce qui indique . . .?*' '**Ce qui l'indique c'est** . . .'

'*Pourquoi . . .?*' '**Parce que** . . .'

'*Comment . . .?*' (in sense of how did someone do something) '. . . **en + present participle**' (by doing)

Work out similar formulae for the other common question forms, and **remember** (i) **to check your cue question word(s)**; (ii) **to answer what is asked**.

Essay work

The **pitfalls** of writing essays in French are (a) trying to be **too ambitious**, and hence (b) **making too many errors**. Knowing that this is so, perhaps from bitter experience, students must learn to accept the fact that their French essays are not meant to have the style or content of their English essays, and to work within a restricted framework. Owing to the fact that students have so often misjudged essay requirements in the past, completely free writing has been largely abandoned for examination purposes in favour of more structured work. Quite often there is a choice between dialogue or narrative. The essay stimulus may take the form of:

(a) **a story outline or scene-setting**;

(b) **a series of** (usually six) **pictures telling a story**;

(c) **a continuation of a story, or reproduction of a story** read aloud;

(d) **a letter**; or

(e) **an account of a simple adventure or incident**.

Indeed, the tendency nowadays is away from the single longer essay (of about 150 words) towards two shorter pieces.

All the advice on prose translation given earlier (pages 178–9) is relevant here (i.e. view the phrases as a whole, maintain consistency, check agreements, etc.) and in addition, **above all**, **avoid** the tendency to think out your essay in English and translate it: that is linguistic suicide!

Steer clear of danger by observing the following rules.

(a) **Plan your work in paragraphs**, with a definite beginning, middle and end. If there is a picture series, this will help you.

(b) For each paragraph **note down key words and phrases**.

(c) **Keep the whole thing uncomplicated.** (By all means show off what you know in the way of polished structures – après avoir ..., avant de, present participle, etc. – **provided** you are **really sure** how to use them.) Otherwise **simplicity** has all the virtues: **write only what you know how to say**.

(d) Considerable effect can be achieved by the **addition** of an **adjective** or **adverb**, devices which incur relatively few risks.

(e) Introduce **descriptive phrases** only if they are **relevant** to the subject and are **correct**.

(f) **Avoid repetition** and **eliminate** superfluous 'he said's, etc. You have few words at your disposal, so **make the most of them** and **do not** significantly **overrun** the required number (up to ten extra should be your limit).

(g) **Do not use the past historic in direct speech**; remember **inversion after direct speech** of verb and pronoun.

Remember that marks will be earned first and foremost for **accuracy** and **relevance**. Flair, style, and individuality definitely come second.

Letters

If you choose the letter option, make sure that:

(a) your 'tu' or 'vous' form is appropriate to that letter;

(b) you maintain consistency of that form, including those adjective and pronoun forms;

(c) you do **not** use the past historic;

(d) you know the correct formulæ for beginning and ending the letter.

Letters should be headed with the **town and date** only on the **right-hand** side, like this:

> *Rouen, le 23 octobre, 1975*

Business letters should begin *Monsieur*, and should end:

> *Je vous prie d'agréer, Monsieur, l'expression de mes sentiments distingués,*
>
> *(signature)*

Letters to friends begin simply:

Cher Pierre (Chère Annette),   and end:

> *Amitiés de   Georges (Suzanne)*
> **or** *Ton ami(e)   Georges (Suzanne)*

Story outline, scene-setting or simple narrative

Here you will probably be asked to write an essay of about 200 words based on an outline like this:

'Votre première expérience sur les skis – le moniteur impatient – il vous arrive un accident – peu après à l'hôpital une nouvelle victime, le moniteur.'

Otherwise the scene will be set for you, like this:

'Un soir, en rentrant d'un restaurant, vous vous rendez compte que le manteau que vous portez n'est pas le vôtre. Dans la poche il y a un collier de perles. Décrivez ce que vous faites ensuite.'

Reproduction of a story *read aloud by the teacher*

For this the candidate will again be provided with a brief written analysis of the story.

(1) Normally this story will carry some kind of punch-line and the candidate should note it down as soon as writing is permitted.

(2) Normal techniques of jotting down key incidents and phrases apply here too; equally the candidate should try to achieve a simpler account of the original story, giving essential details.

(3) Remember to use the tenses of the spoken story.

Series of pictures

Here we offer two typical examples of this exercise. You will be asked to write the story depicted in the series of pictures in approximately 150 words. A possible version of the picture series on the next page might be: **Le crime ne paie pas.**

Le crime ne paie pas

185

Devant une grande maison une voiture luxueuse attendait. Monsieur et Madame Négrault et leur fille, habillés de vêtements du soir, sont sortis de la maison. Un chauffeur respectueux les a salués. Aussitôt la voiture disparue, un cambrioleur a pénétré dans la maison en ouvrant une fenêtre du rez-de-chaussée. Il est monté à pas feutrés au premier étage, où, à l'aide d'une lampe électrique, il a découvert des bijoux étincelants, qu'il a aussitôt fourrés dans son sac.

Fort content il est redescendu au salon où il a pris aussi un plateau et une coupe en argent. Malheureusement en sortant par la fenêtre, il a laissé tomber le plateau, ce qui a fait beaucoup de bruit. Réveillé par le bruit, un chien féroce s'est élancé sur le cambrioleur qui avait très peur. Laissant son butin par terre, celui-ci s'est sauvé, aussi vite que possible, le chien à ses trousses.

Now, referring to the pictures on page 187 (**Un petit détour**) see if you can make up your own story. A few useful phrases are listed below: un poste émetteur = a radio transmitter; un steward = a steward; monter à bord = to go on board; haut les mains! = hands up!; la carlingue = the cockpit; transmettre un appel = to send a message; déguisés en ... = disguised as...; féliciter = to congratulate.

Dictation

As a fixed O-level examination exercise, dictation seems to be losing a little ground, but it is a very useful test of comprehension and accuracy. It is amazing how many candidates do not seem to realise that the dictation passage should **make sense** and that by considering alternative spellings and word combinations from the sounds heard, it is often possible to find sense in what appears to be nonsense.

Of the **three readings**, the **first** is to allow you to **understand** the passage as a whole. Do not dismiss this as a formality – a general picture may help to sort out individual words when dictated later in the **second reading**, which is **spaced**. Similarly the **third** is crucial: it is your final opportunity to check the passage as a whole. Throughout the exercise it is most important to keep in mind **the sense and structure** of the whole piece.

Use your intelligence and **knowledge of grammatical structure** to interpret the passage.

Un petit détour

(1) The problem of the '**é, ai, er, ez**' sounds versus '**ais, ait, aient**' is moderately difficult, but with practice can easily be overcome; use the structure of the sentence as a whole to guide you.

(2) Go through your check-list for accuracy most carefully, ensuring that
(a) **every clause contains a finite verb**;
(b) **every finite verb agrees with its subject**;
(c) **every adjective agrees with its noun or pronoun**;
(d) **present and past participles agree if necessary**.
Be especially careful in cases where an adjective and noun, or subject and verb, are well separated.
E.g. Joli**e**, mais sans le savoir, **la jeune fille** . . .
. . . la voiture, que pouss**aient trois hommes** . . .
Do not be tempted by the proximity of 'la voiture' to write 'pous**sait**'; both **sense** and **relative pronoun** would be incorrect.

Punctuation
Punctuation is **always** given in French:

.	point	:	deux points
,	virgule	;	point-virgule
?	point d'interrogation	!	point d'exclamation
≪	ouvrez les guillemets	≫	fermez les guillemets
. . .	points de suspension	-	tiret
new paragraph	à la ligne	( )	entre parenthèses

Oral examination

Over the last few years the oral exam has assumed an increasing importance in the total mark – 25% and 30% in some instances, which is a very healthy sign. The oral exam is quite definitely **not** one you prepare the night before. One thing to remember above all is that you will gain no credit at all for saying nothing! Your **willingness** to talk will be an important factor in your eventual success.

Your test may be conducted by a **visiting examiner** – who is normally quite human, or by **your own teacher**, in which case it will, in all probability, be recorded on tape.

The pattern of the test, which on average lasts **10–15 minutes**, is usually as follows. Firstly there is a **passage to be read aloud**, and which the candidate will have had time to prepare. This may or may not be followed by a few questions to test the candidate's comprehension of the passage. If you are used to reading in French then you will have little problem: remember that **French intonation** rises at commas, otherwise is fairly even, particularly with regard to individual syllables ('pré-pa-ra-tion'). Remember too that the liaisons **not** to make are after '**et**' (lui et elle) and before aspirate '**h**'.

Secondly, there are **general questions** on topics such as your family, hobbies, holidays, your future plans on leaving school.

These features are **common to most boards** but additionally, according to the board, there may be:

(i) a **description of a picture** or series of pictures which tell a story;

(ii) **preparation of your own topics** of conversation, which means (in theory, at least!) you will know beforehand what you are going to talk about.

(iii) '**role-playing**', the up-and-coming activity for oral exams. This requires the candidate to take the role of (say) a customer in a café, while the examiner takes the role of the waiter.

This leads to an important point concerning **practice** for the oral. If you have a hobby or interest you would be happy to talk about, then it is sensible to practise (in general terms) saying things about that subject (look up vocabulary you may need, etc.). The examiner will be only too pleased if you show initiative in this way.

However, you must **avoid over-rehearsal**, particularly where **prepared topics** are a part of the test. Something which sounds like a well-drilled robot will be **penalised** on the total grading, even though the substance of what has been said may well have been accurate.

Conversation is meant to be a **spontaneous interchange** (given the circumstances!) between examiner and candidate. The oral test can in fact be quite enjoyable if approached in the right spirit.

On pages 190 and 192 are **two picture scenes** typical of the kind found in the oral exam. **Three useful exercises** may be practised using these as a basis.

(1) An examiner is likely to start the conversation by asking open-ended questions of the type: 'Que voyez-vous sur cette gravure?' or 'Décrivez la scène; où se passe-t-elle?' leaving you carte blanche to say what you can.

Phrases for you to use might be: '**A gauche, (droite)**' = on the left, (right); '**à l'arrière-plan (au premier plan)**' = in the background (foreground); '**tout près de . . .**' = very near to . . .'

Dans la rue

etc. To gain maximum credit, give **as much information as possible** about what the people look like, their clothes, their age, what they are doing, what they have just done, etc.

You may then be asked more specific questions such as: 'Que fait la personne près du kiosque à fleurs?' 'Qu'est-ce que le marchand vient de faire?' 'Pourquoi la dame à droite . . .?' etc.

Here you must **listen** very closely to the **tense of the question** and answer accordingly.

The **first exercise** therefore is to anticipate an examiner's questions and give a running commentary on the scene.

Dans la rue

diriger la circulation	=	to direct the traffic;
tendre de l'argent à	=	to hand money over to;
rebondir	=	to bounce;
une moto	=	a motor bike;
un vélomoteur	=	a moped;
un passage clouté	=	pedestrian crossing.

Au marché

un étalage	=	display of goods;
fixer les yeux sur	=	to stare at
faire des gestes	=	to make gestures;
offrir en réclame	=	to have on special offer;
indiquer du doigt	=	to point at

(2) **Secondly** you could try (with a friend) taking the roles of examiner and candidate so that you adjust to the 'interrogation' situation.

(3) **Thirdly** you could imagine what the people in the scene **were doing** two or three hours previously and what **they will be doing** a couple of hours later.

Note You could also use the picture series on pages 185 and 187 to give an oral account of those stories.

Background knowledge

(Series) **Project France** (published by Black & Lippincott)
Looking at France (published by M. Glasgow Baker)
Life in a French Town (published by Harrap)
Life in a French Family (published by Harrap)
(Series) **Destination France** (published by Harrap)
(Series) **Découvrons la France** (published by E.U.P.)
Passeport pour le Passé (published by Edward Arnold)

Au marché

Key Facts Revision Section

Spelling

If you begin by being careful over the spelling of individual words, then you are probably going to learn thoroughly in general terms, and **this** is the key to long-term success. Syllables which are frequently mis-spelt are:
– **eau**; –**eur**; –**euil**; and you must pay special attention to these. As you meet new words learn:
(a) to accept the **gender of a noun** as part of the word;
(b) to check the **conjugation of verbs** in the verb tables (pages 91–7);
(c) to **beware of words closely resembling English ones**.

Articles

The definite article (*le, la, l', les*)
The form '*l'*' is used before masculine or feminine words beginning with a **vowel** or a **mute 'h'**. Make sure you remember the **contraction** of the prepositions '**à**' and '**de**' + definite article, giving '**au**', '**aux**' and similarly '**du**', '**des**'.
The definite article is used **idiomatically** as follows:
(1) in **personal description**, including movement of parts of one's own body, where a reflexive form of the verb is usual;
(2) in **prices and quantities**;
(3) with **names of countries** (**not** when saying 'in' or 'to', however);
(4) with **titles** (royal or professional);
(5) before **abstract nouns**.

The indefinite article
(*un, une, des*)
The singular forms of the indefinite article are also the numeral '**one**'. The plural '**des**' is often left untranslated in English.
The indefinitive article is **omitted**:
(1) when giving someone's **profession or nationality**;
(2) before an explanatory **noun in apposition**;
(3) after '**ni . . . ni . . .**';
(4) after '**cent**', '**mille**', '**quel**', '**comme**' (= as 'a'):

The partitive article (*du, de la, de l', des*)
The partitive article is used principally to express '**a certain**

quantity of', '**some**', but should be reduced to the form '**de (d')**':
(1) in **expressions of quantity**, including adverbial expressions such as 'beaucoup de', etc.
Note 'La plupart' is followed by the **full partitive** and **plural verb**;
(2) **after a negative** (except for after 'ne . . . que');
(3) **before an adjective which precedes the noun.**

Nouns

Certain endings are predominantly masculine, others predominantly feminine. In other instances a feminine form is derived from the masculine. These are worth noting as a guide, but are by no means categoric.
Plurals are normally formed by **adding 's'**, though certain nouns in '-ou' add '**x**'. The plural of '**un oeil**' (= eye) is totally different, = '**les yeux**'. Although fairly rarely found, the plural of '**le ciel**' (= sky) is somewhat similar, = '**les cieux**'.
Compound nouns vary in their plural forms, sometimes changing one, sometimes both parts. Only individual learning of words can be the real guide here.
Proper names never add 's' as in English.

Adjectives

Adjectives must **agree in number and gender** with the noun or pronoun they describe. Masculine and feminine nouns being described by the same adjective take the **masculine plural** form of the adjective.
Feminine forms of the adjective:
It is usual to add an '**e**' to the masculine form (if the word does not already end in 'e'), although certain adjective endings behave differently: '**—er**' becomes '**—ère**'; '**—f**' becomes '**—ve**'; '**—x**' becomes '**—se**'; '**—s**' becomes '**—sse**'; '**—el**', '**—eil**', '**—il**', '**—en**', '**—on**', '**—et**' become '**—elle**' '**—eille**', '**—ille**', '**—enne**', '**—onne**', '**—ette**' (doubling the consonant).
A few very irregular forms must be learned separately, as must the special **masculine singular** forms of two or three adjectives, which are needed **before a vowel** or a **mute 'h'**. N.B. **Compound adjectives** of colour are **invariable** (e.g. 'une cravate **vert foncé**').

Position of adjectives
The normal position is **after the noun**, with the exception of some **very common** adjectives which **precede** it. In certain circum-

stances, mainly for reasons of style or emphasis, you may change the adjective from its customary position. Two adjectives, both of which precede or both of which follow the noun, are joined by **'et'** in the normal position.

Meaning affected by position

About ten adjectives each have **two** very different **meanings**, according to whether they are placed before or after the noun. Needless to say, it is very important to have the differences clear in your mind.

Pronouns

The fundamental point of course is that **pronouns replace nouns**, and must therefore take their **number and gender** from the **original noun**.

Subject pronouns
(je, tu, il, etc. = I, you, he, etc.)
Of the subject pronouns few are deserving of special study since they so closely resemble English usage. Some points you should remember however are:
(1) the difference between **'tu'** and **'vous'**, and the need for care with associated pronouns or adjectives;
(2) **'il'** and **'elle'** can both mean **'it'** when referring to an inanimate object;
(3) **'on'** is used a great deal in French, but is rarely translated by 'one'. It takes the **third person singular** forms in **verb endings** and **possessive adjectives** and **pronouns**.

Object pronouns
(me, te, le, lui, etc. = me, to me; you, to you; him; it; to him, her, it, etc.)
(1) **Except** in **positive commands**, they **precede the verb**. This rule includes all compound tenses.
(2) Where the pronoun occurs with a **modal verb + infinitive**, common sense dictates its position – virtually always **before** the **infinitive**.
(3) The order of two or more pronouns together must be carefully studied from the table given in the main text, page 26.
N.B. **'Le'**, **'la'**, **'les'** are used with **'Voici!'**, **'Voilà!'** to express 'Here he is!', etc. (= **'Le voici!'**).
(4) **Direct or indirect object?** The government of direct and indirect objects by verbs in French varies considerably from English. To be fully aware of these differences is **vital** to correct

handling of French language structure. You must become familiar with those verbs which take direct objects and those which take indirect objects through careful observation and constant practice, e.g. **'regarder quelque chose'** = **direct object** in French; 'téléphoner **à quelqu'un**' = **indirect object** in French.

(5) The pronouns **'y'** (replacing **à + noun', usually a place name**) and **'en'** (replacing **'de + noun'**) need special attention, since they are frequently used idiomatically.

Stressed pronouns
(*moi, toi, etc.* = **me, you,** etc.)

These are used in positions of **emphasis**, where they are **not** the direct or indirect object of a verb. Principally they occur:

(1) giving **additional stress** to an ordinary subject pronoun;
(2) after **'c'est', 'c'était'**;
(3) in **comparisons.**

In a very few circumstances, they are used **instead** of an **indirect object pronoun**, to avoid the combination 'me lui' (or 'nous leur') which is considered both weak and rather clumsy.

Possessive adjectives and pronouns
(*mon, ma, mes, etc.,* = *my; le mien, la mienne, etc.* = *mine*)

(1) The normal rule of agreement in number and gender holds good – the important thing to remember is that the **agreement** is always **with whatever is possessed.** The relevance of the owner is only in determining the **person form** involved (e.g. '**m**on' or '**s**on' = **my** or **his, her** possession; 'la **sienne**' or 'la **leur**' = **his, hers** or **theirs**).

(2) The correct form of the **adjective** must be **repeated** before **every** noun.

(3) Normally a **definite article** is preferred to a possessive form if action is done to a part of the body.

Demonstrative adjectives and pronouns
(*ce, cette, ces, etc.* = *this, that; celui, etc.* = *the one*)

(1) Concerning the adjective forms, remember the '**cet**' masculine form **before a vowel** or **mute 'h'**, and also that the **plural 'ces'** is for **both** masculine and feminine forms.

(2) Concerning the pronoun forms, remember they will never stand alone, but will be followed by:

   (a) **'de + noun'** (to signify possession, e.g. 'John's');
   (b) **a relative pronoun** (to signify 'the one who . . .' etc.);
   (c) **'–ci'** or **'–là'** (to signify **'this** or **that** one').

Note This **suffix** pattern may also be attached to the **noun**

preceded by the demonstrative adjective to express the same distinction between **'this'** and **'that'**.

Note also **'celui-ci'** and **'celui-là'** can mean respectively **'the latter'** and **'the former'**.
'Ceci', **'cela'** (ça') are **neuter** forms, referring to ideas, not a single word, and meaning **'this'**, **'that'**.

Interrogative adjectives
(quel, quelle?, etc. = which? what?)
The use of these adjectives is uncomplicated, but remember the agreement. N.B. These adjectives are also used in exclamations, but are never followed by 'a' as often in English

Interrogative pronouns
(qui? qu'est-ce que?, etc. = who? what?)
(1) for many of the interrogative pronouns there is a short and long form ('qui?' or 'qui est-ce qui?' = 'who?' (subject); 'que?' or 'qu'est-ce que?' = 'what?' (object).
'What?' (subject) has only the one long form ('qu'est-ce qui?') except in set phrases such as **'Que faire?'** = 'What is there to be done?'

It is important to realise in these apparently complicated forms that the **first word** ('qui' or 'que') indicates that the reference is to **people** or to **things,** and that the **last word** is purely a **relative pronoun** indicating that the form, in terms of grammar, is **subject** or **object** of that phrase;
(2) **'which one?'** has the forms **'lequel', 'laquelle', etc.;**
(3) **after prepositions 'quoi'** is used for **things**, and **'qui'** is used for **people**.
Note particularly how **'à qui est . . .?'** denotes possession: **'Whose is . . .?'**
N.B. 'Qui' is always the correct word to use for people, except when you wish to ask 'which one?'

Indefinite adjectives and pronouns
(quelque, quelques = some, any; quelqu'un, quelque chose, etc. = some-anyone, some-anything)
(1) The adjective occurs mostly in the **plural forms** (e.g. 'quelques gens' = 'some people').
(2) You must remember that it is the plural **pronoun** form – 'quelques-un(e)s' – which must be used in cases where you wish to express: **'some** did . . . **others** did . . .'. In this case 'others' is

rendered by **'d'autres'**; thus **'quelques-uns** ont pris une pêche, **d'autres** des raisins' = **'some** took a peach, **others** grapes'.

L'un ... l'autre (plural 'les uns ... les autres') is **'one ... the other'**, **'each other'**. Note particularly 'ils parlent les uns **aux** autres' = 'they talk **to each other'**.

(3) **n'importe** before any of the forms 'lequel', 'qui', 'quoi...' gives the idea of **'any at all'**, making the phrase even more indefinite.

(4) **'each'** is rendered by **'chaque'** (masculine and feminine adjective); **'each one'** by **'chacun(e)'** (pronoun).

(5) **'all'** (adjective or pronoun) has the forms:

tout   (masculine singular or **neuter = everything**)

toute   (feminine singular)

tous   (masculine plural – **'s'**
            pronounced only in the pronoun form)

toutes   (feminine plural)

As an adverb 'tout' is used to mean 'quite', 'very': e.g. 'une **toute** petite fille'. (Note that there is an agreement before feminine forms beginning with a consonant.)

Relative pronouns

(*qui, que, dont, lequel, etc. = who, which, of which, etc.*)

(1) Always introducing a clause, the **relative pronouns** have **'qui'** as the **subject** form and **'que (qu')'** as the **object** form. The reference **subject** or **object** is always to the verb in the **clause they introduce**.

(2) They are **never** omitted as often in English.

(3) **After a preposition 'qui'** remains the form for use with **people; 'lequel'**, etc. (as for the interrogative pronoun forms = 'which one?') is used for **things**.

(4) **'Lesquels'** refers to **people only when following** the two prepositions **'parmi'** and **'entre'**.

(5) **'Dont'** (word order: dont + subject + verb, etc.) is used to express **'of which', 'whose', 'of whom'**. You should be prepared for the necessity of using 'dont' with verbs such as 'se servir **de'**, etc. A relative used with this kind of verb must incorporate the preposition 'de' which is part of the phrase, and therefore can only be 'dont' (**never** 'que').

(6) **'Ce qui', 'ce que (ce qu')'**: these forms are used when **no precise noun or pronoun** is being referred to, but rather an idea or whole group of words. Specific examples should be studied to illustrate this clearly.

N.B. **'Tout ce qui (que)'** is used to convey **'all that (which) ...'**

'Ce' v. 'il'

(1) **Il** (or **'elle'**) is used when relating back to a **noun** or **pronoun already mentioned**, and of which you therefore already know the gender.

(2) '**Il**' is used in telling the **time.**

(3) '**Il**' is used in speaking of the **weather.**

(4) '**Ce**' is used where there is a sense of **definition** of an object (or defining what kind of a person).

(5) In terms of description, '**ce**' is used when a **noun** is **qualified by an adjective**; whereas '**il**' (or 'elle') is used with an **adjective standing alone**, according to this kind of pattern: **c'est un beau chien** but **il est beau.**

Except

(a) where '**it is + adjective**' refers to something of a general nature (e.g. 'it's superb!'), in which case use '**ce**';

(b) **it + is + adjective + verb = c'est . . . à . . .;**

(c) **it + is + adjective + verb etc . . . = il est . . . de . . .;**

(d) '**c'est**' may be used in any tense or mood. The **plural** is **ce sont'**, **'c'étaient'**, etc.

Adverbs

(1) The basic formation is by the addition of '**–ment**' to the *feminine adjective*, with one or two main group patterns diverging from this. In addition there are a few irregular adverbs (**bien, vite,** etc.).

(2) Adjectives ending in '**–ant**', '**–ent**' become '**–amment**', '**–emment**' when adverbs.

(3) Some adverbs have '**–ément**', often where the adjective ends in an 'e' in the masculine form.

(4) **Alternative ways** of rendering adverbial phrases are: *d'une façon* + *adjective, avec* (*sans*) + *noun.*
The context will give the best guide as to the suitability of particular alternatives; as a general rule avoid clumsy long adverbs. *d'une voix* (*d'un ton, d'un air*) + *adjective* may also often be preferred to the one-word form in '–ment';

(5) In several expressions which must be learned separately an **adjective** is used as an **adverb**, but this cannot be applied as a general rule.

Position of adverbs

Usually the position is **immediately after the verb**: in **compound tenses** the short adverbs will **precede the past**

participle. Longer adverbs are placed **afterwards, or** in common with **adverbs** of **time** and **place**, may be placed at the **beginning of the sentence.**

In any case they are **never** between the subject and the verb.

Comparative and superlative forms

Adjectives and adverbs behave similarly here.

(1) The **comparative** form precedes the adjective or adverb with '**plus**' = 'more'.

(2) The **superlative** form precedes the adjective or adverb with '**le plus**' = 'the most'.

(3) After a superlative '... **in** (the class)' is rendered by '**de** ...'.

(4) '**Less**', '**the least**' is formed according to the same kind of pattern: '**moins**' before the adjective or adverb (= 'less'); '**le moins**' before the adjective or adverb (= 'the least').

(5) '**Than**' in comparisons is expressed '... **que** ...' ('moins ... que', 'plus ... que'), whereas the idea of **equal comparison** is conveyed by '**aussi ... que**' = '**as ... as**'.

(6) '**Pas si ... que**' gives the idea '**not as ... as**'.

(7) Irregular comparative and superlative adjectives and adverbs are fortunately few in number:

    (le) meilleur (adj.); (le) mieux (adv.) = better; best;
    (le) pire (adj.); (le) pis (adv.) = worse; worst;
    (le) moindre (adj.); (le) moins (adv.) = less; least;

N.B. Translation of '**the best**' needs special care: is it an adjective or an adverb?

Verbs

Mastery of the verb forms and their usage in at least four basic tenses is essential for even a modest success at CSE level. Any further ambition demands corresponding additional achievement and effort.

Present indicative

This embraces many English forms: *'je chante'* = *'I sing, am*

singing, do sing'. There is only the **single form in French**.
Endings for the three basic conjugation patterns are:

	–er		**–ir**		**–re**
–e	*–ons*	*–is*	*–issons*	*–s*	*–ons*
–es	*–ez*	*–is*	*–issez*	*–s*	*–ez*
–e	*–ent*	*–it*	*–issent*	*–*	*–ent*

Reflexive verbs are distinguished from ordinary verbs only by
the addition of the **reflexive pronoun** (me, te, se, nous, vous)
which have exactly the same characteristics of all other object
pronouns, as far as position goes.

Irregularities of spelling occur with the following groups of
verbs:

(1) certain verbs adopt a **different stem** in the '**nous**' and
'**vous**' forms;

(2) '**–cer**', '**–ger**' verbs need '**ç**' and '**ge**' in the **first person
plural**;

(3) verbs in '**e + consonant + er**' have '**è**' before an
unsounded 'e';

(4) most verbs in '**–eler**', '**–eter**' **double the consonant** here
rather than add '**é**';

(5) '**–oyer**' and '**–uyer**' verbs change the '**y**' to '**i**' under these
same conditions.

It is useful to remember the phrase '**être en train de faire**' to
imply '**at this moment doing**'.

Idioms
'**Depuis**' and '**venir de**' are used with the **present** tense to
express '**has been doing for** ... (time)' and '**has just done**'.
N.B. These are very great favourites with the examiners. '**Aller +
infinitive**' is used to form the **immediate future** as in English: =
'**am going to do**'.

Imperative
The **second persons singular and plural** and the **first person
plural** are used to give commands ('do!' 'do not!') The subject
pronoun (tu, nous, vous) is simply omitted. The **first person** form
renders '**let us do**'.
N.B. '**–er**' **verbs** in the second person singular **lose** the **final 's'** in

the imperative, as does '**va(s)**' = 'go!' (**except** in the one instance of '**vas-y**!').
'**Etre**' and '**avoir**' have **irregular** forms.
Reflexive verbs lose the subject pronoun but of course retain the reflexive **pronoun**. Following the rules for position of pronouns, the **reflexive pronoun** (and any others) will be placed **after the verb** in positive commands, and joined to the verb with **hyphens**.

Future tense

(a) The English translation is '*will*', '*shall do*'.

(b) The **endings** for the future tense are the **same** for all verbs:

−ai	−ons
−as	−ez
−a	−ont

These are **added** to the **infinitive stem** (donn**er**, fin**ir**, ven**dr**−).
The letter '**r**' is always the **letter before the ending.** There are many verbs irregular in their stem (learn these from the verb tables), but all adopt the regular endings.

(c) The verbs which in the present tense doubled the consonant or added an '**è**' do this also throughout the future.

Sequence of tenses

(a) After '**quand**', '**dès que**', '**aussitôt que**' you will often be required to use a **future tense** in French where this is **logical**.

(b) '**Si**' = '**if**' may **never** be used with a **future** tense following. Do not be tempted by an apparent future tense or idea in English.
'**Si**' = '**whether**' may be used in all tenses.

Perfect tense

The usual English translation is '*did*', '*have done*'.

The perfect tense is:
(a) always composed of an **auxiliary verb** ('avoir' or 'être') + *past participle*;

(b) the principal narrative tense for **events** which have **happened in the past**;

202

(c) the past tense of **speech** and **letter writing**;

(d) the tense which recounts **completed, single events** (**not** events which may have begun in the past, but which are still continuing, **nor** repeated events in the past).

The **agreement** (or not) of the **past participle** is **very important**.

All verbs (except the thirteen intransitive verbs and their derivatives, see page 63, **and** the reflexive verbs) use '**avoir**' as their **auxiliary** verb. For the **perfect** tense the **present** tense of the **auxiliary** is used, together with the **past participle** (ending for regular '*–er*' verbs in '*é*', for '*–ir*' verbs in '*i*', and for '*–re*' verbs in '*u*', replacing the infinitive ending).

Many verbs have **irregular past participles** and yet again these must be learned by heart.

The '**être**' verbs and **reflexives** (as listed as exceptions above) use the present tense of this verb + past participle in exactly the same way.
N.B. Certain of the 'être' verbs may take an object occasionally, in which case they change their auxiliary verb to 'avoir'.

Agreement of the past participle
'**Avoir**' **verbs** and all **reflexives agree only** with a **preceding direct object**. This may take the form of (a) **a noun**, (b) **a direct object pronoun**, or (c) **a relative pronoun**. This is a grammatical point which requires alert observation as it is easily overlooked.
N.B. **Reflexive verbs**: normally the reflexive pronoun itself is direct object, thus supplying the reason for agreement of the past participle. On the (fairly) rare occasions where the **reflexive pronoun** is **indirect object**, the **past participle will not agree** with it.

Imperfect tense
The usual English translation is '*was doing, used to do*'.

The imperfect tense is:
(a) a **one-word** tense composed of the following **endings** added to the '*nous*' *stem* of the present tense, *minus* '*–ons*' =

–ais	*–ions*
–ais	*–iez*
–ait	*–aient*

'**Etre**' is the only exception to this, in that its stem is '**ét–**'. Verbs in '**–cer**', '**–ger**' will need to add '**ç**' and '**ge**' in all parts except first and second plural;

(b) a **continuous past tense**, saying what **was happening** when some particular event or incident occurred;

(c) the **past** tense which recounts **habitual actions**;

(d) the **past** tense which **describes people, feelings** or **places**, or **sets the scene** for events which took place;

Thus the imperfect is used **in conjunction with the perfect tense**, but is quite distinct from it in use.

Idioms

'**Depuis**' and '**venir de**' are used with the **imperfect** tense to express '**had been doing for** . . . (time)' and '**had just done**'.

No other constructions will render these two ideas.

Conditional tense

(a) The English translation is '*would do*' (i.e. given certain circumstances).

(b) The conditional tense is an amalgam of two others: without exception, to the *future stem* of a verb are added the *endings for the imperfect*.

(c) Most frequently the conditional is used in connection with an '**if' clause** (giving the condition governing the proposed action in the main clause). The tense of the '**if' clause** is **imperfect**, if it is expressed in English as 'if I *did* . . ., I would . . .'.

(d) The conditional will often be found in **indirect speech** when you are reporting something which someone has said 'would take place'.

(e) After '**quand**', '**dès que**', '**aussitôt que**' you must be prepared, as with the future tense, to use the **conditional** when it is **logical** in the sequence of tenses.

(f) Beware the 'mights', 'coulds', 'woulds', 'oughts'! Check carefully before assuming a conditional tense that you are not needing an imperfect or modal verb. (Consult the 'meaning table' given on page 122 for help with this).

Pluperfect, future perfect, conditional perfect

(a) The English translations are '*had done*' (pluperfect), '*will have done*' (future perfect), '*would have done*' (conditional perfect).

(b) The form of the tenses is suggested by their name; all are **compound tenses**:

imperfect ⎫
   future ⎬ + past participle
conditional ⎭

= pluperfect
= future perfect
= conditional perfect

(3) All the usual **rules** of **past participle agreement** apply.

(4) Take care again over **logical sequence of tense**. 'When I (will) have done . . .' = future perfect: 'as soon as he (would have done) had done . . .' = conditional perfect.

Past historic

(a) The usual English translation is as for the perfect '*did*' but not normally 'have done'.

(b) The form of the past historic is based on *three vowel types*: '*–aï*', '*–is*', '*–us*'.

The **endings** and **verb groups** are:

	–ai		–is		–us
(all –er	–ai	(regular	–is	(all other	–us
verbs)	–as	–ir, –re	–is	irregular	–us
	–a	verbs, +	–it	verbs)	–ut
	–âmes	some others)	–îmes		–ûmes
	–âtes		–îtes		–ûtes
	–èrent		–irent		–urent

Learning by heart is the only way to know whether verbs are '–is', or '–us' types.

(c) '**Tenir**', '**venir**' and their derivatives are the only totally irregular verbs.

(d) Like the perfect tense, the **past historic relates completed**, **single events** happening in the **past**.

(e) The past historic is however a **written tense**, **not** used in conversation or letters (remember this in essays).

(f) The past historic works **in conjunction with the imperfect** tense in the same way as the perfect.

Past anterior

(a) The **past anterior** has the **same** translation in English as the **pluperfect**, '*had done*'.

(b) It is formed from the *past historic* of the regular *auxiliary verb* + *past participle*.

(c) it is **only** used when:
   (1) the 'had done' idea is in a **subordinate** clause, **and**
   (2) the **main** clause tense is **past historic**, **and**

(3) the subordinate clause is **introduced by 'quand'**, **'lorsque', 'après que', 'aussitôt que', 'dès que', or 'à peine ... que'**. Otherwise you will use the normal pluperfect.

N.B. **'à peine ... que'** requires **inversion** of the following verb and its subject.

Use of past tenses

The interaction of past tenses is of the utmost importance. Here is a passage illustrating their different functions and relationship to each other.

'Jules s'habilla vite et descendit. Ordinairement il quittait la maison à huit heures et quart, mais ce jour-là il était en retard. Il avala du café bien chaud, ramassa les lettres qu'il avait écrites la veille et sortit en courant. Il pleuvait déjà depuis quelques heures et les trottoirs étaient mouillés. Bientôt il se précipitait dans l'escalier du métro, mais comme le train sortait du tunnel, le portillon automatique se ferma devant lui. Jules se fâcha. "Tu as raté le train?" lui cria son camarade Paul. "C'est que j'ai dormi trop longtemps," répondit Jules. Mais à peine eut-il prononcé ces paroles qu'on put enfin avancer sur le quai.'

Notes on the above passage:

(1) **'s'habilla, descendit, avala'**, etc.: past historic to denote a succession of single events, complete in themselves;

(2) **'quittait'**: imperfect for a habitual happening;

(3) **'qu'il avait écrites'**: pluperfect to translate 'he had written' (but **not** fulfilling the conditions for the past anterior). Note also the preceding direct object agreement;

(4) **'était en retard', 'étaient mouillés'**: imperfect of description in the past, setting the scene;

(5) **'pleuvait depuis quelques heures'**: imperfect with 'depuis' to show 'had been raining' and **still was**;

(6) **'il se précipitait'**: imperfect used to give dramatic effect, 'soon he was rushing down the steps';

(7) **'sortait ... se ferma'**: continuous action in the imperfect, interrupted by an abrupt event in the past historic;

(8) **'Jules se fâcha'**: his sudden change of mood is on a parallel with something taking place, therefore past historic;

(9) **'tu as raté', 'j'ai dormi'**: perfect tense, since these past events are being told in conversational form;

(10) **'cria', 'répondit'**: back to past historic, since these verbs are outside the conversation. Note the inversion of verb and subject after direct speech;

(11) **'à peine eut-il prononcé':** 'hardly had he spoken' is past anterior, with inversion, fulfilling the three conditions named for this tense in the section above;

(12) **'on put enfin avancer':** past historic, the next thing they **could do** was to move forward.

Present subjunctive
Habits of the present subjunctive

The subjunctive is found very regularly in everyday French. It will not go away if ignored, but it is quite a friendly animal if treated in a reasonable manner!

(a) To form the subjunctive you add these **endings** to the *third person plural stem* of the *present indicative*:

−e	*−ions*
−es	*−iez*
−e	*−ent*

This applies to all verbs of the three conjugation patterns, with very few exceptions. (You will notice that very often this will give forms very similar to the present indicative – tant mieux!)

(b) Irregularities of stem noted with certain verbs in the first and second persons plural of the present indicative will be retained in those persons of the subjunctive.

(c) Irregular verbs are: 'avoir', 'être', 'faire', 'savoir', 'pouvoir', 'vouloir', 'aller'.

(d) The **subjunctive** is a **mood**, not a mere tense expressing what will or has happened, etc.: in general terms it does **not** state **facts** in the way the indicative mood does. It is used nearly always in **subordinate clauses**, where the **main clause** has expressed a point of view of **doubt**, **necessity**, or **emotion**. Inevitably the number of phrases which come into these three categories is very great: 'emotion', for instance, includes joy, sorrow, surprise, fear, indignation, wishing, doubt, etc. All verbs or impersonal expressions coming under these headings will therefore require in a subordinate clause (introduced by 'que') the subjunctive of the verb of that clause: e.g. 'regretter que' or 'il est regrettable que'; 'je doute que' or 'il est douteux que', etc. N.B. **'Espérer'** is the one exception among verbs expressing personal emotion.

(e) Certain conjunctions also indicate use of the subjunctive in the clause following. **'Bien que'**, **'pour que'**, **'à moins que'** and others are in very common use and must be learned by heart. Be careful to remember them too when writing essays!

(f) An additional **'ne'** is placed before the subjunctive verb after expressions of **fearing**, and the conjunction '**à moins que**' = '**unless**'. This is not negative in purpose, and so must not be translated as an active negative!

(g) A few **set expressions** of the type 'Vive la reine!', etc. have the subjunctive in a **main clause**, expressing the wish 'may . . . (something be, happen)'.

(h) The **perfect subjunctive** is formed from the **present subjunctive** of the regular **auxiliary + past participle**: you should use this if the clause is plainly 'past' in sense: e.g. 'It is a pity that you have never met her' = 'Il est dommage que tu ne l'**aies** jamais **rencontrée**.'

(i) The **imperfect subjunctive** is nowadays restricted mainly to the **third person singular** form which can be recognised as the past historic form with a circumflex accent over the end vowel: e.g. 'il donnât' (–er verbs add 't' also), 'il finît', 'il reçût'. Even so it is only in very correct French that you will come across even this form; many people dislike the sound of the imperfect subjunctive (particularly the other persons of the verb) and will use the present subjunctive instead. It is **highly unlikely** that an O-level candidate would need to use the imperfect subjunctive.

(j) **Translate** the subjunctive into English as the sense of the whole sentence dictates, above all making sure the sense is **good sense** and sounds natural in English.

Avoid the subjunctive if:

(a) you know a **noun** which may **replace the subjunctive clause**. There are not an awful lot of these, but 'le départ', 'l'arrivée', 'la mort', 'la naissance' all offer possibilities here;

(b) you can use an **infinitive construction** instead. Here there is one proviso: **both clauses** must have the **same subject**, otherwise the subjunctive clause is obligatory.

The passive voice

(a) The translation is as for the English passive ('*is sung*', '*will be sung*', '*has been sung*', etc.) but as a linguistic device is used less in French than in English.

(b) The formation is also exactly as in English; the verb '*être*' (in the tense required) is used with the *past participle*. N.B. the **past participle** always **agrees with the subject**.

(c) The **tense** required will be that of the phrase had it been **active**; e.g. 'Jean est frappé par Gérard = Gérard frappe Jean = present tense (active or passive).

(d) '**Was hit**', etc. is the only English idea needing care in translation. Is 'was' imperfect? or is it really a 'one-off event' needing therefore the perfect (or past historic)?

(e) The **agent** ('by') is usually rendered by '**par**', except if the reference is not to a particular person or object but is generalised. Usually this is found with expressions of attitude towards people, such as 'respecter', 'aimer', etc. In these cases the generalised agent is represented by '**de**' (Il est **adoré de** tous).

(f) There are occasions in French where the **passive** is **not correct**: these are with verbs where the person-object is **indirect** (this includes for instance all verbs of 'asking', 'giving', 'showing', etc.). Here you **must** use an **active verb form** and if no subject is available use 'on'.

(g) '**On**' is in any case a favourite way of **avoiding the passive** in French. Bear this in mind when you meet it in a passage to be translated into English. It could well be that 'on' + active verb is best rendered in English by a passive form. At least be alert to the possibility.

(h) In other circumstances which should be noted from your reading, the way to **avoid** using a **passive** is to make the **verb reflexive**. But you should only adopt this practice in situations which you know are correct.

In short, do not go out of your way to create the passive in French.

Question forms

Questions may be asked in **three main ways** (politely, that is!):

(1) by altering the *intonation* of the voice (raising it at the end of the phrase, instead of letting it fall);

(2) by prefacing the statement with '*Est-ce que . . .*' (which is a phrase with no worthwhile meaning of its own: it is a waste of effort therefore to struggle to find one);

(3) by *inverting verb and subject pronoun*, and joining them by hyphens.

N.B. If the **subject** is a **noun**, the **noun** is given **first**, followed by the **inverted verb and subject pronoun**, which must be supplied in addition, producing a '**Georges mange-t-il . . .?**' pattern. (Incidentally, do not translate this as 'George is he eating?', which is totally un-English.)

N.B. An extra '**–t–**' is used where the third person singular form ends in a vowel.

(4) **First person inversion** is comparatively **rare**, except for '**Puis-je?**' = '**May I?**' Even here the form 'Est-ce que je peux' is

heard most often, except perhaps in the best and most polite circles!

Inversion (other than in questions)
Inversion of verb and subject is also found outside the area of questions. Principal instances are:

(1) *after direct speech* (usually therefore concerning verbs of saying, or exclamation);

(2) *after certain conjunctions*: 'peut-être', 'ainsi', 'sans doute', 'aussi' (at the beginning of the sentence where it means 'therefore');

(3) after '*à peine . . . que*' which we have already seen used in the section on the past anterior (page 206).

Again it must be stressed that this is a linguistic **device**, a convention to be accepted; it does **not** mean that when you come across examples in French passages for translation you should translate them as they stand into inverted English. **Translation** (no matter in which direction) should aim at producing what is the **acceptable** and **natural** turn of phrase in the **target language**.

N.B. Inversion is **not** necessary in exclamations introduced in French by:
 comme (que) = how! or **combien** = how (to what an extent), e.g. Comme c'est intéressant! = How interesting it is!

Participles

Present participle
(1) The usual English translation is '*doing*', **but** you must be very careful to make sure your '–ing' fits the requirements of the present participle, before assuming this is so. The chances are that it is not, in fact! Translation of the English '–ing' is like a very exclusive club, into which French present participles are rarely admitted!
(2) The **present participle** is formed from the same stem as the imperfect tense (the '*nous*' part of the *present* indicative, from which the ending is removed, leaving the following patterns: '*donn–*, *finiss–*, *vend–*'). To this stem is added the *one ending* '*–ant*'.
(3) **Etre, avoir, and savoir** are the only exceptions to this formation.
N.B. The expected participle of 'savoir' would be '**savant**', which does exist as a noun, meaning a '**scientist**', or '**scholar**' and as an

adjective, meaning '**learned**'. The present participle is 'sachant'.
(4) Verbs ending in '**–cer**', '**–ger**' will yet again need their special forms, giving endings in '**–çant**', '**–geant**'.
(5) The present participle must **either**:
   (a) be a simple **adjective** in function, with agreement in the usual manner;
or (b) have a **verbal** force, referring to the **subject** of the **main** verb, in which case there will be **no agreement**.
(6) The meaning of the present participle may be extended from the simple 'doing' to show '*while . . .,*' '*by . . .,*' or '*on doing*', by introducing the preposition '*en*' before the participle.

N.B. **No other preposition** may introduce a present participle and '**en + present participle**' **must** refer to the **subject** of the **main clause**.
(7) The addition to this phrase of 'tout' (= *tout en + present participle*) **either emphasises** the **simultaneous nature** of the two actions going on, **or implies a concessive attitude**.
(8) '*Ayant*' (or '*étant*') + *present participle* may render '*having done*', with the same restriction on the subject governing it as the other examples.

'–ings' are dangerous!
Do not be tempted to use a present participle form in circumstances which do not correspond exactly to the ones mentioned here. It would without any doubt at all be wrong to do so!

Be specially careful to render the following ideas correctly:
(a) **to hear, see, feel, sense someone doing = voir, etc. + infinitive or voir, etc. + relative clause**;
(b) **adjectives of posture** (sitting, etc.) = **past participle** ('assis', etc.)
N.B. 'Rester assis, debout' = 'to sit, stand for a length of time'.
The corresponding **reflexive verbs** from which the past participles are derived denote '**the action** of sitting down', etc.

Past participles
We have already met the main uses of the past participle:
(1) as a component *part of all compound tenses*;
(2) as an ordinary *adjective*.
It may also serve usefully to:
(3) *resume* a whole '*when*' or '*after*' clause, provided that the **subject** of the **two ideas** is the **same**;
(4) provide a few *conjunctions*, which are used nowadays without any great sense of attachment to their original source.

The infinitive mood

Where '–ing' is not a present participle the correct form is likely to be the **infinitive** in French. In this respect their use is greater in French than in our own language.

The **infinitive** is used:

(1) occasionally *alone* in *printed notices*, or as the '*–ing*' *subject* of a sentence (the gerund in English);

(2) *directly* following on from:
   (a) verbs of motion,
   (b) modal verbs,
   (c) verbs like 'voir', 'sentir', 'laisser' (see page 211, '"–ings" are dangerous'),
   (d) personal viewpoint verbs ('préférer', 'détester', etc.),
   (e) 'faillir' (nearly to have done something),
   (f) 'faire' (to have done, get someone to do for you), 'se faire' (to have something done for your benefit);

(3) after certain *verbs, nouns and adjectives* followed by the preposition '*de*' ('essayer de', 'avoir le droit de', 'content de', etc.);

(4) after certain *verbs, nouns and adjectives* followed by the preposition '*à*' ('apprendre à', 'avoir du mal à', 'prêt à');

(5) after *all prepositions other than 'en'*.

N.B. **Pour** + *infinitive* usually indicates purpose ('in order to'). It is also used with 'assez', 'trop' = 'enough to', etc. **Par** + **infinitive** is restricted to use with verbs of 'beginning' and 'ending' to indicate 'to begin', 'end **by doing** . . .'

Avant always has '**de**' + **infinitive** (before doing).

Après always has the **perfect infinitive** (made up from the auxiliary in the infinitive + past participle). This gives the forms '**après avoir mangé** . . .', '**après être sorti(s)** . . .', etc.

Important: infinitive constructions must share their **implied subject** with that of the **main verb**. If these do not coincide a clause must be used in place of the infinitive (e.g. 'avant que', 'pour que', 'après que', etc. – with all that this may involve . . .!).

Government of verbs

English and French usage are frequently unalike here and (yes, you've guessed) thorough study and regular practice are the only sure ways of sorting things out.

You must be careful that none of the following will trip you up when presented in a context other than a printed list:

(1) verbs with **direct objects** in French (e.g. 'regarder' = 'to look **at**'; 'payer' = 'to pay **for**');

(2) verbs with **indirect objects** in French (how very perverse, you may think) (e.g. 'demander **à**' = 'to ask'; 'obéir **à** = to obey');

(3) verbs implying '**removal from**' (either legal or illegal) (e.g. 'voler **à**' = 'to steal **from**'; 'acheter **à**' = 'to buy **from**');

(4) verbs with the prepositions '**à**' or '**de**' included in the phrase (e.g. 'se souvenir **de**' = 'to remember'; 's'habituer **à**' = 'to get used to');

(5) verbs which take both '**à**' and '**de**' depending on the meaning (e.g. 'jouer **à**' = 'to play a game'; 'jouer **de**' = 'to play an instrument').

Modal verbs

Modal verbs are used very often to give a particular meaning to a second verb (in the infinitive). They comprise the following: '*vouloir*', '*pouvoir*', '*devoir*', '*falloir*', 'savoir'. Their conjugation is frequently irregular and should constitute a special topic to be learnt.

'Vouloir', 'devoir', 'savoir' and 'falloir' may all be used on occasions with an object, in which case they present little problem beyond their conjugation, but it is in the area of **meaning** in their function **as modal verbs** that difficulties often arise. Some main uses and interpretations will be given here, but for a complete picture you should consult the table which was given in the main body of the text (page 122). Where there is a particular tense expressing a certain meaning, this will be shown in brackets; otherwise you may understand that several tenses carry that sense.

Vouloir is used:
(a) to ask for something to be done (present tense);
(b) to say what you would like (conditional tense);
(c) to express willingness;
(d) as a polite request (plural form of the imperative).

Pouvoir is used:
(a) to ask permission (question form);
(b) to suggest future possibility (conditional or conditional perfect tenses);

213

(c) to suggest physical capacity for doing something.

N.B. 'Pouvoir' is omitted where in English we include it in phrases like 'I can hear her singing' = 'Je **l'entends chanter**' (notice that infinitive).

Devoir is used:
(a) to express necessity;
(b) to indicate duty or moral obligation;
(c) to indicate previous arrangements made;
(d) to express an opinion about a situation.

Falloir is used (and **only** in the **third person singular**):
(a) to express necessity in the same way as 'devoir';
(b) to indicate duty or moral obligation.

It is **stronger** than 'devoir', conveying either a greater sense of urgency or a stronger moral obligation or duty.

'Falloir' is also used without a following infinitive, but with **que + subjunctive clause**. To give a real sense of necessity this is often the construction preferred.

Savoir is used:
(a) to express 'to know how to do something';
(b) to express 'to know facts'.

The verb '**connaître**' is used of knowing people, etc. Here the emphasis is on personal acquaintance; personal experience of something if an abstract idea is involved.

Negatives

(1) Negatives in French are composed of **two parts**, which 'sandwich' the verb. They do not sandwich a noun object, but will encompass any **object pronouns** coming before the verb.

(2) The following negatives sandwich the **auxiliary verb** only in a compound tense:

ne...pas	= not;	ne...point	= not at all;
ne...jamais	= never;	ne...guère	= scarcely;
ne...rien	= nothing.		

(3) The remaining phrases sandwich **both the auxiliary verb and the past participle** in a compound tense:

ne...personne	= nobody;	ne...nulle part	= nowhere;
ne...aucun(e)	= not a;	ne...nul (nulle)	= not a single;
ne...que	= only;	ne...ni...ni...	= neither...nor...

(4) With '**ne...ni...ni...**' you **omit** the **indefinite article** before a noun object.

214

(5) With 'ne . . . que' there are several points to notice. Firstly, it is important to place the 'que' correctly. This is the part of the negative giving the meaning (here = 'only'), and 'que' must be placed **before the word** being restricted. Secondly, if 'only' restricts a **verb**, the additional verb 'faire' must be introduced (e.g. Je **n'ai fait que** sourire = I **only smiled**).

Thirdly, if the **subject** of the phrase is being restricted by 'only' (in the sense of 'that alone') then 'ne . . . que' is not possible, and you must use the adjective form 'seul'.

(6) Where the **negative is the subject** of the sentence (as in the case of 'rien' = 'nothing', 'personne' = 'no one', 'ni . . . ni . . .' = 'neither . . . nor', 'aucun' or 'nul' = 'not a') you must be careful to place the 'ne' part of the negative as normal before the verb.

(7) Combination of **two negatives** is possible (except for 'pas' and 'point' which always are used alone). A point to remember here is that the correct **English** translation of **double negatives** is to turn **one** of them to the **positive** (how perverse, the French might say!). This will give a pattern like this: 'ne . . . plus rien' = 'nothing any more'. In reverse you must remember that the English 'not + anything', etc. **must** be rendered as 'nothing' in French (= 'ne . . . rien').

(8) Where an **infinitive is negated**, **both** parts of the negative are placed together before the verb ('. . .de ne jamais y aller' = '. . . never to go there').

(9) If the negative idea ('personne', 'rien', etc.) is used **without a verb**, then the 'ne' is omitted. In other words, the 'ne' **governs the verb**, and the **second part** of the negative provides the sense. Occasionally (with the verb 'pouvoir' and a few others) the 'pas' is omitted, while still retaining the idea of a negative. This **cannot** be done with the other negative expressions.

(10) **'N'est-ce pas?'** has a multitude of meanings and, rather like 'Est-ce que', none of its own. What it means depends on the sense of the sentence to which it is added ('does he?' 'doesn't he?', etc.). **Do not overdo its use**.

(11) Here is a reminder concerning the negative and the partitive article. The normal **partitive** ('du', 'de la', 'de l'', 'des') is reduced to the single form '**de, (d')**' following a negative expression, **except** following 'ne . . . que'.

(12) Two occasions when 'ne' does **not** express the **negative** are (a) in certain **subjunctive structures** (see above) and (b) in **comparisons involving a verb**. 'She gave me **more** ice-cream **than I wanted**' would be rendered 'Elle m'a donné **plus** de glace **que** je **ne** voulais'.

(13) Unluckily for some, a small final point on the negative often

tends to be forgotten . . . that '**si**' i' is used to replace '**oui**' when a question has been put negatively.

Use of prepositions

Correct use of prepositions is a slowly acquired art, since in very many cases it is totally different from English. Here are a few of the major points concerning this difficult topic.

about	(= on the subject of)	= **au sujet de** (or **il s'agit de**)
	(=approximate number)	= **environ** (or **une —aine**)
	(= approximate time)	= **vers**
at	(= at the house or premises of)	= **chez** (**someone's name** must always follow, **never** a place)
before	(= place)	= **devant**
	(= time)	= **avant**
by	(= transport)	= **en** (voiture, autobus, etc.)
		= **par** (le train, avion, etc.)
		= **à** (pied, cheval, etc.)
for	(=future time)	= **pour**
	(= past time)	= **pendant** (or omitted altogether)
	(= have been doing for . . . (time))	= **depuis** + present tense
in	(= in towns)	= **à** (careful with '**au Havre**', etc.)
	(= in (or to) masc. countries)	= **au (aux)** (Japon, Etats-Unis)
	(= in (or to) fem. countries)	= **en** (Angleterre)
	(= time within which)	= **en**
	(=time at the end of which)	= **dans**
of	(= made of)	= **en** (or **de**) (coton)
on	(= on left, right)	= **à** (gauche etc.)
	(= on a winter's day)	= **par** (une journée d'hiver)
	(= on day or date)	= **omitted**
to	(= towards in attitude)	= **envers**
with	(= with a big nose)	= **omitted**
	(= out of (emotion))	= **de** (joie)

216

Everyday basics

Numerals
Cardinal numbers

The numbers 1–20 of course have individual forms, but from 21–69 they follow a similar pattern for each group of ten, e.g. 23 = vingt-trois; 63 = soixante-trois.

You should note particularly:

21 = vingt et un (similarly 31, 41, 51, 61)

70 = soixante-dix	*71 = soixante et onze*
80 = quatre-vingts	*81 = quatre-vingt-un*
90 = quatre-vingt-dix	*91 = quatre-vingt-onze*
100 = cent	*1,000 = mille*

N.B. **Only** when standing alone do '**cent**' and '**vingt**' take the plural '**s**'. Any number following disqualifies the '**s**'!

The numeral '**mille**' is **invariable**; to continue beyond 'mille' (or 'cent'), simply add on 'un', 'deux', etc.: **mille un** (= one thousand and one).

Ordinal numbers

(Are agreeable! – adjectives, of course!). They are usually formed from the cardinal number by the addition of '*–ième*' (take off any final 'e' first).

'**The first**': '**le premier**', '**la première**' is a special form, and you must be careful over the spelling of 'cin**qui**ème', 'neu**vi**ème, and 'vingt et **unième**'.

Ordinal numbers are **not used** in **titles** of monarchs, and **only** with the **first of the month in dates**.

Dates

'On 14th June' is in French '**le quatorze juin**'.

'In 1965' is in French '**en dix-neuf cent soixante-cinq**' ('**mil neuf cent**' is an alternative version).

'In August' is in French '**en août**', or '**au mois d'août**'.

N.B. (a) the omission of 'on' and 'of';

      (b) the use of small letters for the name of the month;

        (c) the use of 'en' for 'in';

      (d) the use of the cardinal number.

You should remember too the unusual '**le onze**' with dates.

Approximate numbers

A noun may be formed to denote an approximate number by adding '*–aine*' to the cardinal number.

N.B. une huitaine = about a week;
    une quinzaine = about a fortnight.

Fractions

Apart from *la moitié* ($\frac{1}{2}$), *le tiers* ($\frac{1}{3}$), *le quart* ($\frac{1}{4}$), the ordinal numbers are used as fractions.

N.B. The **definite article** is used in French where in English we use the indefinite (**a** quarter).

$\frac{1}{2}$ = a **half** something, or something and a **half** is the adjective 'demi' (invariable before a noun to which it is also joined by a hyphen);

$\frac{1}{2}$ = mid = '**mi**' (always before the noun and hyphenated).

Dimensions

These are expressed in one of two ways:

Either (*a*) *avoir* + (*measurement*) + *de long*, etc. A second dimension is joined by '*sur*' = 'by ...'.

or (*b*) *être long* (*etc.*) *de* (*measurement*). A second dimension is joined by '*et*'.

Time

'*Quelle heure est-il?*' and 'A quelle heure ...?' are the relevant questions.

Remember:

(a) always to use 'il';
(b) to keep 'heures' plural (except for 'une heure');
(c) to write 'demi**e**' (except with 'midi' and 'minuit');
(d) minutes past are simply added (no **and**);
(e) minutes to are 'moins' + number;
(f) a quarter past is 'et quart';
(g) a quarter to is 'moins le quart';
(h) 'in the morning', etc. is '**du** matin', etc. (when preceded by a stated time);
(i) 'about' a certain time is 'vers'.

N.B. The 24-hour system is widely used in France.

Age

'*Avoir*' is the verb to use to express age – make sure you remember this when expressing persons and tenses other than first person present tense – many candidates do not! Expressions which are connected with age are:

    être âgé de ...; = to be ... old;
    avoir ... de plus/de moins que = to be ... older/younger than ...

N.B. **Never** omit 'ans' (or whatever is relevant) from the basic 'avoir' expression; *il a quatre-vingts ans* = he is eighty.

Impersonal expressions

The impersonal expressions (fairly obviously) have **no person** as their subject.

(1) They are therefore only found in the **third person singular** form (but with all tenses, naturally enough).

(2) Two constructions are possible with 'il est' used impersonally, as we have seen: **il est + adjective + de + infinitive; il est + adjective + que + subjunctive**.

(3) The number of impersonal expressions is considerable, and therefore must be learned by heart ('*il y a*', '*il se passe*', '*il vaut mieux*' are only a few of the very common ones).

(4) **Weather expressions** are impersonal. Remember that '*faire*' is the verb generally used here, except where a special verb exists. These should be very familiar expressions, and **not only** in the present tense:

il fait chaud (warm);	*il fait froid (cold)*;
il fait beau (fine);	*il fait du vent (windy)*;
il fait doux (mild);	*il fait du brouillard (foggy)*;
il fait du soleil (sunny);	

but *il pleut (raining)* and *il neige (snowing)*.

These form an extremely basic meteorological vocabulary.

N.B. '**C**' on a French tap should **not** give you cold water, despite the terrible rumours about French plumbing.

Various combinations of '**il fait un temps** (or a few other nouns) **+ adjective**' are possible to vary the weather picture.

Vocabulary points

A wide range of vocabulary is essential not only to enable the student to understand the material he is called upon to interpret, whether oral or written, but also for him to have a source of supply for work of his own initiative. In this section of the book only a few generalised points can be made, and it is hoped that the student will consider this as a springboard for personal investigation.

Areas of difficulty

(1) A major problem occurs when trying to express the English idea of *verb + adverbial phrase* (or preposition) of the type 'to go across'; 'to steal in'; 'to climb down', etc. Often such expressions may be rendered in French by a kind of **reverse process**, making

the idea contained in the adverb or preposition the verb, and adding a phrase to convey the idea contained in the English verb (where this is necessary). Sometimes in fact the verb itself conveys the complete idea, and if this is the case, then be content with that! It is amazing how a few basic verbs like 'entrer', 'sortir', 'traverser', 'monter' and 'descendre' can be adapted very simply with the addition of a phrase to cover a whole wealth of meanings. Some examples to illustrate just how easily this can be done are:

entrer à pas de loup	=	to steal in;
sortir à la hâte	=	to hurry out;
traverser en courant	=	to run across;
descendre à pas lents	=	to walk slowly down.

Note down such examples as you come across them in your work and **do not be afraid to use them yourself**. Such expressions create a very idiomatic impression and, used correctly, should bring you credit in an examination.

(2) **Periods of time**
Time periods such as '*day*', '*morning*', '*evening*', where there are apparently two appropriate words in French, create some considerable difficulty.

In these cases, the **masculine word** of the two ('*le jour*', etc.) is used to pinpoint **the time of day it is**, merely as a **point of reference**, and the **feminine word** ('*la journée*', etc.) is used to give the feeling of **the length of time involved** (often to be translated as 'the day-time', 'the whole evening', etc.).

(3) **'To leave'**
Considering the law of averages it is surprising that more candidates do not accidentally stumble upon the correct verb which they need for a particular situation.
There are in fact **three verbs**, commonly confused:
(a) '*quitter*' (which **must have a direct object** – person or place);
(b) '*partir*' (which **never** has a **direct object**). It **may** be used when followed by '**de** and the name of a place' to mean 'to leave' in the same way as 'quitter' does; and it may also be used on its own to mean '**to go**' (**no** object). In this case an alternative verb is the reflexive verb '**s'en aller**' = 'to go', 'leave' (**intransitive**);
(c) '*laisser*', (which means 'to leave behind').

(4) '**Back**' or '**again**'
Candidates often struggle to find a suitable adverb or phrase to express this idea, but very often it can be easily rendered by the

prefix '*re-*' which according to the context, may convey either idea: '*refaire*' = '*to do again*'; '*revenir*' = '*to come back*', *etc.*

(5) 'To take, bring'

A simple rule to remember is that whatever the nuance provided by the prefix used, the verb '**porter**' will refer to objects (its basic meaning is 'to carry', after all), and the verb '**mener**' will refer to people. Hence the following:

apporter	=	*to bring an object here;*
emporter	=	*to take an object away;*
amener	=	*to bring someone along;*
emmener	=	*to take someone somewhere.*

(6) 'To live'

In the sense of 'being alive', the verb to use is '*vivre*' (don't forget your 'joie de vivre'!). Otherwise in the sense of address, location, use '*habiter*' or '*demeurer*'.

(7) 'To look'

This offers a variety of possibilities, the most common of which are:

regarder = *to look at; chercher* = *to look for;*
avoir l'air + *adjective* = *to have a certain appearance.*

(8) 'To return'

Here again we have **three possibilities**, but they do not all mean the same thing:

revenir	=	*to come back here*	(direction **this** way);
retourner	=	*to go back there*	(direction **away from you**);
rentrer	=	*to come or go back*	(usually 'home').

(9) 'Then'

'Well **then**, let me see' is '*eh bien*';
'Then' as a word in a sequence of events is '*puis*';
'Then' meaning 'therefore' is '*donc*';
'Then' meaning 'at that time' is '*alors*';
'Then' meaning 'in that case' is also '*alors*'.

(10) 'A party'

If it is political, it is '*un parti*', but if it is social, it is '*une soirée*' or '*une surprise-partie*'.

Faux-amis

Beware of false friends bringing apparent gifts of words which are very like English words! Their meaning is normally quite different from their appearance.

The favourite red herrings are:

actuellement (which 'actually' means 'at the present time');
assister (which means 'to be present at');
la monnaie (which means 'the change');
la journée (which means 'the daytime');
pêcher (which means 'to fish');
une pêche (which means 'a peach' or 'la pêche' = 'fishing');
passer (which means 'to spend time' or 'to sit an exam');
une pièce (which means 'a room', and can also be 'a play');
user (which means 'to wear out');
des vacances (which means 'holidays').

Quite so! But be sure you know the correct French words for those which the faux-amis so closely resemble in English.

Idioms and everyday phrases

Such phrases tend to be individual by their very nature and must be learned as such. Whichever ones **you** choose to learn as sources of enrichment for your own vocabulary will be a personal matter, but be sure to know **at least** the following.

(1) Avoir idioms

avoir + age	= to be . . . old	**avoir l'air**	= to look
avoir chaud	= to feel hot	**avoir froid**	= to feel cold
avoir raison	= to be right	**avoir tort**	= to be wrong
avoir faim	= to be hungry	**avoir soif**	= to be thirsty
avoir sommeil	= to feel sleepy	**avoir honte**	= to be ashamed
avoir peur	= to be afraid	**avoir mal à . . .**	= to have an
avoir lieu	= to take place		ache in . . .
avoir envie de . . .	= to feel like		
avoir besoin de . . .	= to need		

(2) Faire idioms

il fait chaud, etc.	= the weather's hot, etc.
faire une promenade	= to go for a walk
. . . en voiture, en bateau, etc.	= to go for a car, boat ride
faire la vaisselle	= to do the washing up
faire le ménage	= to do the housework
faire les courses	= to do the shopping
faire son marché	= to do one's shopping (food,etc.)
faire la lessive	= to do the washing
faire la cuisine	= to do the cooking
s'en faire	= to worry

(3) Time expressions

hier	= yesterday	**avant-hier**	= day before yes-
il y a . . .	= . . . ago		terday
aujourd'hui	= today	**ce jour-là**	= that day

demain	= tomorrow	**après-demain**	= day after
le lendemain	= the following		tomorrow
	day	**la veille**	= the day before

la veille au soir, le lendemain matin, etc. = the evening
   before, the following morning, etc.

l'avant-veille = two days before

le surlendemain = two days later

la semaine dernière (prochaine) = last (next) week

l'année dernière (prochaine) = last (next) year

souvent	= often	**enfin**	= at last
huit jours	= a week	**quinze jours**	= a fortnight

Adverbs

The extremely common ones like 'beaucoup de' should be
thoroughly familiar at this stage. Note also:

d'ailleurs	= besides	**presque**	= almost
tout à fait	= completely	**tout à coup**	= suddenly
tout d'un coup	= all of a	**tout de suite**	= immediately
	sudden	**tout à l'heure**	= just now
autrefois	= formerly	**de bonne heure**	= early
plusieurs fois	= several times	**quelquefois**	= sometimes
de temps en	= from time	**déjà**	= already
temps (à autre)	to time	**plus tard**	= later

Prepositions

Note the less obvious:

malgré	= in spite of	**parmi, entre**	= among
sauf	= except for	**quant à**	= as for
faute de	= for lack of	**selon**	= according to
grâce à	= thanks to	**jusqu'à**	= up to, until

Conjunctions

Those mentioned frequently elsewhere are not included below.

cependant	= however	**car**	= for (since)
pourtant	= yet	**parce que**	= because
comme	= as (reason)	**puisque**	= since (reason)
néanmoins	= nevertheless	**tandis que**	= whereas
à mesure que	= as (in proportion to)		

Other study aids in the  series

KEY FACTS CARDS

30p: Woodwork
     Metalwork
     Henry IV Part I
     Henry V
     Merchant of Venice
     Richard II
     Richard III
     Twelfth Night
35p: Latin
     German
     Macbeth
     Julius Caesar
40p: New Testament
45p: Geography – Regional
     English Comprehen-
       sion & Precis
     English Language &
       Exam Essay
     Algebra

45p: Economics
50p: Elementary Mathe-
       matics
     Modern Mathematics
     English History
     (1815–1939)
     Chemistry
     Physics
     Biology
     Geometry
     Geography
     French
     Arithmetic &
       Trigonometry
     General Science
     Additional Mathe-
       matics
     Technical Drawing

KEY FACTS COURSE COMPANIONS

40p: Economics
50p: Modern Mathematics
50p: Algebra
50p: Geometry
55p: Arithmetic &
      Trigonometry
     Additional Mathe-
      matics

55p: Geography
     French
     Physics
     Chemistry
     English
     Biology

KEY FACTS A-LEVEL BOOKS

55p: Chemistry
     Biology
     Pure Mathematics
     Physics

All **KEY FACTS** titles are published by

ibp Intercontinental Book Productions
Berkshire House, Queen Street, Maidenhead, SL6 1NF
in conjunction with the distributors, Seymour Press Ltd.,
334 Brixton Road, London, SW9 7AG

Prices are correct at time of going to press.